Twin Flames Kiss

A True Twin Flames Love Story

Mark Worrall

Claire Worrall

First published in Great Britain in 2015 by Twin Flames Kiss Media
Minor corrections 2016 by Twin Flames Kiss Media

Copyright © Mark Worrall and Claire Worrall 2015

The right of Mark Worrall and Claire Worrall to be identified as the Authors of the Work has been asserted by them in accordance with the Copyright, Designs and Patents Act 1988.

All rights reserved. No part of this publication may be reproduced, stored in a retrieval system, or transmitted, in any form or by any means without the prior written permission of the publisher, nor be otherwise circulated in any form of binding or cover other than that in which it is published and without a similar condition being imposed on the subsequent purchaser. This work is based upon real events. Some names, identities, situation and or locations have been changed to protect the privacy of the individuals involved.

ISBN 978-0-9934620-0-9

Printed and bound by Ingram Spark

Also available as an eBook

Available online, just search for 'Twin Flames Kiss' on your preferred book website.

Twin Flames Kiss Media Ltd

website: www.twinflameskiss.com
music: www.twinflameskiss.com/music
email us: markandclaire@twinflameskiss.com

cover: Mark and Claire

Preface

When we met in 2009, we started to joke from the very first day that it was as though we were 'twins', for, among other things we were noticing that we seemed to know what the other was about to say next and seemed to have some sort of deeper psychic connection. It became so apparent, that we started to look online and discovered 'twin flames' (or 'twin souls').

As we read whatever we could find, it seemed there was a common description of what 'twin flames' were, but it also seemed to vary for each couple experiencing it. After moving homes and in together we felt compelled to write about our experience, to add our small contribution to the body of knowledge out there about 'twin flames'. It might not ring true with some, but to others for whom it does, it just might help them understand what they were experiencing a little bit more, and that they are not alone.

We also began looking back at our past life events and relationships, now understanding some in different ways. Maybe when we are suffering in our lives, we are also learning, growing, and/or helping others around us to do the same.

We felt a compelling urge to write about both, so created a simple website, www.twinflameskiss.com, to share our experiences and thoughts with others by writing and posting some articles.

We received many responses from people thanking us for talking about some topics no-one else appeared to be talking about, and how it had helped them realise that they were not alone in their thoughts and experiences. We also received many emails from people telling us their very personal stories and situations, and asking for our advice. Encouraged, we started writing and publishing more articles.

Certain questions re-appeared in many emails we received, so instead of writing many similar responses back, we eventually realised that putting them all together into a book might be more helpful. It might assist others also going through dark times, as we once had, and offer some encouragement to not give in, whilst also discussing the intensity of the Twin Flame relationship and our amazing experience of coming together.

It wasn't easy reliving a lot of deeply hurtful experiences so that we could write about them. Mark wrote 3 chapters and then stopped to wait for Claire, it took her eighteen months before she was ready to write her first words. When she finally started writing, it became clear why it was such a difficult task for her.

If the pain of reading some of the dark events we had to endure matches that of writing about them and becomes too much, you can always jump ahead to chapter 29, and go straight to the beginning of our meeting and Twin Flame love story.

During the next five years we wrote and edited and re-edited the content many times over, with sections being added or rewritten, and others completely deleted. In one of the last edits we removed over 140 pages. Many of the difficult situations we did include are just examples, we could have included many more that happened, but in the end decided not to.

These are our experiences and our opinions, they are honest and true, we hope they can be of benefit to others and help them realise in dark times to not give up, there could be better times ahead.

"...and when one of them meets the other half, the actual half of himself, whether he be a lover of youth or a lover of another sort, the pair are lost in an amazement of love and friendship and intimacy and one will not be out of the other's sight, as I may say, even for a moment."...

— Plato, The Symposium

1 – PONT des ARTS

(The Padlock Bridge)

Mark:

Paris. December, 2013.

Dawn is breaking, as we stumble out of Hotel Regina and onto the Rue des Pyramides. The memory of French champagne and a night of making love still lingers in each other's eyes, as we flash a playful smile at each other. Past the gold statue of Joan of Arc, we flag down a taxi on the quiet streets and jump in, asking for the "Pont des Arts". We think we have nailed it in French, but the driver's face just gazes blankly back at us. We obviously haven't. Instead we try, "The padlock bridge"? Then magically it's "Oh, wee, wee", and off we go.

He takes us around the Palais des Tuleries Gardens and back up along the banks of the River Seine. A golden dawn is breaking through, so the drive is swift and easy in contrast to the usual chaos of daytime Paris traffic. As we arrive, we jump out in excited anticipation, and oops, in our eagerness almost forget to pay him.

The sign on the steps says, 'Pont des Arts'. We joke that it must sound different in French and walk up the few steps holding hands. Staring in awe we are stopped in our tracks, for along both sides of the bridge the entire steel mesh fences shimmer gold with a million padlocks put there by lovers. As we walk along to get a closer look, we see that every centimetre of the fences on both sides are covered from the hand rail right down to the ground with a sea of padlocks. So many, there are hardly any gaps left to squeeze one more on. People have even locked padlocks onto padlocks, or onto lamp posts, just to get theirs on somewhere, anywhere, to join the communal sculpture of love.

We stroll beside them, seeing couples names and dates going back many years. There is an energy of pure love reaching out to touch you as you walk along - feeling it, like nowhere else.

While it is still quiet, Claire slips our gold shiny padlock out of her coat pocket and writes 'Mark and Claire 15-12-13' with an indelible black pen on one side. On the back, I write 'www.twinflameskiss.com', our website where a few years earlier we had felt compelled to start writing a few articles about our long and often painful journey towards each other.

We wait for some early morning walkers to cross the bridge so that we can be alone long enough to complete our contribution. Other couples arrive and seem to have the same idea as us. They stand with the same look of awe on their faces as we had, taking photos and video and soon look like they too are searching for their own spot to attach their padlocks.

I attach ours, squeezing it into one of the few remaining gaps. I catch a waft of Claire's perfume in a breath of enchantment and my heart starts to quicken. It suddenly reminds me of last night with her French black seamed stockings smothered in black nylon lingerie and high heel shoes. I lean her up against the lamp post, beside where our padlock is attached to taste her dark red lips, and then capture the memory forever with a few photographs and some snippets of video on my phone.

Claire tosses our keys into the river with a chink as they descend, followed by a tiny splash as they sink out of sight, down to the bottom and onto the top of the piles of other keys that must be down there too.

We stand there taking in the energy of so much love, beaming at each other in such a special moment. No wonder people love Paris, the city of love. A token of our love, our tiny contribution to a work of art gleams forever in that communal sculpture of love on the famous Lovers Bridge, with all of the other lovers' padlocks.

We later edited together the photos and video and set it to music Claire had composed, sharing it on our website at 'www.twinflameskiss.com/OurJourney/Pont-des-Arts-The-Padlock-Bridge', hopefully to inspire others to dare to dream also. It is possible.

Love is all we are here for. Love is what everyone is truly looking for in life when you break it right down. Our love is so rich, intense and permanent, a padlock seemed so fitting to express the intense union of our love. There is no pretending no honeymoon period, as in previous failed relationships. We love each other intensely, and for the first time in our lives, we can be who we truly are, without being punished for it. It is so liberating, so fulfilling, so exciting and so sexy being filled with such an adrenalin rush. It really is the ultimate drug.

But it was not always like this. It took each of us fifty years of struggling through difficult, abusive, manipulative, and at times horrific experiences and relationships, driving us to the depths of darkness, to the edge of life itself even, before we were finally ready to be with 'the one'. At times we were brainwashed that we were damaged and worthless, by manipulative partners who avoided looking inwards at their own issues, by putting all of their energy into pointing the finger at us instead.

Every time we were beaten down, deceived, lied to, cheated on, stolen from, discarded or abused, we would slowly somehow piece ourselves back together, and eventually recommence our search for 'the one'. Like an unstoppable program in our souls, we were both driven to search on, seeking out our one true love. Just like in the movie Titanic when Rose finally met 'the one', Jack and the rest of the world simply stopped and they just had to be together. All that went before was no more, and all that mattered was being together. We found it too, and seriously believe everyone else can, which is why we wrote this book. We wrote it to encourage others still going through similar dark experiences, not to give up seeking 'the one'.

This is a glimpse into each of our spiritual journeys and of how we sometimes gently, sometimes abruptly, did the inner work needed on ourselves through many very painful experiences, trying to learn something from them and turning them around into something positive instead. We would often repeat the same mistakes many times over, before having the realisation of learning to always choose love over fear. Hopefully others can learn from our mistakes, and find 'the one' for them quicker than it took us. Both of our journeys lead to looking for the answers within, instead of outside of ourselves, learning to love the self without being selfish, of taming the id and transforming the ego into the Higher Self, learning when to do work, when to fight and when to just let go, and not staying in destructive or passionless relationships.

We are 'Twin Flames' and this is our story.

"Humans were originally created with four arms, four legs and a head with two faces. Fearing their power, Zeus split them into two separate parts, condemning them to spend their lives in search of their other halves".

— Plato, The Symposium

2 - THE FEELING OF YOU

Claire:

I always knew that Mark would come, yet he was not to be my first love bursting with pimples and testosterone and school yard fumbling. He was to be my last love, my one and only true love and the final masterpiece of my life worth waiting for. Mark was to be a real man, not like the others I was going to fall for, who felt so much younger than I, no matter how old they were. He was to be strong and tall, both physically and emotionally, who would make my jaw drop down, because he would be so damned attractive to me. He was to be 'the one' to make me flush, as he played tango with my eyes across the room, and to take my breath away every time he would speak my name, because even today, my heart still beats faster whenever I hear his voice, or watch him walk across the road as if he was a complete stranger.

You may think I am just talking about romance, but you are mistaken, for Mark and I share something deeper than just physical attraction, which continues to sizzle and spark on another dimension altogether, somewhere within the kingdom of the soul. We even experienced this oneness as a mysterious gift when we first connected, which was long before we actually physically met. It was as if he had instantly used a secret key to unlock a private room inside my soul, which nobody else had ever known was even there before, let alone entered.

Even when I was just a child, I knew he was out there in the world for me, so strong was the feeling of him. I can still remember it, together with the first twinge of longing for him.

I must have been only three or four years old at the time, because I was on a cot mattress in my mother's bedroom. I was vividly aware that the man of my dreams was a little boy out there in the world somewhere too, breathing the air in and out at the same moment with me.

"I know you're here now", I clearly remember whispering to him.

"I don't know your name yet, but I know you are alive somewhere out there with the moon, and one day we will be together and live happily ever after".

I would often wonder, if he was watching the moon at the same time, whilst it mysteriously followed me around, wherever I was going. I decided that even if he could not see it, that the moon could see him, and we were mysteriously connected by a shimmering ray of silver thread. Whilst I could not actually see my true love, I could always feel him and that perception helped me to recognise him forty odd years later, but only after two divorces and numerous unrequited love affairs first.

As you can imagine, after so many failed relationships, I had that sinking feeling of being pretty hopeless for many years, believing I had to pretend that I was happy, when my relationship was in reality a living hell. I felt that there was something intrinsically wrong with me, and so I set about transforming myself from within, hoping to make that old feeling of not being good enough, finally go away.

But now I have started at the end and if I continue telling it all upside down like this, you will not understand what we both had to learn about ourselves, and about love, and what transpired before the great love of my life could finally come into it without me sabotaging that relationship too. It was such a beautiful clear day though, when I finally realized that l was no longer separate from everything anymore, but part of the great oneness, which everything is.

Like an odd piece of jig saw puzzle that was in the wrong box, I never fitted in at home, so I rather felt separate from everything and everyone. I was the youngest of six children. My oldest brother and sister were born in mum's previous marriage and then she adopted my other brother and the twins. My oldest siblings were much older than I and were busy getting on with their own lives, so I did not really get to know them when I was small. Jana and Birdie were seven years older and the three of us shared a bedroom together. They were identical twins and had their own secret relationship, so naturally I felt like the odd one out.

They say it is always easier being the baby, because you are spoilt, but that is just not the case about my childhood. At least not when your mother is dying of cancer and you don't trust your father, because of the terrible things he does to little girls when no one else is around. My happiness came from outside of myself and depended primarily on my mother's moods. For the most part, I was on edge, as if I was being trained passionately to survive, whilst being hunted down ruthlessly at the same time by a highly trained mercenary. Her treatment of me taught me to use my gut instinct, as if it was my only hope for survival. Sometimes, I was quiet and carefully watchful like a spy, as she bound my mind up in chains and tortured me as she played with it, for I was never allowed to relax and just be myself. Not ever. Over the long period of time, which was my childhood, I learnt to discover that pain was carrying me across an invisible bridge to my soul, where the journey from the core inspired me to become my own mother, encouraging the small child within to finally grow up. It was my own way of finding some peace within the violent war of my life and to actually gain a sense of control about who I really was.

My parents were strictly controlling and devoutly religious, and they used to threaten us with the wooden spoon relentlessly to keep us in a constant state of fear. My mother spoke in an irritable tone, as if she resented us most of the time, except when we were in the company of others. She never revealed to other people the real person she was with us behind closed doors. They were avid church people and my father was an Elder, so they were highly respected pillars of the community, which seemed to pose a huge contradiction to me. They demanded respect, or I would get another hiding if they thought I had looked at them the wrong way, or had spoken in the wrong tone. I learnt to live on a sea of egg shells, and if I had not become expert enough at sensing the smallest of shifts in my energetic environment long before my mother's voice was ever raised, the thrust of a wooden jam spoon quickly stung my legs again before I could say I was sorry. Hence, I became super sensitive to the invisible energy of different places and people, knowing that something else entirely was always going on underneath the facade of every day chatter.

I would have loved to have grown my hair long and worn it in a soft and feminine way like the other little girls, whilst dressing up and playing with makeup and nail polish, but my mother forbade it, and cut my hair short, right up to my ears instead so that I looked just like a little tom boy. But I never acted like a boy. Perhaps she did this, because she was aware of what my father was doing to Jana and Birdie the twins, although she never admitted it. I'd like to think in retrospect that she was trying to protect me, by trying to keep me looking asexual.

She would gather me up sometimes and sing to me,

"Claire, Claire Buchholz is no good. Chop her up for firewood. If she is no good for that, give her to the old Tom cat"!

Over and over she would sing that old song and then she would laugh and pull me up close for a peck on the cheek and tell me to run along. The melody still haunts me today, so I guess she programmed me pretty well to have low self-esteem. I ask myself over and over the question which still troubles me. Why would any mother want to treat her child like a worthless little bird locked up in a cage with its wings clipped, so that it never learns how to fly? It just seems so cruel to me now, and as I reflect upon it as a parent. I have to wonder if she was silently suffering from her own wounds to reflect such darkness to me and perhaps she was treating us the way she felt about herself.

When you are a child, it doesn't occur to you that your parents are sick, or that they are transferring their own inner fears onto your emotional map. All I knew, was that it felt like I was trapped in the pages of a wicked fairy tale. Sometimes I would simply run away from reality and into my own thoughts and dreams, where I was beautiful, and where I was adored by my beloved. I could see the world through my own self-created vision, pretending to dress up in grandma Flo's lingerie and jewels, and parading up and down the bedroom in her imaginary stockings and pearls with lipstick smudged across my mouth and lavender cologne splashed over my frock in an effort to make myself more worthy of being loved.

Whenever I was just being myself, my parents would repress me with another hiding, so it was easier to act like I was someone else. I thought this treatment was normal and I tried to do exactly what I was told, although my bruises would often prove that I failed. I pretended to be lots of other imaginary people, to try and figure out what sort of person they wanted to love instead of me, which only served to keep my creativity buzzing and flowing most of the time. My mother would often catch me sitting on the step outside the kitchen and fling the window open to find out who I was talking to. Then she would irritably tell me off, because I was only talking to myself by throwing my voice around so much in an effort to create characters of all ages and different accents. She would yell in that prickly tone of hers, which always made me jump like I was doing something wrong again.

The back door of our house led down a step onto the veranda and my father made a special little glass knob, which he placed just low enough, so that I could let myself in. I remember being rushed to go inside one day, probably just to have a pee. As my arms were busy carrying toys, I grabbed the knob with my mouth and tried to suck it open with one mighty gasp. The three inch nail attaching the knob to the door was already loose and was sucked down into my throat lodging precariously like a wobbly bullet. If I screamed for help or breathed in any further, I realized that the nail would kill me, but if I gagged like I was going to vomit, I thought that I may be able to eject it without causing too much harm to myself. The question was did I want to live or die? That little voice was quite plain to me and if I had known the difficult journey I would take in the years ahead, I wonder if my decision would still be to stay? The effort to just let go seemed to be so easy, yet I chose to fight to save my own life instead.

I would often hide in the back seat of our father's 1932 Rolls Royce, which he had immaculately restored along with his other veteran, vintage and classic cars. It was just like the one in the film, 'The Yellow Rolls Royce', and I kept it as my special place to ponder things over in, or whenever I needed to simply run away from feeling worthless and afraid and back into my own fantasy world again.

I would often sit in the back seat wondering why I was ever born and what I was meant to do here when I grew up. Nobody seemed to have a clue and I was amazed considering my mother and father knew the answers to everything else. It seemed to me that I was here to find my true love and to create beautiful music and exquisite spaces, living in peace and happiness. I remember one time imagining that I was a beautiful lady dressed in floating layers of black chiffon with seamed nylons and high heeled shoes, all wrapped up in a soft white fur coat, whilst smoking a cigarette positioned in a long silver holder. I decided to carefully apply my mother's dark red lipstick in the mirror that was inlayed into the polished woodwork at the side of the back door, and powdered my nose as well with her softest new powder puff, which I had secretly borrowed without asking her.

The imaginary chauffeur was just waiting to be told where we wanted him to drive us to, as I wound down the window that separated the front and back seats. My love and I had been sipping imaginary French champagne in tall crystal flutes, which were stored in the built-in wine cabinet, secretly hidden in the back compartment with us. We were nestled on plush cream velvet seats holding hands and entwined like a painting of rapture displayed on the ceiling of the Sistine Chapel.

"Where to my darling"? I pretended to ask in my most eloquent of English voices. We found ourselves gazing into each other's eyes, and I almost drowned in the pleasure of the electricity, pulsing through my heart and into my groins, knowing at the same time, my love was too, because I imagined his face was all flushed pink, and his eyes were flashing fearlessly with a hint of something that I could not touch with my fingers.

Suddenly Jana abruptly swung open the back door of the Rolls, saying "Come on sis, what are you doing sitting there all alone for"? She had been watching me quietly for God knows how long, before bursting into my fantasy and scaring the living daylights out of me.

"Mum's looking for you and she can't find her new red lipstick".

Well one day 'the one' and I would be together forever, I reassured myself. After all, I could dream couldn't I? He and my piano lessons were all that I had to keep me sane, and I was a woman now. I was eight years old, and I had already finished my very first period for heaven's sake.

"Into the bathroom young lady" my mother spat, as she grabbed onto one of my earlobes and dragged me across the back porch, with the wooden jam spoon banging around my bare legs as we went. They always used the bathroom to make us wait to be punished, and hit us with our panties hauled down around the ankles. I think they used this tactic to keep us vulnerable and weak, just by making us feel naked and exposed, and sometimes the embarrassment was more painful than the actual hiding. More severe punishment required the strap, and for that we had to wait in the garage for our father to come home from work, stripped right down to our undies, until he decided to deal with us.

My mother permanently set the punishment in our house, and if she wanted to pass the deed of administering it on to my father she did. He had little say in it. He simply did as he was told, and we were expected to do the same. Barely would he throw off his hat and coat after a day's work, than he would be dishing out punishment for what he had little understanding of what it was for. Then we would be sent to bed without any dinner, bottoms blazing and legs still burning from the thrashing. Our mother always said that it hurt her more than it hurt us, but we never believed her. Not in a million years. She seemed so authentic in her power over us, being the Queen of The Dark Shadow, and I was absolutely terrified of her.

If we did not grovel back and say we were sorry within a few minutes, she would hit us all over again until we were truly very sorry, for goodness knows whatever had upset her. In this case it was the lipstick and her powder puff, and I promptly apologised and told her that I would never do it again. A great flood of tears welled up and fell down my cheeks, and I prayed that she thought they were genuine and from sheer remorse, rather than from the absolute dread of enduring that pain all over again from another hiding, which was the outright truth of it instead.

It never occurred to me that they were being violent with us at the time, only that we must be bad – very bad, and that we deserved to be punished. Sometimes our bruises were so raw, that they bled and soiled the sheets, and when our pillows became so damp and covered in tears, she would storm in demanding that we all stop crying, or there would be yet another hiding. We were never allowed to cry, and I never understood what we did wrong most of the time, believing that I must be the child of the devil and would burn in hell when I died along with the twins. We were kept in that constant state of fear and worthlessness and as a consequence, the twins emotionally shut my parents out and turned to each other, whilst I turned my loathing of it all inwards and punished myself.

My childhood nightmare continued, with not being able to spontaneously throw my arms around my father, and smother him in kisses, or sit on his lap for that matter, developing a natural father daughter relationship. The shame and repulsion of him made me feel like I was the one, who had something wrong with me instead, and it was not about him at all. It may have been a blessing, if like my sisters, I simply chose to dislike my father, keeping him separate from my heart and my conscience, but the truth of the matter was far more complicated, for I was torn with a plethora of mixed feelings for him, which was intensely overwhelming. He was such a kind man and generous, which only made my belief that he was cruel to my sisters so hard to swallow. Whenever he read a bedtime story to me, I would rush with tenderness for him and then as he lent down to kiss me and give me a hug, I would suddenly be repulsed. I was the wicked one nurturing aversion for him, without ever understanding that it was my natural intuitive nature, warning me away from ever becoming physically close to him. I did not understand these contradictions and simply bashed myself up about it instead by feeling guilty most of the time.

The burden of these mixed emotions and my guilt about them slowly consumed me. On one hand the church was telling me to honour my mother and father, but on a gut level I did not know how to, which only reinforced my belief that I was bad and would go to hell when I died. What was wrong with me?

Why couldn't I be affectionate like other children to their parents? I was also ashamed of being his only flesh and blood, whilst constantly being reminded that the twins were not like me by my posh grandmother Flo, because they were adopted, and she insisted they call her Mrs. Buchholz, whilst I simply called her Grandma. I could never understand why she would always refer to them as my step sisters. To me they were my real sisters, regardless of whose blood they had.

I often heard them whispering about what our father was doing to them in secret and I would feel that it was all my fault somehow. Birdie finally plucked up enough courage to talk about it with our mother, but that trust was misplaced, for Birdie suddenly disappeared, and we were told that she had been sent away to live with the nuns. Jana and I were terrified that something dreadful had happened to her and later we discovered that she had been abused with shock treatment as punishment for telling lies about our father and was living at the nunnery indefinitely. When Jana was asked if our father was doing the same things to her, she quickly denied it, even though she told me that he was, because she was too damned scared of being sent away, imprisoned and tortured as well, poor darling.

Birdie's courage to stand up and say the truth, regardless of the consequences remains a mystery to me today. Her bravery in standing up and speaking the truth to my cruel parents puts her in the realm of a heroine and I always admired and respected her immeasurably for it. It is only through speaking opening about such things can they be stopped and dealt with.

Our mother demanded the truth, yet she was also the one teaching us all how to blatantly lie through our teeth by creating so much fear of the consequences if we were to be honest. Hence, the sharp edge of her axe continued chopping us all up into little pieces of firewood so to speak, leaving us all with wounds so deep that they bled for many years of our lives. I do not know how the others managed, because we all literally fled from each other as soon as the opportunity arose, but my own survival depended on learning how to love and value myself back into a state of continuous healing, regardless of her mind control. My wounds still bleed sometimes, just when I think they have finally healed, I suddenly burst into tears for no apparent reason and I wonder if the others have similar post traumatic symptoms too.

My mother never asked me if he ever touched me like that, or mentioned anything sinister about my father at all. She was already programming me to believe that he should be placed high up on a pedestal, being the Elder of the church and a thoroughly decent man. Who the hell was I to question my own parent's word on the matter for goodness sake? For a very long time I didn't. My parents' mind-control over me was so powerful that I constantly felt worthless and small. Speaking up never crossed my mind, for my spirit had already been crushed.

After Birdie came home from the nunnery, my parents referred to her as being a psychopath and tried to turn the rest of us against her. She had come home without a lot of her memory, and she naturally seemed really quiet too. It took me many years to realize that my mother's denial of what my father was doing meant that she did not have to change anything about herself. She could simply point the finger away from the truth, labelling Birdie a 'liar' and continue being passive aggressive towards us all. She epitomized a great dark energetic archetype, pouring out her wrath upon us in an effort to protect her own denial, without having to leave her marriage.

All I could do at the age of ten, was to learn to be like my mother and hide in the dark shadows of the feminine psyche by denying the truth and pretending that everything was wonderful. I was frozen with fear. I simply did not know how to face the demon and I believed it was all my fault that everyone was so unhappy anyway, which was a very heavy burden for a child to carry without being able to openly talk about it to anyone.

To help me survive, I would run away, dreaming that I could fly to 'the one'. Nearly every night, I would drift up into a swirling mist and effortlessly move my body against gravity to astral travel to him. I would soar above the chimneys and rooftops to a place far away, where snow covered fields like icing on a Christmas cake and where my true love waited for me on a splendid white horse, amongst the ruins of an ancient castle. I dreamt of being surrounded by the colour of winter, where everything was simply black and white and ever so pure and simple. Layers and layers of white chiffon wrapped me up like a present for him, as I floated with the wind above a rocky cliff overlooking the wild ocean. No matter how many times I went there in my dreams though, I could never see his face, or know his name, yet I knew his soul and could sense how it felt to be close to him. We would fly amongst the seagulls in the moonlight, as they ascended above the sea, their cries reminding me that it was time to return to the reality of my life again. That fog would curl around my heart like a magic spell and I would be carried by a silver thread of moonbeam back to my bed again. The sadness would anchor me back to earth when I awoke, because I had returned to the nightmare of my life. Every night, I would will myself to go back to where the dream had left off, but it never did, until the present day that is, where the dream continues as my actual life here in England with him instead.

The first time Mark took me to Tintagel Castle, the ruins seemed so desolate and eerie, as the wind howled around us and a mysterious mist, which could have been cast by an ancient medieval spell, seemed to crawl up from the sea out of Merlin the magician's cave below. When Mark gathered a bunch of wild flowers that he had picked for me and placed them into my hand, I realized in a moment of awe, that this was the place I had astral travelled to in my dreams when I was just a child long ago, and that I was staring right back into the beautiful face that I could never picture, but could always remember the feeling of so perfectly well somehow.

Other children did not seem interested in romance at all. Perhaps they were just happy children, being light hearted and having fun and just being themselves. They seemed more allergic to the opposite sex, than attracted to each other, like they had leprosy or something. Everyone that is, except Kerrie Smith, the prettiest girl I knew. Kerrie liked boys a lot, and boys liked her back. She was so popular with them, that I was completely mesmerized by it. I wondered what she had going for her to attract so much attention from them, besides the confidence that almost blinded you that is, because she sparkled so much with it, and she also had that bewitching ability to hold direct eye contact with any boy she wanted to for at least ten seconds, without going red in the face. I would rather die, before I would have the nerve to do something as terrifying as that.

I first met her at kindergarten, where we were buzzing with excitement, because Patty Bugsby had invited all the children, including the boys to her fifth Birthday party. Everyone that is, except Kerrie Smith. Perhaps Patty was jealous that Kerrie was so popular and did not want her to come, but whatever the reason, Kerrie was not happy about it, and so she gathered up all of the invitations and hid them inside her bag. If Kerrie wasn't going, none of us were going. As we assembled on the navy blue floor mats, with crossed legs and straight backs, gazing up at the teacher, we watched in silence to see how she was going to find the infamous 'Birthday Invitation Snatcher'.

"The person who stole Patty Bugsby's birthday invitations only has nine fingers" she said quietly.

Everyone was silent except for Kerrie, indignantly counting her fingers out aloud one by one, because she was sure that the teacher was mistaken.

That is how Kerrie earned the reputation of being queen bee amongst the bad girls and I secretly admired her, wishing that I simply had the guts to do whatever I wanted to as well. My mother soon heard about her, after gossiping to Mrs Bugsby down the hill, and was somewhat unsettled that Kerrie was also in my first class at school, remaining there for the duration of my entire primary school years also. She forbade me from socializing with her out of school hours, because she was afraid of her powerful influence over me.

At least when I was at school, my mother was out of earshot and I could be more of myself. One day after art class, Kerrie and I were selected to clean up all of the dirty paint brushes down at the troughs behind the shelter sheds.

We weren't best friends, because I was too much of a goodie goodie and she was too popular to hang out with me, so I was really surprised when she shared her deepest secret with me, confiding that her grandfather regularly did sexually inappropriate things to her when she was just three years old. My body stiffened and I suddenly had the courage to tell her about what my father was supposedly doing to the twins. She seethed with anger and her eyes flashed with the same feeling I was having also. "Fucking bastard"!

"Yeah. Bloody bastard" I hissed, trying to mimic her passion and distaste.

"Say 'fuck' Claire", she urged, as the red paint swirled around the bottom of the trough and mixed with all of the other shades creating a sludgy brown mess.

"ffff………….uck", I spat, trying earnestly to say the "uck", with the smallest emphasis as I could muster, letting the air waft loosely out over the obscenity.

"No!! Say FUCK!" continued Kerrie with so much verve, she made me start laughing really hard and it felt so good.

But no matter how much I tried, the word never sounded the way Kerrie made it sound, and she accused me of just being too ladylike. We laughed about it for ages, until one day, I mastered it enough to be my favourite word in the dictionary, whenever I needed to vent.

There was a kind of mutual respect between us after that day and Kerrie decided we should become blood sisters. So, one afternoon out in the school yard we bravely pricked our thumbs with a safety pin that Kerrie unhooked from her hem and then she mixed our blood together whilst chanting, "Blood sisters forever". She was dancing around like a primitive savage until half the school had gathered around us, thinking we were both bonkers.

"Yeah blood sisters forever". I mimicked bashfully, wondering what the hell I was getting myself in for.

Every Saturday we played basketball in the winter and softball in the summertime together, which was far away from my mother's eagle eye and ear shot. Whenever I arrived home, she would always cross examine me though. Her deep blue ocean eyes would chop me up all over again, and I would attempt to soften her with an affectionate cuddle. That was my way of disarming her, for I was discovering my own 'Dark Shadow Feminine' emerging and I was becoming expert at emotional manipulation. I thought I might push the boundaries and attempt to make her feel sorry for Kerrie, by whispering the story she had told me about her grandfather.

As with Birdie, my trust in her was misplaced. Taking out her compact, my mother slowly powdered her nose in an obvious effort to calm herself. I watched her close the compact with a snap and then she closed her eyes and shuddered, as if she had just heard a demon snicker, as he watched her silently squirm from the darkness.

3 - ACROSS THE ROOFTOPS

Mark:

England, 5th of August 910AD, the Anglo Saxons defeated the Danes in the Battle of Wodensfield, a major turning point in British history leading to the Vikings withdrawing from Britain. Wodensfield is today called Wednesfield, a rough working class village in Wolverhampton, and is where I grew up.

In the heart of the Black Country, the birthplace of the industrial revolution, the heavy steel industry sprawled out in every direction, to the tune of the clanging of metal beating on metal, and thick grey choking smoke clinging to the air in a perpetual haze. It seemed like it was always raining, and dark and drab. But it all depends how you look at it, even grey comes in a rainbow of different shades, and I grew up to love my roots, the rain, the greyness, and still do. I love the wind on my face, and while others complain, I love the freezing cold weather, the snow and the ice, but then, I was also always very much the black sheep of my family.

'Out of Darkness Cometh Light' is the motto of my home town of Wolverhampton, and little did I realise just how prophetic those words were later going to turn out to be. It was December and the final days of the conservative and classy 1950s. The refined and respectful sophistication of the prior decades, along with values like integrity and honesty were all about to come to an abrupt end, and disappear into the past forever. Society would be stretched to opposite ends of the spectrum, often replaced with grunge and 'whatever' attitudes, ruthless commercialism and profit orientated economics, behaviours repeatedly refined and exploited over the decades right up to today.

I was brought up from an early age to be a quiet boy and not to speak until spoken to, to be a wall flower, a grey person, seen but not heard. I was conditioned to be polite in the extreme, to always to say please and thank you, open doors for adults, and to naturally give up my seat on the bus to women or elderly people. I was disciplined to be a boring background person, to keep quiet and out of everyone else's way, and I excelled at it. Hence, I grew up without any social or conversational skills and throughout my childhood would blush bright red as soon as anyone tried to talk to me in even the simplest of conversations, and unable to talk back. I thought that's how all children were raised and never questioned it. I compensated for being socially inept by becoming a good listener, and a thinker. I seldom missed or forgot anything others talked about as a result. Instead of spending my time talking, I would spend it processing what others were saying or doing, their motives behind it and the effects of it on others.

My favourite word was always 'why?' I wanted to understand everything. How do the television pictures get to the television? Through signals in the air, yes, but how - it's just air? Why doesn't a ship made of steel just sink? Why does water boil? Why? Why? Why? My parents quickly grew tired of it and from an early age I would soon get the same blank response from them… "Zed".

I would often ask what 'Zed' meant, but they wouldn't ever tell me. Eventually I realised it just meant, 'shut up and stop asking' and used to infuriate me. I stopped asking and would sit and try and work out the answers for myself.

At home if we did something wrong, it would be the wooden spoon, a slap of a hand, or worst of all, the cane around our legs. If we were really in trouble, my dad would do the slapping and it would hurt like hell. I seemed to have a habit of doing or saying the wrong thing and frequently in trouble. There would always be a rack with two or three canes in, kept within easy reach, and after a few hidings, the canes would start to split. If a split one was used, it would also nip at your skin as it made contact, biting into your leg as it left, making it all the more painful. One day I remember merely saying the word "damn", and was promptly dragged into the bathroom and a bar of soap was shoved in my mouth to wash it out for swearing, and it wasn't the only occasion. How things have changed within just half a lifetime.

I loved football. It's in my blood. My dad started taking me to see the matches at Wolverhampton Wanderers when I was six years old. My pocket money each week was always two shillings, and the admission price to matches just happened to be two shillings as well. I would be made to make a choice: either keep my pocket money to spend how I wished, or use it to pay for my admission to the match. It was a big choice for a six year old to make, but also an easy one, because I loved going to watch the Wolves. It was purely miraculous that the very week the admission price went up to two shillings and sixpence, my pocket money went up to two shillings and sixpence as well.

Back then sitting down was only for the rich. We would stand on the barren terraces on cold concrete steps, with only the odd steel bar to lean on, in the midst of the black and grey sea of overcoats of the grown up men. I would have to take a wooden box to stand on so I could see the game and we would have to be there hours beforehand to get a good spot. The men on the terraces would always make room for the youngsters, welcoming us in as one of their own, as if being initiated into a special brotherhood. In the cold, drab, grey air of winter, it would be two hours of standing on frozen icy concrete steps holding onto cold steel bars, with my hands and feet going numb from the cold, in the snow, sleet or rain. If I was lucky we'd get a hot cup of Bovril at half time to thaw the blood out. We all loved it, men would moan and complain and groan, but it would always end with "see you next match" and we would all be back for more.

At school, I noticed how some kids were pushy, always taking advantage of other kids with a quieter disposition, to get what they wanted. They would be the first to speak up and not afraid of a confrontation to selfishly argue for what they wanted if challenged. The rest of us would get out of their way, or be pushed aside. Having been brought up to always think of others first, it felt like they were another species to me. It seems the ego starts early in life and they were already on their journey to becoming the 'takers' in this world, and the rest of us the 'givers'. It's always intrigued me how those personal traits and idiosyncrasies start so early on in life, and go on to become more and more deeply rooted throughout growing up. Freud calls it the 'id', that part of our consciousness that is all about getting what we want. Is it something genetic we are born with, or a behaviour we learn? Maybe it is a ticking time bomb we bring with us, programmed from birth, that one day will blow up and force us to finally face up to and discover empathy?

Whenever I stumbled across the laundry basket with something nylon sitting on top of it, particularly nylon stockings, I would be drawn mesmerizingly towards them, as if pulled in by some cosmic tractor beam. I was unable to resist touching and feeling that glassy smoothness and the unique and delicious smell that it had all of its own. It was as though there was something programmed deeply into me about it, but I did not know what. At the mere age of only five or six, there was absolutely nothing sexual about it at all. Well, nothing I knew of or understood consciously at the time. Freud might disagree. Decades later, I would discover how it would play its own special part in meeting 'the one', as if we had both brought our own secret keys with us into this life, to one day help instantly unlock the door to each other.

I always felt there was something really important about girls. I was mesmerised by them from a young age while all the other boys at school did not really seem interested in them at all. Girls gave me a rush of excitement and I felt constantly drawn to them, but not just any. I was always evaluating which ones I was attracted to, as if I was looking for someone specific without even realising it. At that age, there was nothing sexual about it, consciously, for me anyway. Freud might disagree with that as well. I had no idea sex even existed, for back then it stayed unspoken about until you were old enough to be told by an adult, unlike today.

Occasionally the other lads might show some curiosity with girls just long enough to flirt with them and get a quick kiss, only then to instantly loose interest. They would be straight back with the other boys gloating and laughing their heads off at their conquest and no longer interested, another male adult trait that starts very early in life. Or is it a childish one that lasts into adulthood? It was not a kiss I wanted though, I wanted more. It was as though I was looking for something and someone special, as if it had been programmed into me from the very beginning and I was on a quest to seek her out. I didn't know who she was, but it was as if I would recognise her when I found her.

Crazy things happened to me in my childhood. One day my dad dazzled us one day with a magic trick, putting a piece of foam under his handkerchief and making it disappear, 'abracadabra', only to re-appear in his hand from behind my ear, or somewhere. In the end he showed us his slight of hand, and after he left I tried it by myself. I put the foam under the handkerchief said 'abracadabra' and lifted the handkerchief up and it was gone! That's not how it worked, so where was it? I looked everywhere and eventually found it in one of my pockets, and I know I didn't put it there. Magic does happen.

I remember constantly feeling as though I had a white ribbed transparent tube coming out of my lower back, like the flexible tube on a vacuum cleaner, only thinner, white and transparent. If I ever became aware that I had turned through 360 degrees somehow, such as by walking right around a table, I would feel absolutely compelled to turn 360 degrees the opposite way, to 'unwrap' it as soon as I could. No one knew what I was doing, or ever noticed, nor did I ever tell anyone for fear of ridicule as even I realised how stupid it was. Eventually around the age of seven or eight I forgot all about it… until adulthood. I was also obsessed by 3. Things had to be in 3's, and then groups of 3's. At times I thought I was just nuts.

At night I would have the same recurring dream, over and over. After going to bed and falling asleep, I would wake up and find myself floating up above the roof of our house in the darkness, feeling lighter than a feather, looking back down at the roof tiles below. It was surreal, as if I was a spectator in some wild LSD induced hallucinogenic dream I had no control over.

Slowly, I would start to float off, head first and face down and always in the same direction. I can still to this day clearly remember looking down from high up and vividly seeing our back garden pass underneath me, as I silently glided through the darkness of night and headed off over the back fences. Once I crossed over the gardens at the back and over the roofs of the houses behind ours, I would float onwards into the darkness… and then nothing, for at just at that point, my memory would go completely blank. Always.

The next thing I would remember would be returning back over the roof tops later in the night towards our house, always from exactly the same direction I had left. Once I remember returning with chocolate bars stuffed in the pockets for some bizarre reason, and I was usually alone when I returned, but not always. As an adult my mother commented a number of times how they used to wonder where I got all the chocolate bars from when I was a child and how they would find them hidden all over the house, and I would wonder too. As I reached the roof above my bedroom I would stop for a moment, look down barely making out the roof below in the darkness, before whooshhhh, I would be back in bed, briefly wake up, look around my bedroom and fall instantly back to sleep again.

It was a dream that I had over and over, but it never felt like it was a nightmare, for I was never scared. It seemed something very natural and familiar to me and I remember being perfectly at ease with it, whenever it happened, which was frequently.

At the age of ten, just as life was sedately chugging along in an average kind of English suburban working class way, my dad suddenly decided to uproot us all and migrate to Australia on the other side of the planet. It had never been mentioned before and came like a bolt of lightning.

We were soon sitting in an office in Birmingham in front of a man from Australia, being interviewed about going to live there. I remember him leaning over his desk and asking,

"So why do you want to come to live in Australia?" My dad started to answer and the man immediately interrupted him and said,

"No. I'm asking your children. They're who we want".

Back then, children were not asked. Your parents (that is, father) did what he wanted, and you were told what was going to happen and you just went along with it, and that was that. There was none of this "we can't move because of Jimmy's schooling" you hear all the time today. If your parents wanted to move, you changed schools. At the interview we said what we had to, knowing it was what my dad wanted. I didn't want to go, and back home as meekly as I dared, said so. In return I just received that parental blank look back and was otherwise completely ignored. My opinion didn't matter. There was no discussion, we were going, and so was I. We became 'ten pound Poms,' as it cost £10 per adult to go, with the four children free, and were soon booked on a ship.

Before we knew it, the day approached to leave and for the final couple of weeks we went to stay with my Grandparents in Castlecroft, a leafy part of town. Every so often, someone in the house would openly burst into tears and we children would look on somewhat bemused, not really understanding the gravity of what we were about to do. In 1970 air travel was only for the rich and we were going on a five week long ship voyage to the other side of the planet. As far as my grandparents knew, they would never see us again.

On a sombre winter's day in February 1970, we set off, boarding the train at Wolverhampton railway station at the crack of dawn, heading for the Boat Train to Southampton docks. There were so many people emigrating then that they ran special trains direct to the docks. We found out years later that after seeing us off, both pairs of Grandparents sat on the platform for two hours crying their hearts out, believing they would never see us again. To them, they were saying goodbye to us forever, their own children and their four young grandchildren off to the other side of the world, never to be seen again. It must have been a horrific experience for them, and I still think about it.

After travelling all day, late on a grey drizzly afternoon the boat train finally pulled into the sheds at Southampton docks. We got off, were walked through a shed and straight up a gang plank and into the small dark hole in the middle of a massive white wall of steel, otherwise known as the Sitmar liner, Fairsky.

We did not even get a chance to see what the ship looked like from the shore. It was just a blur and we were on board before we even realised it. I had never even seen a ship before and had spent the last couple of months annoying everyone asking how big a liner really was? No one could explain it other than saying 'huge', and it had been burning away at me for weeks about just how big 'huge' actually was? Now I knew.

Before we had a chance to even get back up on deck, we could feel the ship moving. We raced back up just as we left the wharf and slowly sailed off down the Solent. I still remember standing on the back deck, watching England, my only home, disappear into the lovely grey drizzling rain, heading for a land we knew nothing of, wondering where we were going and what lay ahead. It was surreal. Nearly all of the passengers on board were migrants, new world settlers heading off into the unknown, leaving family, friends and all they had ever known behind them, for an unknown land on the other side of the planet. It was like being at a wake for a funeral, people standing there in a drab sombre silence, in family groups looking dazed, numb, quiet, some openly sobbing, watching our beloved England slowly fade away. The only home we had ever known, our culture, our people, families, fading slowly away into the grey mist.

During the first afternoon on board as we headed down the English Channel and out of English waters, we wondered what all the flat paper bags hanging over handrails in lobbies and on stairwells were for? What a strange thing to do we thought, as people started asking each other what they were for? By the next morning, we found out. After a rough crossing of the Bay of Biscay during the night, people were coming up from their cabins and suddenly grabbing for the paper bags on the handrails, hastily burying their faces into them, before hurriedly heading straight back down to their cabins again. Okay. So that's what they are for, and it wasn't long before I was reaching for one too.

We stopped at Las Palmas and then sailed down the west coast of Africa and through the Doldrums, where there was no wind and the sea was flat like shimmering glass as far as you could see. We would watch the wake behind the ship ripple right out to the horizon on either side in perfect symmetry. We would watch the garbage bags constantly thrown over the side, drift off into the distance, and we would watch the raw sewerage come out of pipes low down on the side of the ship just above the waterline.

"I wonder who did that one?" we would ask each other as we turned around and looked at the adults sitting on the deck, trying to match them off, as kids do.

We could regularly see flying fish rising out from under the bow, and sharks zig zagging back and forth following the ship, and the occasional whale.

There were three meals a day on board and if we missed any of them, we went without, as you couldn't get food from anywhere else on the ship. A couple of times, we went to the dining rooms and noticed the white tablecloths were strangely all wet, and assumed someone before us must have spilt something. Then during one meal, the waiter came over and picked up the water jug and much to our surprise, calmly poured it all over the table, explaining there was some rough weather on the way and it helped stop the crockery from sliding off and onto the floor. Now we knew. When the rough weather did arrive and the ship rolled from side to side, as we looked over to the lower side the restaurant windows would go underwater, and it would be the sky and clouds out of the other side, then as it rolled back the other way the other side's portholes would then go under water. People would quickly lose their appetite and hastily leave.

There were no shops on board like there are today, we eventually discovered the only food you could buy in between meal times was fruit cake from the bar, but only adults could go in the bars to get it. There was also a tiny room on deck, more akin to a broom cupboard, which would open at 1:30PM every day for an hour and sold a few hygiene related necessities, some toys and trinkets and more importantly, chocolate. People would be queuing for ages before it opened each day to get their hands on a much sought after bar of chocolate.

Every few days, one of the other boys' parents would buy them a plastic football from the broom cupboard shop and word would go around that a game was on. Before long, a big mob of excited boys would gather on the children's deck at the back of the ship. We would pick teams and play for hours around the kiddies swimming pool, around the playground items and the many support poles. Full time would always be, when sadly but inevitably, someone would kick the ball overboard, and we would all race to the railings and watch as the bright bobbing orange plastic ball would slowly drift off in the ship's wake behind us, and eventually completely out of view. We would all give whoever kicked it overboard a glare, and then dejectedly slowly head off in separate directions… until word went around that someone had been able to talk their parents into buying another ball, and we would all excitedly race down to the back deck and another match would soon be on.

After leaving Cape Town and a very rough night rounding the Cape of Good Hope, we set off across the Indian Ocean, next stop being this Australia place. A couple of days out, a passenger fell overboard. It was 1AM and as the ship swung around and went into a search pattern, everyone was immediately ordered back to their cabins over the tannoy, as the crew began a roll call to identify who it was by a process of elimination. The stewards knocked on every cabin to take a roll and account for who was and wasn't there, and the names of those not in their cabins were soon being called out over the ships tannoy, until they eventually responded. The entire ship was woken up by the loud announcements which continued for hours throughout the night. Eventually, one name was being called out over and over and obviously wasn't responding, then it just went quiet.

The ship carried out the compulsory six hour search required by international maritime law. We could feel it sharply turning left and right as it executed a search pattern, sweeping the dark seas with search lights and any other light they could turn on it, but he was gone. He was ex-Royal Navy and a strong swimmer so they thought he might have had a chance. However, when you fall overboard in the middle of the night, just in front of churning propellers, with sharks always following not far behind, in the middle of the Indian Ocean thousands of miles from land, and have also been drinking heavily, the odds really aren't very good. It was a sobering reminder to us all that you do not have much chance surviving if you went over the side, and death was always only a couple of steps away, just over those railings. The thought of bobbing away in the middle of the ocean in the blackness of night and surviving, watching the lights of your ship slowly disappear off into the distance leaving you floating in complete blackness all alone, was utterly terrifying. The search was called off after six hours and we sailed on.

The next day, the atmosphere around the ship was very subdued. At midday, the ship slowed and did a full 360 degree circle, as we all watched his shocked wife and four children throw a hastily assembled wreath overboard onto the sea. The on board photographer tried to photograph it, like everything else that moved and he might be able to make a quid out of, until the Captain ran screaming at him to go away. A man, a husband, a father, a son was dead and gone forever. A wife was suddenly a widow, and his four children now fatherless. This time yesterday he was walking around the ship and none of them would have ever thought that he would be gone forever in less than twenty four hours. It was a sombre reminder that death could always be just around the corner for any of us.

Further on across the Indian Ocean a hurricane raged, so we had to divert south to go around it. We headed further and further south, far out of the normal shipping lanes, and passed by a remote uninhabited island called the Isle of St Paul in a desolate area of the southern Indian Ocean. Even today, I often notice that it is not on a lot of maps and keep it in the back of my mind as being a place to run away to.

We passed three fishing boats and the Captain's voice from the bridge of the Fairsky came over the tannoy announcing that we were sounding the fog horn to salute the brave fishermen, who every year travelled all the way from Japan to fish there.

"Brrrr. Brrrr. Brrrr".

No response. The Captain said that they should normally reply and wondered why they had not? We soon wondered if it was due to the long v-shaped line of bright orange buoys, trailing behind either side of us, as we swept one of their fishing nets away with us.

We finally reached Australia and docked in Freemantle and were greeted by the biggest brightest blue skies and most brilliant sunlight I had ever seen. A few more days sailing and late at night, we finally cruised in towards our final destination, Adelaide, in South Australia. It looked barren and desolate in the darkness, as we slowly sailed up the Gulf of St Vincent closer and closer in to land, with yellow street lights illuminating miles of huge pine trees. Soon the aroma of smelly seaweed on the foreshore reached us, and we could see rusty old wharf sheds, and a railway station with train carriages you would more likely see in an old Wild West cowboy movie. I heard one man nearby say "I'm glad we're not getting off here", as he turned away with a wince.

By the time I had gone to bed and closed my eyes, I was already dreaming of a new adventure in a new world, which was waiting for us all in the dawn of the new day.

4 – BIG BLUE

Mark:

We had left England in the cold depths of winter, but here in the Southern Hemisphere it was mid-summer. Australia was like nothing we had ever seen before. Everyday there were big blue skies, brilliant blue, without a single cloud in sight all day. The ground was dry and dusty and the faded grass brittle from the blistering heat. It was like standing in an oven and under a giant spotlight at the same time. Being so open and spread out gave it an unfamiliar feeling compared to cramped built up towns and narrow streets I was used to back in England, with wide roads, some up to twelve lanes side by side, and open skyline views to beautiful hills or the crystal clear sparkling blue sea. In the barmy warm evenings the chirping of thousands of crickets would echo everywhere, and we would try and acclimatise with bottles of ice cold soft drink and ice cream.

We had only been there about three days, when my dad left us in the parklands while he went into the city to the bank. My mom asked an elderly lady if we could sit on the park bench next to her. After sitting down she turned and said, "Are you Poms?" My mom replied with a smile, "From England? Yes", gleefully thinking it might be her first conversation with a local. The lady retorted, "We've enough of your sort over here already" as she turned the other way, abruptly terminating any conversation. We wondered what we had done, and why we were not welcome. It was our initiation into how it felt to be an immigrant.

There were creepy crawlies and insects everywhere, like nothing I had ever seen before. It seemed everywhere you looked closely, there would be something alive and crawling along, and we were warned some were dangerous and not to touch any. Everything seemed to either swarm, be big, scary, or poisonous, and then there were the reptiles.

Walking along paths sometimes we would often hear something moving in the dry grass nearby. We would stop and listen, looking at each other with bulging eyes as we could clearly hear something slithering along, and then we would take off scurrying along as fast as we could. My parents bought a small house in Para Hills West, and whilst viewing it one day, as usual we kids were made to wait outside at the front. As we waited I suddenly saw a snake appear from around the side of the house and slither along the front and up onto and across the front door step. I went inside and called my parents and the agent out. My sister was holding the pushchair with my youngest brother in at the top of the sloping driveway and when she saw the snake she screamed and for some reason let go of the pushchair. We all watched as the pushchair rolled down the drive in slow motion straight towards the snake, until someone rushed over and grabbed hold of it at the last minute. We had only just got here and were coming face to face with snakes already.

After we eventually moved in, we would regularly go and play in a small gully which was about twenty foot deep and fifty foot wide, with thick leafy bushes along the bottom. We would play crawling across a thick iron pipe straddling it. It was only two doors up from our house so we thought it would be ok. When mom got to know the Aussie neighbour who lived in the house right next door to the gully, she pointed out that the gully was infested with deadly Tiger snakes and had wondered whose children had been playing in there. We were promptly banned from going back. You always had to be on the watch out for snakes, neighbours would find them in garden sheds or wrapped around children's bikes, even indoors in children's toy boxes and curled up in toilets.

The family evenings at home were just about watching whatever my dad chose on television, and boring. The only excitement was if a liner was at Outer Harbour, in which case we would all pile in the car and drive out to see it. In those days they would often let you on board, so we were able to go onboard many different liners. One night he offered to teach me to play chess. I was only about ten or eleven years old at the time so it wasn't in any stretch of the imagination an even game. We would play every evening after tea and as much as I improved, he always beat me. Always. He would never pretend to let me win the odd game to give me some encouragement or confidence, he would grind me into the ground every game. Regardless, I never gave in and became even more determined to one day win a game, but I never did.

A work colleague of my dad's was into all sorts of 'alternative ideas'. He insisted he had seen a UFO land in a field about 400ft away from him over in Western Australia, and said he was so close to it he could see occupants inside through portholes. My dad said he was a fruit cake and it had done something to his mind. He was searching for answers and each month would read a huge amount of paranormal type books. He would then give my dad a small cardboard box full of books he had read, hoping my dad would read them too. My dad wasn't interested, he would accept them out of courtesy and just dump them in the laundry outside on top of last month's box.

One night Eric von Daniken's 'Chariots of the Gods' was on television and I watched it utterly spellbound as it tore my perception of what our true origins might be apart and opened my mind right up. Maybe much more really has gone on in our history than we are taught at school? I started to wonder if things are being kept from us, intentionally hidden, or by denial, and if it's up to us to find the real truths. I suddenly felt a desire to start reading and went outside to the boxes of books and looked through them. I wasn't interested in all the satanic or paranormal ones, but wanted to know more about ancient history, UFOs, and aliens. Each month I would go through the new box and pull out all the interesting ones, and devour them. I soon started to open up to other possibilities about the universe, life and why we are here. An open mind is always the first step to progress.

Things were deteriorating domestically with my parents, they were fighting and having regular rows, screaming and shouting at each other. My dad would blow his fuse and some nights would violently throw all the saucepans that were cooking on the stove against the wall and then storm out until the early hours. Mashed potatoes and peas would be left stuck all across the blue kitchen wall, looking like fluffy white clouds floating across the sky, as they bled brown with gravy running down. We kids would just sit there in silent disbelief, absolutely terrified.

Every night for the following couple of weeks he would work late, or just stay out, creeping in well after 11PM, long after he knew everyone else would be in bed, but I would lie awake until I heard him. I remember my mom confiding in me that she was afraid he was seeing someone else when she found black tights that weren't hers in the glovebox of the car, but he just told her he bought them for straining paint. I was terrified at the thought of them separating or divorcing and can empathise with how children must feel when their parent's relationship starts to fall apart. It is always earth shattering to them, but often they just don't say anything.

We were always scared of his volatile temper and if we did anything wrong, our mother would always use him as her ultimate threat, saying that she would tell him about us when he got home if we didn't do as we were told. That usually did the trick. Putting fear into peoples' minds with just words is such a powerful weapon.

My father was a total introvert, which explained why I had been brought up that way. There was no socialising or parties, or ways of learning how to talk to people who weren't family. They would get invited to a neighbours party, and my mother would be excited about it for weeks, but by the time the evening came he would always find an excuse to not go, so nor would she, and we would see her face drop in disappointment. He was only ever focussed on what he wanted to do and everybody else had to just follow along. I can't ever remember receiving any affection, or loving, from him. I couldn't ever talk to him about life, or anything personal, or emotional. It was sad really. There were no hugs, or praise or any encouragement and the only connection we ever had was football. Instead it forced me to become emotionally independent from a young age, but sometimes it would have been nice to have at least known that he loved me as much as I loved him, and that he cared. But if he did, he never showed it, and never has.

It seemed I could never do anything right by him and he was always looking for me to slip up, which I seemed to do all too often. One small example was the night he bought a rare treat from across the road at the shops, a box of After Eight dinner mints, and we were allowed exactly one each. The next night when he came home from work he was furious, in a rage insisting someone had stolen some, and as always, he was adamant it was me. To prove he was right, he went over to the shop and bought another box to compare it with. As he counted the contents of the two boxes out, I stood there terrified of them not matching, but he discovered that there weren't any missing at all, and stormed off and hid in his bedroom the rest of the day, furious with himself for being wrong. But there was no apology for being incorrectly accused or the terror he put me through.

Each day I would go off to school and be given exactly 23 cents to buy a 23c pie for lunch, but I would often see my sister walking around at lunchtime with a 23c pie, a cake, a drink and sweets, or an ice lolly in the sweltering heat. She told me one day that mom would wait until I had left with my 23c, and then she would give her a $1 most days. It used to hurt and left me wondering what I had done wrong, but I never said anything or complained.

Three years flew by and soon we were back on another ship, the 'Ellinis', sailing out of Melbourne bound for England. I can't even remember why my parents decided to go back to England, my dad just decided, as usual, but this time there were no complaints from me. We had a cabin on the lowest deck at the back, below sea level and right above a propeller shaft. The entire cabin shook violently and it was like living in an industrial sieve twenty four hours a day, every day, for five weeks. We had dozens of little folded up bits of paper squeezed behind mirrors, door frames, cupboards, anywhere, to try and stop things from shaking, rattling and reduce the noise. It was so bad, that my father blew his top one night and dragged one of the medical officers into the cabin at 3AM and told him to come in, shut up, and listen, and asked him how we were supposed to sleep in the racket? The medical officer immediately authorised unlimited sedatives for all of us for the rest of the voyage.

This wasn't a migrant trip, so there was no school. Although I was only thirteen years old I spent all my daytimes on the outside decks alone and usually up on the top at the front, watching ships pass us and the forever changing weather and sea for hours and hours on end. It was just too good to miss, so I was out there every day in all weather, experiencing every bit of it that I could.

After stopping in Sydney we set sail off across the Pacific, stopping at Auckland, circling the outer edge of a hurricane and then off across the vast blue Pacific Ocean towards Tahiti. I'll never forget Tahiti, but for all the wrong reasons. My dad said I could pop back on board to post some postcards which must have took a mere two minutes. As I came back down the gang plank, he was coming up after me, absolutely livid with anger and face red with rage, the veins twitching in his forehead, and spitting his words as he shouted at me for holding him up. He slapped me around the face so hard that the crack rang out right across the docks and everyone on the dockside below turned and stared up at us. The rest of the day I withdrew into a state of isolation and silence, my face half red and stinging.

After stopping at Acapulco, then passing through the Panama Canal, we sailed to New York. Up the Hudson River we pushed through huge slabs of two foot thick ice, grating along the steel hull, as they gouged paint off the side of the ship. Leaving New York we headed off to cross the North Atlantic in mid-winter, not realising what was waiting for us out at sea.

The next day as soon as we awoke, we could feel the ship being thrown around by a raging North Atlantic outside. When we walked outside on deck we literally looked up at the tops of the massive waves roaring past, being driven by a ferocious wind as a gale raged all around. The waves were just enormous. They rolled past relentlessly one after the other, hour after hour, all day and all night, each one hitting us like a steam train slamming into the side of the ship, and frequently as loud, pushing us right over each time. The frothing white wave tops were being whipped off into spray and sand blasted the ship, as it heaved violently from side to side and simultaneously ploughed up and down. We endured going over each passing wave that rolled underneath us, each a micro journey in its own right, as it threw us from one side to the other side, and then up and over and down. It was absolutely terrifying. The wind screamed around the ship, turning the heavy external doors into guillotines, which would easily amputate a foot.

It was announced we were in a force 10 gale, and before long, all of the decks were closed off and no-one was allowed outside. Ropes appeared across all of the foyers and you had to hang on to them, or a wall, to be able to walk anywhere. At times you actually could not walk across an open space without being thrown to the floor. Walking down the corridor, I would be thrown against the left wall, and then against the right wall, against the left and then the right, all the while, going up and down at the same time. A lot of people just gave up and stayed in bed in their cabins all day, it was easier than trying to walk anywhere. One crew member told us that the ship was currently rolling at 18 degrees, which didn't sound like a lot, until you try and stand on it. 18 degrees to the left and then 18 degrees to the right, meant it was going back and forth 36 degrees each time. He then told us that 19.5 degrees was the ships limit, after which it would just roll right over. Something we would have probably been better off not knowing until later.

The storm went on for four days, and there were people with terrified looks everywhere you went. You could see some people actually mumbling away prayers under their breath. We all would have done anything to get off at that point, but there was no going back. One day as we were sitting in the main ballroom with a few hundred other passengers waiting for bingo, the only entertainment not cancelled, the ship seemed to roll a bit further than usual and just hung there, and I could hear people gasp waiting for it to start to come back. It hung and hung and hung. Suddenly the entire contents of the main lounge gave way and everything and everyone slid right across the floor. I remember my father just saying "this is it", as we clung on tightly to our lounge chairs as they slid right across the floor, just like in one of those old black and white liner disaster movies, crashing into the port wall with everyone else, thinking we were about to die. There were tables, chairs, two or three hundred people and all the carpets they had all been on, piled up against one wall. We only slid from the centre to the side, which was bad enough, but others had slid from the opposite side all the way across. The ship hung there for what seemed like ages keeping us pinned in a big pile, before eventually coming back up. People were screaming, some with broken bones. It was mayhem.

We all prayed to God to see us through and I am sure, even those who did not normally believe, or pray, started praying as well. The storm raged for four or five days, but it felt like a lifetime. We were so relieved when we eventually got close to land, and it finally started to subside. None of us would ever be the same again.

5 - SECRETS AND DREAMS

Claire:

I remember when Daisy, my beloved grandmother died, as if a little voice had plainly told me that she had gone. The frequency of everything was different that morning, like a feeling you have whenever the birds stop tweeting for some unknown reason. She was very old and the kindest and gentlest lady in the world, who loved to bake cookies and cakes for us all, and she was also entirely deaf.

Sometimes she would shuffle into the garden and stand beside me as I crouched at the pond, whilst trying to save the insects that were drowning on top of the water with a stick. She would smile without saying a word, whilst gently nodding her head, whenever I rescued the odd butterfly or little ladybird. We built a simple language based on kindness to connect and perhaps that is how my sensitivity and empathy was gently nurtured. I could never understand why she would just stare endlessly watching me play the piano when she couldn't actually hear anything. She always said that what I played was very beautiful and that she didn't need to hear it, because she could always see the music flowing though my face and hands as I touched the keys. Now I realise that she was reading my electromagnetic frequency, as today, I might read a stranger's energy the same way.

Most of the time she would be tending her little patch in the garden, or tucked up on pillows in bed fast asleep, with Renny, her red Abyssinian cat all snuggled up and purring loudly on her comfy tummy. I used to think she was so funny, because I would often find her sitting up in bed fast asleep, completely oblivious to the heavy metal music screaming out from the telly after the news she loved to watch was over, when of course, we were never allowed to listen to that sort of music in the house.

I think I was able to cope with the harshness of everything at home, because Daisy was just so pure and gentle. I loved her so much and she gave me the appreciation of what immense grace and beauty was, in comparison to the violent energy around me. Her death taught me that just being here as a soul filled with light and love is sometimes enough, for Daisy's energy raised the vibration of everything else around her, helping to balance out all of the dark energy elsewhere in the world and I wished that I could radiate love just like her too.

Not long after she passed away, I had a terrible premonition that my mother was going to die imminently also. Even though she was cruel to me, it was terrifying to think of life without her, because my own life and happiness was so dependent on her. I was very upset about it and she tried to reassure me by saying that I could confide in her about absolutely anything. When I told her about my vision, she laughed and said I was just being silly and that it was all just my over active imagination again. Only I knew that it wasn't.

The following years remained lonely and filled with sadness, especially when my two older brothers and oldest sister married and left home. Even though I did not have much to do with them, their missing energy left a vacuum and I became even more introspective. My mother soon found a lump in her breast the size of a pea and was diagnosed with breast cancer.

The twins each had boyfriends and Jana's boyfriend would unbutton my blouse and touch my breasts and buy me a block of chocolate every time he came to see her, as if he had every right to touch me like that. He would always bring two blocks of chocolate, one for my mother and one for me. I wondered why he never bought my sister any and even after they married and moved away, he would continue to touch me like that. I was twelve and I was trained to be submissive and do exactly as I was told whether I liked it or not, or else I got a hiding. I never realized my brother in law was actually blackmailing me to keep my mouth shut about it. Once again, I was frozen with fear and just went on pretending that everything was fine.

I would sit at the piano for hours practicing my little pieces of Bach and Mozart and I would lose myself in the imaginary world of fame and music and other bohemian people, all of whom I pretended loved me just for being myself, until my mother would harshly call me out of that world for something wrong she had found out I had done yet again.

I went to Methodist Ladies College for my secondary education, which took me two trains and a tram to get to every day. One afternoon coming home from school, I spotted Kerrie and her new friends from High School in the carriage joining mine. She was wearing tons of eye makeup and smoking and swearing and I felt so self-conscious dressed up in my gloves and hat and looking all prim and proper in my private school girl's uniform, that I was too embarrassed to even to say hello. I kept my head down and closed my eyes, hoping that she would not recognise me.

We seemed even more different from each other than before and I was so relieved when she jumped off the train without saying a word to me. She seemed so happy and casual, whilst my life was so formal and serious. There were piano lessons and guitar lessons, flute lessons and theory lessons, tennis lessons and choir practice, madrigal singing group and orchestra practice and then my usual school work. I adored the stage and was often cast in multiple roles in drama. I couldn't wait to dress up and wear the makeup and wigs, which allowed me to create a new character with a new voice, being free to be someone else for a little while - anyone else but me. I loved to sit at the piano and perform for the recitals in front of lots of people and their applause and adoration overwhelmed me. So much love seemed to come from total strangers and scarcely any seemed to come from home, so I decided that I would become an actress and write music one day and that was simply that.

Amongst other things at that time, my mother had found the Seventh Day Adventist Church, which she and my father became unbearably dogmatic about. The Pastor would come to visit every week and sometimes he would bring his son Lesta, who became one of my closest lifelong friends.

Whilst my parents would have their Bible study, Lesta and I would talk about our passion for music. Sometimes he would bring his guitar and his giant Marshall stack and sit at the end of my bed and play for hours with the same frequency as my soul. Its magic would float around me, reaching into me through the barriers and walls I had built around my heart to defend myself, nudging me to remember who I really was underneath all of the layers of protection. I would often refer to him as my white flame, because he was such a pure light of inspiration to me. He thought that I was just putting him up on a pedestal, whenever I expressed my admiration for his work, yet in reality I was quite aware that he was the perfect mirror into my own special uniqueness. We were equal. By loving his music, I was allowing myself to love my own originality too.

Jana and Birdie were both married and had left home by now, so my parents insisted that I join the church with them. My mother's cancer was progressing and I became deeply aware that she was getting worse and that she now needed a miracle to save her life. One morning, when I was on my knees praying around her bedside with my father, she shocked me by saying that it was no use praying for her, because she was going to die.

"But mum you have to believe, really believe, so the miracle can happen. I believe in miracles mum and if you can't believe too, then it won't happen. Please mum, please don't just give up?"

"People with cancer die Claire", she said frankly and I was so sad that she did not have any hope or enough faith to call the miracle into being and wondered how real going to church was, if she couldn't even believe that God could save her.

She called me to her bedside one afternoon in an effort to have a final little chat with me.

"Promise me that you will never be an actress and that you will never wear eye makeup Claire".

My heart sank unbearably. All I ever wanted to be when I grew up, was an actress and to wear smoky dark eye shadow and black eye liner. She knew me only too well, yet this was simply her dying wish.

"Ok mum", was all I could whisper.

"And you have to tell your father to paint the house and things like that", she continued, hoping to lessen my disappointment of never realizing my dreams. I nodded, but the tears were already in my eyes and burning my face. I really was worthless. My mother had constantly programmed me so.

"Never ever let a man touch your legs above the knees. He can touch your breast, but never your legs. Do you understand"?

Little did she know, that I already grasped more about these things than perhaps she cared to acknowledge. I was fifteen years old and already dating my first husband. I had discovered many secret pleasures of my own, but above the knee of all places? Really, my sensitivity in succumbing to pleasure did not include the top of my legs. My mother was obviously sharing her own weakness to temptation, which made the corners of my mouth curl upwards in surprise.

"Yes mum".

When she died there were no tears in my eyes at her funeral, but I discovered that I could cry through my fingers at the piano instead. I would sit there in the darkness, pouring out my soul and purging my mind of all the sadness that was trapped and pent up inside of me, until it bubbled over and exploded out into my hands and into music, as if the demon was being exorcised into something beautiful at last. In fact the sadder I felt, the easier the music flowed out from inside, becoming the language that I could express myself through completely, without getting into trouble for it and I was grateful that my father never hit me again.

We were both invited to the Pastor's house for dinner, shortly after my mother's death. Lesta's mum and sisters were really musically talented too, so his mum asked me to play one of my original pieces on her beautiful piano. A well-known Lecturer from the Conservatorium of Music was also there for dinner and when she heard me play the piece I wrote, after my mother died, she asked my father if he would allow me to be her student. I was offered a scholarship to leave school at the end of the year and study for a degree at the Conservatorium full time at the very young age of fifteen. I was thrilled by the chance to take my most hoped for opportunity of a lifetime being invited into university at such a young age. When I asked my father about it, he said that I had better ask my boyfriend, because ultimately, it was up to him, to which his answer was an emphatic "no" and that was that. I was merely moving from one sphere of control to another. I was devastated and that old feeling of worthlessness consumed me yet again.

My father soon arranged for me to have a holiday overseas with my piano teacher and another student of hers in Singapore for two weeks, which is where our teacher went every year for her Christmas break. When we arrived, her friend, who she said was our tour guide, picked us up at the airport and drove us to the hotel, which had bars on all of the windows and was very old and damp and unbearably hot. There was no air conditioning and the stench of something that had died, clung to the air and made us feel sick all of the time. The other girl and I could not stomach eating the local food, but we found some fresh pineapples at the market and just ate those for the entire time we were there.

Our teacher left us and checked into the Shangri La a few days later, much to our horror at being abandoned in a strange country. We just locked ourselves in the hotel room and stayed there, because we were too scared to go out again. Then one night when we were both in our beds falling asleep, the tour guide let himself in with a key and raped me in the darkness. It is only now that I wonder where he got the key from and have to ask if it was the spare one our music teacher had, as they seemed to be more than friendly towards each other.

The other girl remained silent in her bed for the entire nightmare, even though I was struggling to kick him and to push him off me. When he had finished with me, he simply left, leaving the door unlocked as he went. I just cried into the pillow until I couldn't stand it any longer and got up to run a bath. I felt disgusting. I already felt dirty inside out from breathing in all of the grimy air and after being touched that way, I felt even more putrid, which did not go away even after I soaked myself in that corroded old bath for over an hour.

Like me, the other girl must have either been too scared to scream, or was simply asleep, for that was the reason she gave me when I asked her why she didn't try to help me the next day. I never spoke about it again, but when our piano teacher returned to take us all back to the airport to go home, the tour guide was with her, his dirty fingernails and sleazy smile giving me the creeps all over again, warning me with that look I had seen before in my brother in law's eyes, to either shut up or else.

I didn't tell my boyfriend, or my father about it, for I was much too disgusted and ashamed, thinking once again that I must have done something really terrible to have caused him to have been so repulsive to me in the first place. I just kept the secret locked away, as if it was just another viper slithering around with all of the others trapped in the snake pit of my head instead.

6 - THE WOMAN WITH THE BLACK HAIR

Mark:

We only lasted six months back in England, house prices had gone through the roof so my parents didn't have enough money to buy. We soon reached the crossroads where all they had left was just enough money to get back to Australia where there was work for dad, or be stuck in England where there wasn't, and unable to buy a home. There was no choice.

All over again, I was saying goodbye to my roots, my relatives, my home, my culture and I was back on the boat train bound for Southampton docks and on another ship journey half way around the world. This time we boarded the 'Australis' for another five week voyage at sea with no idea what lay ahead after we arrived back in Australia.

I spent every day out walking the decks again, watching the moods of the sea and weather forever changing, sometimes calm and serene, and sometimes raging full of anger, as though it was some giant manic depressive entity with a life all of its own. Down the Atlantic Oceans, around Africa, and out from Cape Town across the Indian Ocean. The Indian Ocean was very rough, huge waves rolled past and squalls of rain danced around us all day. I would watch the black columns across the sea in some sort of bizarre race, each seemingly with a mind of their own, until one would intersect with us and pour rain down, until it passed and I would watch it move away.

I would stand for hours on deck, in tune with the sea, feeling the rhythm of the relentless waves. Every seven to eight minutes, one would be just a bit bigger than the rest, and the ship would roll over just that bit further, and hang there just that fraction longer. I would grip the hand rail a little bit tighter and then it would eventually slowly roll back upright, accelerating as it came further back up, and then the sequence would start all over again. I often used to wonder how the Captain knew what was safe and what was not.

Before long, we were back in Adelaide again and I was off to high school. It was another three years fancying feminine girls with black hair, as my search continued.

At high school with my two best mates Craig and Graham, both from England, I started to shed my shyness and embrace a rebellious side. Craig was football mad too, and we used to go everywhere together and stay over at each other's houses. He was outgoing and an extrovert, the opposite to me, and would engage anyone and everyone in conversation. Hanging out together some of it started to rub off and we used to run around the neighbourhood at night and get into all sorts of trouble and strife while each of our parents thought we were safely at the other's house.

We would ride on our bikes everywhere and sometimes on the way back from the local town centre if I was in front, Craig would speed up just enough to overtake me and be in front. Then I would speed up a bit and overtake him back, then he would speed up even more to get back in front, and then I would, and then he would, and we would end up peddling like mad in a masochistic ego induced race overtaking each other for the next five miles home. We would arrive there gasping for breath and pouring with sweat, absolutely exhausted. After doing that two or three times I started to realise how stupid it was, and how easily our ego allows us to be drawn into an unnecessary duel just to prove who is the biggest, fastest, strongest and most stupidest. I eventually decided it was actually stronger and more interesting to resist and not be drawn into these alpha male games. It was more of a challenge not to respond to these testosterone fuelled 'whose got the biggest dick' type of challenges. It isn't that easy as a teenager, it's practically a way of life for so many young adolescent males, always trying to outdo others. I discovered it is much more beneficial to save your energy and aggression and use it in a controlled way, but only when you really need to. Even today driving on the roads as I slowly overtake a slower car, I notice they sometimes suddenly speed up, their ego kicking in as they try up to avoid being overtaken, and it reminds me of those teenage bike races. I have a little grin and let them go on ahead.

Craig and I started fancying the same girl, and to my surprise I asked her out first, and even more of a surprise when she said "yes". But it wasn't long before she dumped me as she really fancied Craig, so I then started going out with one of her friends. Her dad insisted he meet me to give his approval. He was a Vietnam war veteran and everyone seemed terrified of him, maybe it was all the Vietnam War knives and weapons he had brought home and mounted on the wall in his office. I passed, but when the long summer school holidays came around she told me to stay away from her house as she had to look after her cousin coming to stay from interstate. On the first day back at school I was promptly dumped, and discovered the cousin was actually a 'he', nearly twice her age, and while staying he had introduced her to sex, and they had been having sex every day. So much for her father's heavy handed vetting of boyfriends to protect his daughter's precious innocence, whilst a member of his own family, a relative, was fucking her daily in his own home behind his back. He was so focussed on being suspicious of outsiders, he didn't even think to look at his own family members.

I couldn't wait to be old enough to leave school and get on with my life. I wasn't learning anything academically at school and it all seemed like a waste of time. I had decided I wanted to be a fighter pilot and you needed a good education in Maths, English and Physics (whatever that was), and none of us were getting one. I used to go to the library some lunchtimes and find books on this physics thing, to read and try to start teaching myself. In the end, out of sheer frustration Craig and Graham both left school and joined the navy and begged me to join too, but I refused. I'm glad I did. One went in saying he was going to be a missile operator only to be assigned as an administration clerk, and the other saying he was going to be a diver, and ended up a cook. The last I ever heard of Graham was that he was in a military prison somewhere in the outback of Western Australia.

My dad was already plotting another move back to the UK and one night I was complaining about not learning anything at school and was thinking of applying to the navy too. I think he was afraid I was going to screw up his plans and he suggested if I went to England immediately, I would be there just in time to start the new school year. I couldn't get "Yes" out quickly enough and within two weeks was flying back to England on my own.

Back in the mid-1970s flying still wasn't a common thing to do for most people, especially a sixteen year old on their own. It was the first time I had ever been to an airport, never mind fly, and on top of that I had to change flights by myself. I flew from Adelaide to Melbourne and got off and followed the list of written down instructions I had to change flights and check in.

I waited there all day for my flight to England and back then the journey would have about four stops along the way.

As our British Airways 747 approached landing in the Iranian capital, Tehran, the pilot warned us not to take any photos, as if anyone did, they could be removed by the local militia officials and the airline would not be held responsible. As soon as we had stopped taxing, the plane was immediately surrounded by men dressed all in black with long black beards and holding AK-47 machine guns as the doors were opened and the heat poured in. While the plane was refuelled three men dressed in black militia clothing boarded at the front and slowly walked down the aisles of the plane, staring intensely at each and every passenger directly into their face and slowly moving along a row at a time, as though they were looking for someone. It was very intimidating. You could feel the tension among both the passengers and the crew, anxious people exchanging nervous looks and wondering what was going to happen next. Everyone just sat there silently, sweating and willing the refuelling to be completed as fast as possible. When we finally took off there were loud cheers and clapping all through the plane, as soon as we were airborne.

Back in Wolverhampton, I quickly enrolled at an adult education college to start some serious education. I hated myself for still being introverted and shy. It felt dysfunctional, limited, restricted, and made me determined to do something about it, so I made a concerted effort to be more outgoing.

My fantasies moved to a more adolescent level. In one I would be walking down a suburban street, when I would notice one particular house with a classy feminine middle aged woman in her forties or fifties, with a curvy mature sexy body, and she would call me over. She was always dressed totally in black,

black blouse, black skirt and black high heels and she would have that jet black hair of the woman I had always seemed to be searching for. Not natural black, but that extra deep dyed black look. As I got closer, I could see she had long dark red nails and heavy makeup, dark red lipstick and lots of thick dark black eye liner. She was always very feminine, with a wicked sexy twinkle in her eye and smile to match. She would ask me to come in and help her with some household problem, which I was unable to refuse. I would always notice she was wearing black seamed nylon stockings, but then that was because she would always make sure I saw, as if she already knew me. It was strange how the fantasy lasted for so many years, and its intensity would never wane. Who was this woman with the black hair I was mesmerised with I used to wonder? It ran all through my teenage years, as though I subconsciously knew she was out there and would come into my life one day.

I finally had 5 'O' levels and went to an interview with a RAF officer in Birmingham for joining as a pilot only to be told no-one is selected with just the minimum requirements. They wanted 'A' levels which would mean another two years of studying, which I really didn't want to do. So I applied for the Arctic Warfare Unit of the Royal Marines instead. After doing the entrance tests the Petty Officer told me I had easily passed but if I really wanted to be a pilot I shouldn't give up as they needed them badly and they were much harder to find. He then proceeded to give me a personal dressing down, telling me I should get a haircut, buy a suit, learn to sit upright properly in a chair and look switched on and focussed. He said he would hold onto my application for the next three months, and all I had to do was call him anytime and I would be on a bus and off to basic training in Devon within two weeks. When I walked out I was furious about his lecture, but I looked at myself and soon realised he was quite right and I did all the things he suggested.

I had to wait for the next school year to start, so was stuck at home unemployed, just like my parents and sister. It wasn't long before my father started screaming at me to "go out and get a job and bring some money home". I used to wonder why it was only me he picked on when there were four of us there unemployed? It was the same story again, I was the black sheep of the family and first to be picked on and never allowed an easy time.

I found a job sawing steel girders in an engineering factory. All day long, lifting heavy steel girders around and sawing them into precise lengths, and they had to be exact to the millimetre. In winter it wasn't much fun working in a big open steel factory with ice cold heavy steel everywhere. Your muscles would be tight from the cold air and sub-zero temperatures, the ice cold steel could just stick to the skin of your fingers and rip it off without gloves and you always needed to be alert to avoid injuries. After six months I injured my back and left.

I soon had another job as a labourer, building rugby pitches in Telford Town Park, not realising I would be digging trenches in the rain, ankle deep in mud. Not exactly a lighter alternative, but I daren't sit around at home like the others did. The boss would ask us to dig a trench to find the end of a pipe and we would dig down four foot and along ten yards and find nothing. "Oh, dig another trench over here but in that direction this time", he would say. We would dig away and again find nothing. "Ok, can we dig one over here heading this way?" he would ask, as we rolled our eyes at each other. It felt like some form of punishment. But it was still easier than lifting heavy steel girders around all day and nice to be outside in the weather. I eventually got sacked, which shocked me as I was always a hard worker, but it was a lesson in the reality of adult life not being fair. I later found out it was due to the foreman having promised his neighbour a job, so he sacked who had been there the longest, which happened to be me. I went straight down to the jobcentre and by 5pm I had another job to start the very next day.

This time it was industrial cleaning, and with the naivety of a teenager, I had no idea what that really meant, nor even thought to ask at the time. I was picked up by a minibus load of big blokes at the crack of dawn and we were driven to a huge old heavy industrial factory in Birmingham. Two of the men grabbed a double extension ladder and extended it up to its maximum length and then put it up against one of the round steel columns that held the roof up. "Up you go. You'll need this" I was told, as a paper mask was thrust into my hand. The two men held the ladder so it wouldn't rock or slip against the round column, and I must have climbed up at least thirty or forty feet. The higher I climbed, the harder it was for the two men at the bottom to hold the ladder in place, with my weight at the top getting heavier it would start to slide off one way or the other against the round column, but I kept on going up. At the top, three of us inched our way across narrow steel girders, without any safety harnesses, where we found high pressure air hoses. We put our masks on and started hosing the thick dark red dust off rafters as far as we could reach, and after a while I asked the others what it was. "Iron oxide dust", one bloke said. "Aye good for ya. Causes cancer I 'eard".

We stopped for a break, not that we could go anywhere, or even sit down. I looked down and there was a huge steel tank of dark liquid directly below us, with tiny bubbles all over the surface.

"What's that?" I asked. "Acid", was the reply. "Fall in there an ya dead".

A few hours later the boss came in and I heard him shout "What's that fucking kid doin' up there? Get him down now, 'e's too young". So I inched my way back along the girders and back down the ladder and was given other jobs to do. The next day I was told to fetch a broom that had fallen onto a dusty roof above some offices, so I got a ladder, climbed up to the roof of the offices and, not thinking, just walked off across the dusty roof. Crash! I didn't realise, and no-one told me, the roof under the thick dust was just thin Perspex and I went straight through it. Luckily I had quick reflexes and caught the beams on either side of me with each hand as I passed through them. I was left hanging there in mid-air with my legs dangling into the office below. I quit the next day. Not so much because of the danger, but the two hours it took in the bath each night to get clean and all the thick muck out of my knotted up hair.

Eventually I started at a sixth Form College, to study what the air force wanted: 'A' level Maths, Physics and English, and a few other 'O' levels to fill out the time. One of the lads in the advanced maths class was asking for new people to come along to their chess club, so one day I went along. I turned up in my heavy metal leather jacket, long hair and ear ring, and they all gave me the usual strange looks. After asking me slowly if I knew the rules, their number one player decided he would use me to loosen up on, and make sure I knew who was number one there. As we started playing he seemed more interested in organising who he would play next and chatting to others, but as I slowly started to take his pieces from him one by one I slowly got his attention. The room fell silent as the other lads started to gather around and watch with shocked expressions on their faces as I beat him. No-one else would play me after that, so I walked out and never went back again.

The evenings at home would consist of watching television. Everyone would ring off in the weekly television guide what they wanted to watch, and in the gaps it would be whichever was the least popular program on. I could only take so much of it. Most evenings I would be in the kitchen studying, and after that would often go up the banks onto the lookout, and just sit there in the dark, for two or three hours, by myself, just thinking about life and the world and stuff.

Two years later I had my 'A' levels and applied for the RAF again, and went off for selection. I got through all the hard parts, the medical, IQ tests and interviews, but failed, and told I was very close and invited to try again in another two years. But that meant either going to university or starting a regular job. Back home I gently floated the idea of going to university and my father was absolutely furious, and blew his top, screaming at me that I was "afraid to get a real job". I thought I had already proven myself by working in a steel factory, digging trenches and climbing thirty foot ladders without a harness on over acid baths? I had always thought all parents would love their kids to actually *want* to go to university, and be capable of it? He was completely against it.

I applied for university places regardless. I needed to get away from home, and live in the big city, so I only applied for places in Birmingham and London. I was pulled like a magnet to the built up buzzing of a big busy city metropolis, where throngs of people milled about and was open all night. When it finally came around I packed my bags with what I could carry and caught the coach to London, leaving home for the first, and last, time. Maybe I might even meet that woman with the black hair there?

7 - TWISTED FAIRYTALE

Claire:

My taste in men was atrocious. I was definitely not a good judge of character in that department, but then I never had a worthy male role model in my life whom I truly admired or looked up to. Instead, I would look to rock guitarists and movie stars with square jaws and steamy eyes. They were the ones with bad boy edges and gutsy dispositions, fast cars and sharp minds and they were definitely not the sort I would want to take home to meet my father.

My boyfriend was also a Seventh Day Adventist, the same denomination my parents belonged to, so I figured that he must be a good choice, being a fine Christian boy and all. Besides, my mother had asked him to always take care of me for her before she died, and he had agreed, so that was that really. He also played the guitar, which was pretty cool and one day when I angled a cowboy hat across his brow and took a photo, I discovered that if I squinted my eyes a bit, I imagined he was actually a dead ringer for Robert Redford, my favourite movie star at the time. So, here I was going out with someone who looked like a movie star and acted like a rock star. I was pretty happy and by the time I was eighteen, was proudly wearing an engagement ring and planning my dream wedding. It was time to leave my disturbing childhood behind me along with my friends and escape to the future, where I could live happily ever after in my very own fairy tale at last.

Things suddenly took a turn for the worse though, one month before the wedding. I was at the hairdressers having a bridal rehearsal, whilst my fiancé decided to fill in the time waiting for me by milking petrol tanks from the local car park at the railway station. I was definitely not into stealing or anything like that and I would have said so, if he had of told me first what he was up to.

Two undercover policemen were patrolling the train station in plain clothes, as there had been a surge of break-ins at that car park over recent times. They were eyeing him very carefully through a couple of pairs of binoculars and when they saw the syphoning hose, thought it was actually a wire instead, believing he was the culprit breaking into the cars. They came running towards my fiancé, preparing to arrest him, but when he spotted two strange men running after him, he jumped into his car and nearly ran both of them over, as he raced to get away, without thinking for a moment that they were actually policemen.

He was charged with assault with a weapon, theft, loitering with intent, and escorted off to jail one month after my wedding day. He also lost his driver's license, so he could not drive in the State of Victoria for twelve months. I was nineteen years old and an emotional wreck. I decided not to tell anyone in the family except Jana. I moved house close to where she lived interstate, to a little country town over the state border in New South Wales, where nobody else would wonder where he was and I knew he could drive once he got out of jail. I don't know what actually happened whilst he was locked up, but when my husband was eventually released, he was never the same person again and he never talked about it to me either.

His temper seemed to be a time bomb, which sat right at the surface, just waiting to explode at any moment with me. My first experience of it happened when I wanted to play some music.

There had been a drawer sitting on the piano stool and as I bent down to lift it onto the floor, he snarled at me.

"If you drop that, I'll smack you one".

Without thinking that I was doing anything wrong, I simply dropped it a couple of inches from the floor and he wacked me in the nose so hard, that I heard it crack and blood just poured out everywhere and down my throat.

My nose was leaning to one side and the blood just would not stop, so he ended up taking me to hospital. I told the doctor that I had an accident playing tennis, so that my husband would not be charged with assault. Eventually, I had plastic surgery to rebuild my nose and soon contracted an infection, which made my nose bleed relentlessly. It was back to the hospital, where I had to have blood transfusions and it gave me time alone to ponder what I was going to do about my marriage.

My husband swore that he was so sorry and that it would never happen again, if I did not make him so angry next time. How easily I was reeled in, for his hooks had made their way into my old conscience, where I was so good at bashing myself up and being submissive. He blamed me for losing his temper, as did my parents when I was a child, for their own lack of control over themselves.

It also occurred to me that he just wanted to control me and whenever I pushed back and simply asserted myself, he became frustrated with his own lack of power over me, lashing out and abusing me, instead of being able to communicate his emotions verbally.

The church taught us that the male is the head of the family and something started to niggle away at me about it. At the same time, my religious conscience also pleaded with me to forgive him and so like a good Christian wife, I suppressed the nagging thoughts of conflict and resumed our relationship, as if nothing sinister had ever happened within it at all, because that is how I thought forgiveness worked. I remained in this state of denial, where I was actually living a massive dark lie, because my inner map of normal boundaries was in so much conflict and confusion. I was being taught one set of principles and yet I was also starting to develop my own, based on what felt right and what felt wrong in my gut.

The brutal episode of my broken nose was just the beginning of such violent behaviour, which continued to chip away at my relationship and also to my faith in the church over the following three years of my life, yet at the same time it slowly started to uncover the real Claire, whenever I would question the principals that I had been taught. I never lost faith in God per say, it was always just the doctrines of the church that my instinct was becoming uneasy about. My belief system was beginning to shake and crumble, yet I continued to hold on believing that in some foolish poignant way, everything happened for a reason and would all work out for the best somehow.

I tried to keep my mouth shut and get used to the violence and aggression, but sometimes my husband would literally try to strangle me whenever he got angry with me, and he would hit me in the head so hard that I would see stars. Every time following these episodes, he would promise that it would never happen again and each time I would believe him a little less and forgiveness would be more difficult for me to give him. I was beginning to create my own set of boundaries and beliefs, which resonated with a tiny voice within and I felt that forgiveness is not necessarily the right thing to do in every situation.

I would be left feeling so numb, after these episodes, that the only way for me to move forward emotionally, was learning to block the memory of what had just happened. If I really thought about it to try to understand what was actually going on, I would just want to retaliate and hurt him back as much as he hurt me, like telling him I did not love him anymore, using my Dark Shadow Feminine ploys of emotional manipulation.

I thought that marriage was for life and mine was becoming a gloomy prison, where playing head games to make him suffer was the only way of getting him back for being so abusive to me. He was violent with his fists and I was equally violent with my tongue.

We moved back to Melbourne and when my first baby came along, I suddenly realised that playing out these Dark Shadow Feminine war games with him was no longer an option. It was time to grow up and be the best mother I could be to my precious little baby son, Jensen, which did not mean exposing him to our negativity. Whenever his little cry called for my attention, I would rush to gather him up, vowing to love and protect him with everything I had.

One afternoon when our baby was quietly sleeping, my husband dragged me by the hair into the bath and bashed me in the nose again until I bled profusely.

"Where are my car keys?"

"I don't know!"

"Oh yes you do you fucking slut. You can't fool me, now where are they?"

"I honestly don't have your bloody keys. You must have lost them somewhere" I yelled, thinking he had completely lost his mind.

I remember running for my life to the sanctuary of the neighbours' house next door, believing my son was safer sleeping in his room, as my husband ran the bath to clean up the blood screaming,

"Where's the evidence now Buchho?" His terrifying laughter chilling me inside out, as I slammed the front door behind me.

Then the police arrived and I was beside myself, because Jensen was still next door and I was too frightened to go back inside alone to get him. I honestly thought my husband was going to kill me. I could not understand why he had just snapped like that. I certainly had not taken his keys, because I had my own car and I remember worrying not about myself, but what he would do to Jensen one day as well if we stayed together.

After the police had spoken to my husband, they returned to the neighbours and berated me for causing such a spectacle. My husband had successfully fooled them into thinking that I was the one who had created the drama in the first place. I tried swallowing my anger, as the police escorted me home again, where I found my husband to be all smiley and cheery, which really did my head in. To my relief, Jensen was still sleeping soundly and I shuddered, as the chills began to take over my whole body like an aftershock following a devastating earthquake.

The next day he was rather sheepish and glum.

"Oh sorry, I thought you were going to steal my keys and I remember now, I hid them in the peg container under the sink in the laundry so that you couldn't".

I rushed to the laundry to empty the peg basket out and when the car keys scattered onto the floor with a clunk, I just couldn't believe my eyes. I was mortified and struck dumb, as to what was really going on inside that head of his and wondered how even the police could have been so gullible to believe his lies, over my sincerity for their assistance.

Not long after, I heard the phone ringing and when he answered it, his voice was guarded, instead of naturally assertive like it normally was when speaking to friends or family. Then just as I knew somehow that morning when Daisy had died, my gut dropped and my heart raced faster, as adrenaline pumped through me. I crept into the hallway, wrapped in a towel all dripping wet, because I had jumped out of the bath. I strained to hear what he was whispering in such an intimate tone and wondered who in hell other than myself he could be talking to like that. When I could not make out exactly what he was saying, I walked straight into the kitchen, where he was. He hung up immediately, without even saying goodbye. I never questioned him about it, because I expected him to lie to me and he never told me who he was talking to either. My intuition conveyed to me what was really going on and I could not bear the jealousy that was nagging at my thoughts. The lessons from my childhood to trust the unspoken language of the frequency around me had been learnt, and I honoured what I was being told by it.

As soon as he was out of the house, I found the evidence. Love letters were neatly stashed away inside his brief case and I suddenly realized that my marriage was well and truly finished this time. As I collapsed onto the floor, I could hardly breathe from the sheer shock of my fairy tale shattering, and once again the feelings of worthlessness gripped my solar plexus like a boa constrictor and was slowly squeezing the life out of me for what seemed like the final kill.

I crawled on my hands and knees to sit outside on the back step, taking in some deep breaths, but I just wanted to curl up and die instead.

I gathered Jensen up and reluctantly stayed at my father's house for a few days, until I found a nice two bedroom flat upstairs at the back of a house on a busy road close by. I was working at the tax office in Melbourne and Jensen was now a gorgeous one year old, being looked after during the daytime in a crèche run by the local council. I was struggling with a sense of sadness in being such a failure as a wife at only twenty two years of age and was also unsure of how to be a proper mother, considering I was also still only a child really and there was no one I knew that I could bounce with about it in my life. Sometimes I would feel so low, that I would shut down and not be able to function, but nobody else would know, because I would always smile and pretend that everything was fine.

My husband had been constantly making death threats to me at work and he was not showing up at the arranged meeting place to have access with Jensen, or paying me any money towards maintenance either. My own money was enough and I didn't really care for his anyway. I was terrified of what he was going to do to us physically though and prayed that we were both kept safe from harm. I remained as vigilant of my surroundings as humanly possible, feeling like the KGB casing out an enemy in a foreign country most of the time.

Twisted Fairytale

One evening, when I arrived to pick up Jensen from the crèche after work, I was told that his father had already been and taken him, even though I had specifically given instructions to never allow this to happen, because he had been threatening to kill me. I was edgy and panic stricken, because I didn't even know where he lived, or if he was even capable of caring for my little boy.

The police were not much help either, saying that there was nothing they could do, because he had done nothing legally wrong. He was my son's father after all and the death threats were only threats. They could only do something after there was actual bodily harm. I was shaking with pure rage and fear at the same time, feeling out of control and victimized. The law was protecting the bully and accusing me of being just a silly, paranoid mother. They advised me to go home, have a nice hot cup of tea and plan to see a family law firm about formal child access arrangements as soon as possible.

Needless to say, the night was horrific, as I endlessly tossed about in a sleepless state of anxiety and tears, but I determined to be strong and went to work as usual the next day, hoping to hear from my ex-husband as to when and where I could pick Jensen up again. However, that afternoon, I received an urgent telephone call from my landlord instead. He had come home from work at 3PM, only to discover that my son was screaming his lungs out, strapped inside the baby car seat and abandoned on the stairs to my flat for God knows how many hours on his own.

When I rushed home, Jensen was still in a frenzy and it took us both the whole evening to calm down enough to sleep. As I held him in my arms and kissed his little blonde head, I vowed that I would never let anything like that happen to him or us again. I found myself shaking and asking someone deep inside of me, who the hell I really was. Like calling to the dead in the wind, I never expected the response. What the hell was I doing here and where the hell was I going in my life? Mysteriously the answers swarmed about my head and gathered into the silence. Suddenly the knowingness became so clear and strong.

I am Claire.

I am here to be the best mother possible.

I am going to leave my job and teach piano, so that I have enough money to stay at home to care for my gorgeous son.

And then I fell asleep. Moreover to the music, I had discovered the voice of my first sovereign self, oblivious to the notion that I had just made a tiny hole in the fabric of my mother's design of what she thought she had created of me. With little more than a slight tug on the loosened thread, her whole masterpiece would be unravelled into nothing but tatters, the consequence of which would be the beginning of finding out what I was really made of instead.

8 - COMPROMISE IS THE ANSWER

Mark:

Leaving home was like beginning a whole new life, only this time in the adult world. I had waited for so long to be in control of my own life and no longer being told everything I could and couldn't do to meet someone else's expectations and standards. I never went back, I never asked for handouts, nor to borrow money from my parents, no matter how desperate I was. Ever.

I moved into a hall of residence with a couple of hundred other students. For most of them moving there seemed to be a big family outing, with flashy Range Rovers parked right outside their blocks, with stereos and box after box of home comforts being unloaded by proud parents and siblings. I bet they hadn't been accused of going to university to "avoid getting a real job", I mused to myself.

In London I had privacy for the very first time. Growing up I had always had to share a bedroom with one or both of my younger brothers, with their constant coming and going and noise. Solitude is so good for the soul. When you give yourself true peace and quiet, you embrace your Higher Self. You can listen to your soul, which is who you really are and which always speaks from love, unlike your mind and ego which so often speaks from fear and drives you to do bad or selfish things. I didn't think of it in these terms back then, but now I realise that is what I was doing, having a conversation with my soul.

London was everything I had heard it was and a whole lot more. I couldn't wait to go out exploring, so while the other students were only focussed on bonding with each other, I went straight out on the town exploring. One night I ended up at the Hammersmith Odeon to see a heavy metal band, rock music, long hair and leather jackets everywhere, alcohol, deafening noise and explosions, I was with kindred spirits. Awesome. Welcome to London I thought.

After a few days I went grocery shopping for the first time and bought all the things we were never allowed at home growing up. Chocolate biscuits, Frosties breakfast cereal, soft drink - all the "no" things. Growing up a snack in the evening would usually have been cold toast left over from breakfast, or a couple of broken plain biscuit pieces. I could even buy takeaway food now if I wanted to, the only 'takeaway' I had ever had was the occasional fish and chips from the local chip shop. Chinese takeaway, pizza and wine were nothing special to the other students, but we never had any of them back home.

One evening I put my first load of washing on in the communal laundry, used normal powder, set it to hot, turned it on and left it going. Well, no-one ever told me you're not supposed to use normal powder in an automatic. Before long, someone appeared asking who was doing their washing as they really should go and take a look. All the people in our communal lounge looked out of our windows across the yard and let out howls of laughter. As I headed over I could see a three foot high white wall of bubbling suds forcing their way out of the laundry door into the yard. Inside the suds had piled up even higher and I had to hold my breath as I felt my way to the machine to find the knobs to turn it off. When I finally got my washing out my brand new maroon jumper had shrunk and looked like it was made for a ten year old, and all my white clothes had turned pink. Well no-one told me you shouldn't use hot water for coloureds. So they all had to go straight into the bin. I seemed to have a habit of learning how to do things the hard way.

Our first party was a 'wear something blue' party, and we joked afterwards that even the police were in blue. A girl in our block took a fancy to me and we started seeing each other. I was attracted by her maturity in comparison to most of the others around. She was bubbly and extroverted and the others considered her the 'mother' of our block. In private I soon discovered behind closed doors she would go completely flat, as if a big 'on/off' switch had suddenly been switched to 'off'. At first I obviously worried it was me, until one day she told me she "sort of suffered from depression", "occasionally". Apparently it had been an ongoing problem and her mother had been constantly asking her if she had told me about 'it' yet, and was worried how I would react when I found out.

It was the first time I realised that people aren't always the same on the inside as they may appear on the outside, regardless of how they may act in public. You can never really tell what is going on inside someone else's head, or in their life, or what they are really thinking or feeling. People can be dealing with all sorts of issues and carrying all sorts of burdens they are struggling with, often very private ones, psychological issues, physical pain, emotional trauma, and yet show no obvious signs externally of them. They can appear happy, when they are really far from it. Ordinary people, whose paths we cross in our daily lives are often the greatest actors that ever lived, as they act out a public persona which is nothing like who they really are, or what they may be going through, or having to deal with, not wanting to burden others, and are totally convincing. We all do it to some extent. Who hasn't put on that Monday morning act at work when asked, "How was your weekend?" only to lie through their teeth "Good", when in truth it was bloody awful? 'Don't judge a book by its cover' as the saying goes, none of us really know what is going on in someone else's life unless we have walked in their shoes, and we should always consider and respect that. It was a valuable lesson I would carry with me forever.

A few months later I started to notice my girlfriend seemed to have more and more 'appointments' with old girlfriends during the evenings and we started seeing less of each other. When I finally confronted her about it, she told me her student friends had been telling her she could 'do better' than me and she happened to agree. It was a rather blunt way to put it. I felt like a old worn out jumper being tossed out to make way for a newer and better one. I tried to cling onto us, but eventually realised it takes two to make a relationship work, but only one to end it. If one ends it, no matter what the other thinks or feels, or how much we want to cling onto it, there is nothing we can do about it, it's gone.

I had only been at university a few months when my mother rang to say they had decided to move back to live in Australia again, and asked if I was coming with them? My Dad didn't discuss it with me at all - he had already left. Even though I was only scraping by on a student grant, I was independent for the first time and loving it. I was standing on my own feet now and old enough to decide for myself, so politely declined. They didn't seem very concerned, and off they all went. They were doing what they wanted to do, and I was doing what I wanted to, so I had no issues about it.

Two years passed, and I applied for the Royal Air Force for the third, and what would be the final time due to my age. I was doing well again until I was asked in the interview: "If you were ordered to kill someone and you knew it was wrong, would you still do it?" I told them "I wouldn't do it if I *knew* it was wrong". Wouldn't anyone I thought? I was taught at school about the Nuremburg trials after World War 2 and how human beings did terrible things to other human beings during the war, murdering and exterminating millions of innocent people, and how the perpetrators in the courtroom tried to defend their actions with the excuse that they were just 'following orders'. No, I wouldn't kill someone if I 'knew' it was wrong, and would hope no-one else would either, even in our armed forces. So my dreams of the last ten years to become a pilot came to an abrupt end.

We are all encouraged to grow up and aim high… little Johnny wants to be an astronaut, little Mary wants to be a ballerina, and we encourage it (well, most parents do). It's great to dream and we learn many things along the journey striving for them. But the reality is that Johnny often ends up sawing steel in a factory and Mary an accounts receivable clerk at the tax office. To have your childhood dreams crushed by the reality of adulthood and be forced to face having to do something mundane for a living, is much harder to face up to. I find it quite sickening when I read about multi-billionaire golfers being a 'hero' for playing on with a slight knee injury, while there are people all over the world homeless, in poverty and working in terrible conditions, with crippling injuries, being paid a pittance.

It is depressing at first when our childhood ambitions get squashed, but as we mature, we eventually realise it is actually not what is important. Our lives are not about what job we do, how much money or property or shares we have, what model car we drive, what designer clothes we wear, how big our house is, how much we save for retirement, or how much fame or authority or power we can get. Many people think that is what life is all about. It's not. Some even believe that is all life is about. It's not. They become so obsessed at reaching for these materialistic possessions, that they lose their real purpose for being here.

The drive, obsession, outright greed for money and adulation, sends many people into some very dark places, and out of their fear of not attaining them, they will do the most selfish and despicable things to other souls to satisfy their own ego. Some who do actually achieve their highest ambitions and materialistic desires, then stand there on the top of their own personal mountain of 'achievement', rich, famous or powerful, still with a hollow feeling inside, wondering why they still feel so hollow? It is as though there is something missing in their life and it often takes them a lifetime to work it out. Many people never do. For many of us it takes a life changing crisis, a shattered dream, an illness, a betrayal, a divorce, a death, losing all our money, to wake us up to what is really important and it's none of the above.

When we are 16 we think we are an adult and understand the world and other adults. We want to be treated like and adult, have all the good parts of adulthood, but still have the best parts of being a child. Then at 26 after going out in the adult working world, we realise how little we actually understood back at 16, but we know now. Then at 36 after experiencing good and bad relationships, and then parenting, we learn more, and realise even back at 26 we didn't really understand, but we do now. Then by 46 after dealing with 16 year old teenagers, and often divorces, the death of peers and many other dramas, we finally start to truly understand, and realise that even back at 36 we still had a lot to learn.

Sooner or later most of us eventually work it out, but not all.

There is a reason why so many cultures look to their elders for wisdom. Some don't even consider you and adult until your 40s. They have travelled the journey already and understand what is truly important and meant to be learnt along the way. You just don't realise when you are young and only have dollar signs or fame in your eyes. You just have to listen to the elders, learn to listen to your inner self, your soul and it will tell you what really matters.

One day I was mooching through the spiritual books in a shop when I picked up a book about Out of Body Experiences and freaked out. It had an illustration of someone's soul leaving their body and floating up above, connected back to their physical body by only a thin transparent tube coming out of their lower back. As if that wasn't enough, it then had pictures of them flying off across the rooftops, and left me wondering about that transparent stupid tube thing I had when young, and those childhood dreams of floating out through the roof and across the garden at night. Were they actually more than just dreams?

I moved to another hall of residence to be able to focus on the end of year exams, as the first two terms had been one long party, but it was too late. I failed the year by 2%, and it was probably for the best, as Electronic and Communications Engineering really wasn't for me.

The three month summer holidays arrived and all the other students went back to their families to be pampered and go on holidays. I had nowhere to go, so stayed on in the empty halls of residence with a handful of others. I took one of the only jobs quickly available, a nightshift job working from 6PM to

8AM every night, operating injection moulding machines that made the little plastic insides of toy cars. It was strange going to work at 5PM when others my age were preparing to go out and have fun for the evening, but I needed the money to repay my usual end of term overdraft.

One evening I didn't have to work, back at the halls where I was staying I went down to the bar and bought a drink and went outside alone and sat on a bench looking up at the stars. After a while a girl followed me out and sat down and started talking to me. I had seen her around the halls a number of times, always in high heels and wearing makeup, things that I loved, and many guys eyeing her up. She seemed nice to talk to and we got on really well and within a few days we were seeing each other daily and in a relationship.

I wanted a close, affectionate, loving and sensual relationship and she said she did as well, but it seemed to be a challenge for some reason, as if there was a block there. Eventually she revealed to me that she had some serious unresolved 'personal issues', which she would never fully reveal, and she would regularly just explode and storm out. From a lot of the things I had read and heard, my belief system had been moulded into believing that every relationship is about 'compromise'. No-one is perfect for any one of us, so it is a matter of finding someone as close to what we desire, and then resolving the differences via compromises, learning to live together. The more we compromise, the better chance we have of making a relationship work. 'Compromise' was the key to a happy relationship!

I tried really hard to face the issues she had and help her overcome them by being supportive and understanding, but she would regularly lose her temper, explode and completely trash my room. I would sit there in silent disbelief as she would throw everything not screwed down all around like confetti. When she had finally finished, she would just walk out and catch a train back to her mother's, …or ask if I wanted to have sex? My room would look as if a hurricane had blown right through it and she would never clean it up afterwards. It would do my head in trying to work out what was going on in hers. Each time she would trash my room I would wonder if I should be getting angry, or turned on? It was such a head fuck.

I had to twist arms and talk my way onto a new Science degree course at Westminster University and knowing it was my last chance, finally switched my academic brain on. I dedicated my life for the next three years to studying and focussed on nothing else. It was hard work and long hours. I would stay in my room studying away, sometimes right through the night until dawn to get assignments completed, while I would hear the other students outside in the common room drinking and laughing and larking around all evening, just like I had the previous year.

I felt a huge sense of achievement after three years when I walked away with an honours degree in Computer Science. I took up a role I was offered by Marconi Avionics and ended up working on the software for the radar for the Tornado fighter jet for the Royal Air Force. Within a year I had six developers reporting to me and was responsible for the software on a £25 million automated radar test rig. That's a lot of responsibility for someone so young, but I was good what I did and had already learnt more than the others about how all the software worked.

Over the next six years our relationship would frustratingly just yoyo back and forth between splitting up and getting back together, hot and cold, on and off. I found it hard to believe anyone was truly 'the one', or 'perfect' for any of us, and that a relationship is never a perfect match. It can only work if both parties compromise. Compromise is the answer. Give and take. That's the key. A funny thing often starts to happen though when you live by the compromise mantra and one party is being more compromising than the other, things just start to slide and you eventually find yourself being taken advantage of, things you do as compromise soon become the norm, and are then replaced with new demands. Slowly it grinds you down as you lose who you really are and become engulfed in a cycle of just trying to please the other party and bit by bit, end up under their control. Even if you could please them 100% of the time, by constantly compromising, where does it leave you? You end up just being trampled underfoot. It's a place I ended up so many times in relationships and just didn't realise at the time that I was as much to blame for allowing it to happen as they were.

The final straw came when she went to Greece on holiday without me, and came back clearly very coy about some male encounters. It wasn't hard to fill in the few blanks that she wouldn't. That was the end for me, so I finally stood up for myself and said, "enough". There were just too many things missing and after six years and making so many compromises, it wasn't getting any better, only worse. I decided we should free both of us to try and find someone who we would be happy with, without having to make so many compromises. She was so accustomed to the usual cycle of getting back together, it was ages before she actually realised I really meant it this time and the yoyo-ing finally stopped.

After all the dust settled it was such a relief. I was happy and sad. Personally I felt like I had failed and wasted six years, particularly the last four, always trying to compromise, yet at the same time was so much happier feeling free and me again. I wondered if I was just plain stupid to have stayed in such a relationship for so long. Were those six years just a big waste of my life? And hers? Or were we supposed to have learnt from them? I agonised for ages over when do you work on a relationship and compromise over the differences and issues, and when do you just say it's just not working and get out? It was going to take decades to really learn the answer to that one. I hope reading this helps anyone else going through the same situations, realise sooner than I did when it's time to let go and get out.

I was in the adult relationships arena now, where we try and navigate our way through a minefield, searching for true happiness. Every aspect of every relationship becomes a learning experience, even if we don't realise at the time. Sometimes we are actually the teacher, helping our partner learn, sometimes we are the student, but most of the time we are both. We are both growing, and as we become older with more and more experiences, we also become wiser. Relationships are where we learn and grow. We could give up and sit at home and avoid them entirely, saying we are happy being alone, but we would learn very little. We would have checked out of the whole experience, out of fear of failure, fear of getting it wrong again. We grow through the pain of failures in relationships, learn from them, and then move on to take that knowledge with us, hoping the next one will be 'the one' where we find true love and utter bliss.

9 - THE MYSTERIOUS MAN

Claire:

My father agreed that it would be better if I stayed at home to look after Jensen and was really supportive in offering us the granny flat, where Daisy and Grandma Flo had both lived years prior, rent free at the back of his house for some added protection from my ex-husband. The offer had been too good for me to refuse, as I was very much afraid for our safety, realizing if anything happened that the police were not going to get involved with domestic issues. I was also seeing a family law court barrister to attend to my affairs, including a restraining order in an attempt to secure some protection as well. The access arrangements were also put into place, which my ex-husband just ignored.

I decided to post an advertisement in the local newspaper to test the market for potential adult piano students and was amazed by the positive response. The decision was made to finally make the move back home. I quit my job and my sister Jana offered to drive down from the country to help me move.

Just as everything was all packed up, she suggested taking Jensen in her car, as mine was pretty full of boxes and so I agreed. A little voice in my head told me to go via the back streets to my father's house instead of the direct route on the busy main roads, where I would often speed around the corners. As I took the second bend through the back streets, the wheel nuts dropped off each of the wheels at the same time and all four tyres fell off the car and rolled down the road. I stopped after a couple of metres with just the bare metal scraping on the bitumen, creating sparks which flew up and about everywhere. It was lucky the car stopped in the gutter without any injury to me or the car, but if Jensen had been with me and I had raced normally through the main roads, there may well have been a very different outcome. It was clear that it was not an accident, for someone had deliberately loosened the wheel nuts on purpose. Jana said that she had seen my ex-husband walking down the street carrying a white ice cream container the previous evening and did not want to say anything, because she did not want to upset me. He used a white ice cream container to carry his tools around in, so I quickly realized that he had just attempted to kill me.

I decided not to attend church anymore, because l did not want to be hypocritical and I did not believe the doctrines resonated with my own inner truth any longer. My father being an elder stirred up a lot of anger within me as well and Jana's husband who used to buy me chocolate when I was a teenager, had also become a born again Christian. He had been convicted for indecent exposure as well and I wondered if all paedophiles hid behind the stony cold walls of the church somewhere out there in the world. I wanted to be a part of the Church, but I just felt I was being a hypocrite if I belonged as well.

I was not prepared to pretend anything for anyone anymore, not even for the Church. It seemed to me that some of the doctrines were put in place because the Church just wanted to control us and we were just the victims. Why had God given us the power of choice then I asked myself? Why had he given each of us a unique set of fingerprints like snowflakes – beautiful images of unique expression, if we were all meant to be the same?

The sermons were fused with "Trust and obey" and "Thou shalt not…". Everything seemed to be about control, such as being preached to about burning in hell and sinners and the devil and the perilous times to come. All was fear based and guilt ridden. Nothing so sweet and tender as who I imagined my God to be was ever delivered within the sermon. And so I listened to that little voice inside of me once again and I quit the church and I never went back. I still did not quit God – just the church. The sermons were all about God being somewhere outside of ourselves up in heaven somewhere and I had surrendered to all things outside of myself for long enough. It was time to experience 'me' and that is exactly what I committed to do.

I just wanted to be a normal person and be happy. Kerrie and Lesta started to keep in touch again after ten years. Lesta had never been into the Church like the rest of his family, so we'd often meet up at the pub and have a drink and a good old laugh as well.

Kerrie's grandma went to my father's church and when she told Kerrie that she hadn't seen me in a while, Kerrie decided that she would love to catch up. She was still uptight about being molested as a child, because her mum continued to stay in denial about it. We spent hours together talking about our opinions of the world and discovered that we actually shared so many similar views and philosophies. After all of those years, we had become more alike. I was more casual and less serious and she had become more serious and philosophical somehow. We declared that we were soul sisters reminiscent of the day when we mixed our blood together and swore on our lives that we would be there for each other no matter what.

My friendship to Kerrie allowed me to experience myself like never before and I was able to shift some negative emotional patterns, which had stuck since my early childhood. I thought I would surprise her with a visit one time and so I put together a meat platter to give her. When Jensen and I arrived though, no one was home, so I let myself in the back door and left the platter in the fridge instead. Kerrie never mentioned it to me and initially I felt really angry about it. I asked myself, why I was so upset and realised that I had only given it to impress her and to feed my own ego, looking for the obligatory 'thank you', and not because I wanted her to have it simply because I loved her.

It taught me something about unconditional love and I decided that from that moment on, if I did not give for the joy of just giving, I was not interested in giving at all. The other aspect of that lesson was that I learnt not to point the finger at someone else, whenever I experienced that negative feeling, enabling me to change the programme inside my head, and from then on, whenever I did experience something unpleasant, I focused on looking inward to change something about myself, instead of blaming the other person for it. Step by baby step, I was reprogramming myself to be the woman I wanted to be, at the same time being very conscious, that this would not please my mother one bit, if she were still alive, for I was undermining her programme of who she wanted me to be.

I think the actual process of teaching music was so healing for me too, in experiencing my true authentic self at last, because I was constantly pouring myself out to my students and working with them on such deep energetic levels by drawing out their own unique and creative natures, which was so rewarding for them to experience also. The space that I had grown up in as a child, which had always felt so sad and dark and depressing, was now filled with light and music and the infectious giggles of Jensen's voice made me glad that life was turning at last into a very special place. Every day my heart would melt, as my precious little boy would present me with a miniature pink rosebud that he had carefully picked out of the garden for me all dressed up like Superman. I had never known what it was like to love someone so deeply and completely and adored how fulfilled I was to hear his soft little voice call me mummy.

I was also beginning to encounter some other unfamiliar aspects of my personality, as they emerged in the company of a mysterious man with a foreign name and a devastating smile. He worked at the local music shop, where I bought my sheet music from for my students. He played the bass guitar and I would want to dissolve, whenever he spoke to me. I was so nervous around him, that I never allowed him to know how I felt, although he always seemed to entertain me for an hour or so every time I had to visit the shop to buy more music for my students. My colleague, on the other hand, (who was also my last piano teacher) would only take a few minutes to complete her order. She told me that he always seemed really attracted to me, yet he never told me so. Kerrie used to say that perhaps he was equally terrified of me, which made me laugh of course.

Over a period of about two years, I discovered that there was something very curious about him, or us I should say, because sometimes he would just come out and say exactly what I was unmistakeably thinking. I never knew if I was the sender of these thoughts or in fact the receiver, but it only made the intensity between us seem stronger and all the more terrifying. This connection tapped us both on the shoulder in the most unlikely of places, where we would bump into each other accidently miles away from the music shop or from home, as a series of coincidences. But the most mysterious experience happened when one night, I found myself astral travelling over power lines and down to where he lived, even though I had no idea where that was, because I had never been there before. His parents were both standing next to a sleek, red sporty looking boat in the driveway and when they saw me approaching them, they quickly started shaking their heads at me and gesturing ferociously with their hands for me to go away. It felt so real and I was so scared that I quickly flew back over the power lines, only to notice that the mysterious man had flown up to be there beside me too. The next day, I told Kerrie about it and she said that she knew that his father had a butcher's shop near her house and that I should go and check it out to see if it was the same man.

My heart jumped into my throat, as I stood outside the shop window, because the mysterious man's father whom I saw the night before with his wife cautioning me to keep away from their son, was busy serving customers in front of my unbelieving eyes. It was the same man. It proved to me that astral travel is a real phenomenon and that my experience was definitely not a figment of my own imagination or just a dream. I could never have conjured up that face in a million years and it haunted me for a very long time to say the least.

The next time I had to get more sheet music, the mysterious man had vanished and had apparently found a new job in the city somewhere. The chances of ever seeing him again were so slim, that I tried to put him out of my mind, returning to my music and to teaching my students again instead.

Two of Jana's girls were also coming to me to learn the piano. They lived in a rural town in New South Wales some six hours away and they both went to boarding school. Once a week they would both come and stay with me for the night and we would talk together about all sorts of things, including how scared they were of staying in the main house with my father. I delved further as to the reason, thinking my sister had simply filled their heads with all the stuff they had made up about him when they were children. However, the second oldest niece started shaking and burst into tears. She described in detail what my father had done and tried to do to her many times when they were alone. She confessed that her little sister and brother were also being abused. I could not believe my ears. How could this be happening? Everything my twin sisters had warned me about my father, must really be true and I felt so sick about what to do with this new information. I simply made a bed up in the flat and contacted my sister. We decided to meet half way in the car the next day, driving three hours each and meeting in a service station to drop my niece back to her parents. That was the best I could do. I felt so ashamed and so powerless and so afraid. Perhaps I could just forget about it and maybe it would all just go away and that is exactly how I chose to move on, as I drove back home again completely in denial of my father's secrets.

"Like mother like daughter", I thought I heard the demon snicker with a chuckle, and then I closed my eyes and shuddered without giving it another thought.

10 – VISITED BY ANGELS

Claire:

I could never understand why I was able to perceive the unusual, except that I was aware that there was something else going on underneath the hum of the ordinary. One morning, I was enthralled by two white doves spiralling up slowly outside my window in the lounge room and I felt that I could hear angels singing at the same time. I say that I felt, because it was almost like being amidst a clairvoyant and clairaudient vision. I was actually part of the vision and not outside looking at it from another space or time, like my experience when I had a premonition about my mother dying. I was not afraid or even aware at the time that I was experiencing something so extra ordinary until I turned away from the window and actually saw them and it definitely was not a hallucination.

Time seemed to slow right down and stretch out like a never ending field of flowers inside a beautiful dream and I seemed to be caught somewhere between the tick and the tock of the pendulum swinging on the clock in the kitchen. This feeling of time standing still or slowing right down is exactly how I feel when I am most emphatically drawn to sit at the piano and compose a piece of music, almost as if when I am inspired, I slip into another dimension, where time stands still just long enough for me to complete my work. However, I had never before heard anyone else singing or felt that I was being visited and told what to write until that moment.

Their voices made my hair stand up on the back of my neck and on my arms and legs as well, because it was so very, very beautiful. I felt completely bathed in love, as the euphoric light frequency of their voices lifted my heart into their realm. I do not know how many there were, because they seemed countless, but they were gathered around the ceiling above the piano with their wings overlapping each other, gleaming with pure translucent white light and every colour of the rainbow radiating brilliantly through them. I was just so happy. Thousands of celestial voices seemed to be reaching not just my ears, but into my soul, restoring the glow of my chakras to resonate with their own neon hues, and so my whole essence was electrified and my whole being vibrated with the grandeur of their chorus. I felt inspired by their beautiful white light wings and was moved to tears with sheer gratitude that they were sharing such beauty with me all alone in the lounge room where Daisy once sat in her chair with Renny the ginger Abyssinian cat.

All I could think about was to get to the piano and work out what they were singing. The key was C# minor, which is not a key that I would ordinarily write in, as every key is raised a semitone and takes more concentration than other keys.

I was spellbound by the sheer structure of the composition, for the chorus began two octaves higher than the voices of the core melody and hung like an ethereal mist over the melody. Then another host sounded like a great boom of thunder rumbling and cracking out underneath and opening the tonal spectrum up to a great crescendo in the depths of the lowest bass notes that was audible to my senses. As the haunting melody developed, the other ethereal mist of voices seemed to cross over and into and under the main host of the melody, which was sung by another mass of angels, so that the music felt like it was interwoven with sweeping threads of magic silver and golden light voices. It was as if the music was alive and luminous, yet it sounded so simple and it was difficult to work out how to play on the piano. When I had finished learning it, I was suddenly very tired and the room fell back to normal, as I heard the clock distinctly ticking again in the kitchen.

My encounter with the angels was over, but it was never forgotten. I am still struck with wonder at how special it was that they had chosen to share with me such a divine experience.

Throughout my life, whenever I have felt sad or negative, that piece of music seems to lighten my spirit, as if I can time travel right back to when they were actually there in Daisy's lounge room and I am hearing that music all over again for the very first time.

11 - DIVORCE? IT WON'T HAPPEN TO ME

Mark:

I hadn't seen my family in ten years, they were now living in Woomera, a government run rocket base town way out in the Simpson Desert in South Australia. I went to visit them and realised my brothers and sister were now all grown up and thought it would be nice to spend some quality time together as adults. I decided to put my promising IT career in England on hold and go and spend a few years down under with them, so I applied to migrate back to Australia on my own.

Some Fridays after work I would drive up the motorway to the West Midlands and stay at my Nan's for the weekend and go to a Wolves match. She always loved seeing me and would sit and tell me about her life, about her great, great uncle, who was a radio officer on the Titanic, stories about living through the second world war and being bombed, and I would ask about how the weather was when she was young compared to how it is today. She would talk about my grandad and how devotedly in love they had been all their lives, and since his sudden death she was now just waiting to be back with him once again.

While there, I would often catch up with my best mate, Jim and we would go out drinking and to night clubs. One week Jim insisted on arranging a blind date with a girl he worked with. I said "no way" and told him not to, I had plans to go and live overseas, but Jim could be pushy and arranged it anyway without telling me. I got on really well with her and she seemed to be all the best of things I had found in prior relationships, but this time even more feminine, kind and gentle, less aggressive and stable, and seemed really keen on me. She had recently broken off an engagement and moved back in with her parents, with whom she told me she fought with regularly.

I had only known her about six weeks when my phone at work rang one afternoon. She asked if she could come and stay with me as she had rowed with her parents again and was moving out? Being put on the spot at work all I could say was "Erm, err, ok", to which she replied she had already loaded her car with all her belongings and would be at my place in a couple of hours. Gulp. She had calculated I wouldn't say no, so suddenly I found myself living with someone again without even really deciding if I was ready to, or wanted to.

A year later my permission came through to live in Australia, but I was in a serious relationship now and decided to not go. When I told her she absolutely insisted I should still go, and told me she was "really keen to come too". So we went and settled in Adelaide, I got a boring programming job at a bank, we got engaged and then married. Her parents flew over from England for our wedding and stayed with us. As usual, it wasn't long before my wife and her mother suddenly exploded into screaming at each other for no apparent reason, and they packed their cases and just left. Other than a letter to her telling her she should come back to England (alone) and find someone for a real wedding, that was the last we heard from them for many years.

My childhood sleep adventures changed direction as an adult. I would often have two or three vivid dreams a night, in colour and great detail. Some would be of events that I would later sit in shock and watch on the news, and others of locations or events I'd never been to, but would one day find myself at, months, or even years later. Some nights I'd wake up with sleep paralysis, I could see, but would be completely paralysed, unable to move even a millimetre. Terrified I had died, I would fight with all I had to move something, anything, unable to even reach my wife next to me. Eventually I started to try and relax and experiment with it, trying out different things when it happened, and I proved to myself it wasn't a dream.

Life became a constant struggle financially. Each week after paying our bills we would often only have $30 left. Sometimes, my wife would go out and find a job to help out, but she wouldn't last more than a month before she wouldn't like someone at work, or the way someone spoke to her, or being watched over, or checked up on, or questioned by a manager, or just the work itself, and would resign.

Over at my parents' house there always seemed to be a drama going on, and always with my dad or youngest brother at the centre. Sitting around every day with nothing else to do made it some form of sport to them. When I would hear outright lies being told involving me, I would be forced to have to go down there and confront them about it and put things straight - something my dad hated. He was never open to discussion, and couldn't take any form of criticism. He would blow his top and storm out, and then try and accuse me of being a trouble maker.

I started to hear some really ugly things, such as one of their favourite pastimes when I lived in England had been to spend an evening 'running Mark down', where they would sit and say the nastiest things about me behind my back and laugh about them. My other brother told me he witnessed them doing it and said he found it revolting and without cause.

We eventually had a little girl. I was the first to see Liana's head pop out into the bright lights of this world, as if being awoken from a cosy warm bed on a cold winter's morning by someone switching on a bright spotlight. It was surreal and the most amazing experience of love, to suddenly see this new life you had both created arrive into the world.

Liana refused to breast feed, other than the first few days in hospital, so she was bottle fed and so I did the feeding as well. I would stay up every night to do the midnight feed, and then get up extra early in the morning and do the dawn feed, before heading off to work. I would walk in tired and exhausted in the evening, and be handed Liana by her mom, told she'd had enough for the day and needed a break, as she went off to bed to relax, as if she thought I had been relaxing all day at work.

I started to reflect on how life was going. I had moved back to spend quality time with my family, yet except for my sister, I hardly ever saw them. We started asking ourselves, what the hell were we doing struggling away in Adelaide? If we invited my parents up, mom was always keen, but dad would moan that they couldn't afford the fuel, only to later discover they had instead driven over to my sister's, who lived five times further away. Eventually our patience ran out, it was time to return to England. My wife then dropped a bomb shell on me, she had decided she was never going back. Period. It shook me to the core, for I had made it clear before leaving England that I was only going for a few years. So as usual, I compromised, and just fitted in with what she wanted. Instead we moved interstate, to Sydney. We didn't complain or cause any fuss, or upset anyone by saying why we really were leaving, but it was disappointing. We had to do what was best for the three of us now and so left.

After two years in Sydney, things started to ease financially, but as that got better, our marriage started to fall apart. Liana's mom was fanatical about giving 100% of her time and energy to the baby, and never had any left for our relationship. I had become a 9-5 zombie living purely to work, provide and parent. We moved home at least five times in the first three years, as Liana's mom would suddenly decide she didn't like where we were living anymore, and demanded we move. So we would. We always seemed to be packing or unpacking.

One night Liana was in her cot and coughing from the asthma she had developed, it was my turn to get up and check on her. I staggered half asleep down the corridor in the dark and towards her room. I stood in the darkness at the door and there hovering just above her cot was a brilliant sparkling dark blue ball of light about the size of a golf ball. It was only there for a second or two, I blinked and it vanished. I quietened Liana down and went straight back to bed and to sleep. I didn't tell my wife anything about it as she was already upset about other paranormal things that were going on in the house, hearing footsteps and kitchen cupboard doors frequently opening and closing in the middle of the night. I thought I must have imagined it anyway. The next night Liana was coughing again, and it was my wife's turn to check, so she got up and went down to her room. When she came back she woke me up all freaked out and said "You'll never believe what I just saw! There was a small bright blue ball of light hovering over Liana's cot when I walked into her room". I shot up in bed and realised the night before wasn't my imagination at all. I told her I felt the light was a kind energy, maybe it was Liana's guardian angel watching over and protecting her, so it was a good thing.

Our marriage and relationship had all but died. My wife's obsession with being a mother constantly resulted in her claiming to be too tired to ever have any 'us time', ever, and so life became more and more depressing. I needed love, affection, enjoyment and excitement, even if only occasionally. I would get up at 6AM on weekends and would take Liana straight out, so her mom could have a lie in bed, in the hope that would help get us some time in the evening, but it didn't. She suggested hiring a cleaner once a week, so she didn't have to do house cleaning. That didn't change anything either, nor did her suggestion to hire a gardener so we didn't have to do the gardening on the weekend. The weekend would still end up filled with a long list of chores to do and still no 'us' time.

Whatever she asked of me, no matter how tired or exhausted I was, if I didn't do it straight away, she would be back within two minutes scolding me that I hadn't done it yet, and storm off saying she would do it herself, and my heart would plummet, knowing she would be in a bad mood for the rest of the day, and that would be her excuse for not having 'us' time that day.

She would ask me to go to the shops to get milk and when I returned would be asked "Where's the bread?". I'd tell her she didn't ask me to bring bread, and she would insist she did. It happened so many times, eventually I would just apologise for my failing memory and go back and get what I had 'forgotten'. At times I thought I was just falling apart. When she started mocking me and telling everyone else what a bad memory I had, I decided to try something different. Secretly, I wrote down a list before leaving, and double checked it with her just before I walked out the door. I discovered to my dismay when I returned that I was being accused of forgetting things that weren't even on the list. I soon realised it wasn't my memory at all, she was forgetting what she had asked me to get, and I had just allowed myself to be blamed all too easily.

Recently, Claire wanted to show me a little insight into her past, about what her ex-husband used to do with her. She sat me down to watch the 1944 Ingrid Bergman movie 'Gaslight' about how a husband tries to convince his wife she is losing her memory, when she actually isn't at all. "Shh Paula, you've forgotten again", he would say in the movie, as his wife profusely apologised for having such a bad memory, when he'd never even asked her in the first place. As Claire sat there uneasily squirming at her own memories of being put through the same, I was uneasily squirming too. I had forgotten all about it until we watched the movie. It is really about low self-esteem, doubting yourself too easily, allowing yourself too quickly to take the blame for something that wasn't your problem at all, because you're a giver, from someone else quick to point the finger of blame at you, content to trample you underfoot to avoid looking at themselves.

Our marriage was now fast disintegrating and the rows were becoming worse and worse. Sometimes we would have a row and my wife would go and systematically smash all the crockery in the kitchen, throwing it against the walls, one piece after another. Liana would be in her bedroom hysterically crying her eyes out, and I'd be in there on my knees beside her bed, patting her and trying to calm her down as we both jumped at each plate smashing against the wall in the kitchen. Sadly as much as I refused to accept it, the end was near.

For a long time Liana had been the only reason keeping me there, I just couldn't bring myself to break up our little family. I was still driven on by the belief that relationships were all about compromising, even in a passionless marriage falling apart. I clung on as much as I could, because I truly wanted to save it. It was heart breaking watching it disintegrate, nothing I did seemed to change things, I felt so powerless to stop it. It takes two to make it work and the reality was two of us weren't trying.

Eventually Liana's mom demanded we separate, and reluctantly I agreed, even if just to stop the fighting for Liana's sake.

We all go into our first marriage thinking they will be for life. We all think we have found 'Mr Right', or 'Miss Right', 'the one', the person we will be with for the rest of our lives and grow old with. It is put up on such a pedestal to us that absolute fortunes are spent on first weddings, the bridal showers, hen parties, bucks parties, gift registries, grand receptions, hundreds of guests, trendy and expensive photographers, videographers, photo shoots, exotic honeymoons and all the trimmings that we just have to have, because most of us expect it will be the highlight of our life. It is usually quickly followed by getting the biggest mortgage possible, buying the biggest house, the biggest car, a second car, and so it goes on, tick, tick, tick down the checklist. Before long, it's parenting time and the desire, pressure, to have children, from friends and parents. You can easily end up feeling your life is no longer in your own hands as you work your way through the big checklist of life, slowly shackling yourself down with the chains of debts and commitment, until before you know it that is all it is.

When people see marriages around them failing, they look down on them, arrogantly thinking it won't happen to them. You must have something wrong with you, mine won't fail. I remember people I knew looking down on me like I was a failure, some sort of loser, when my marriage was disintegrating, as if it was something infectious and they were afraid they would catch it too. We ignore the statistics that tell us that more marriages fail than succeed, not believing it will ever happen to us. We think it will only happen to others, the losers, until one day it happens to us too. Then we have to face up to the same devastating reality. I noticed most of those friends who looked down on me all those years ago are now divorced too.

Alone now, I didn't have anyone to talk to, or lean on for support. The friends I did have, if I tried to talk about it, would soon switch off and clearly not want to talk about it. They didn't want to know about someone else's marriage break up. "Just forget about it and move on" was the flippant advice usually dished out, as they quickly changed the subject to something banal and irrelevant, as I ached and emotionally disintegrated inside searching for answers I couldn't find, needing someone to talk to about it. It's one of those things in life that you just can't empathise with how it feels unless you have actually lived through and experienced it yourself.

The prospect of only seeing my daughter every other weekend and half the school holidays, I calculated, would now result in me only seeing her about 18% of the rest of her childhood. I hadn't been a cheat, a drunk, on drugs, or broken any laws, I hadn't been violent, or abusive, yet I would miss out on 82% of her childhood for no fault of mine. That plunged me into an even darker abyss. I loved my little girl and was distraught at having her just ripped away from me literally overnight, as if only her mother mattered and I was disposable as a parent, just for being make, other than when it came to money of course. Why should her mother see her 82% of the time, and I only 12%? And, have to pay her? What happened to sexual equality? Or is it really an implicit admission the sexes really are not equal? The law was all about protecting mothers and children where fathers just deserted them, and rightly so, but had no consideration for good fathers wanting time with their children. I would never see her come home from school again, nor be able to help her in the evening with her homework, or have tea and play around having fun after work. I was distraught.

One evening on the way home from work I reached absolute rock bottom. With no reason to rush home anymore, no smiling little girl happy to see me when I got home, I stood teetering right on the edge of the train platform at Wynyard railway station. I watched in a daze as a train's lights shone up the kilometre long tunnel as it hurtled up towards the platform. All I could think of was stepping off in front of it, and ending the pain. I had had enough. It hurt too much. I just stared into its light in a daze thinking how I wanted it over, I wanted this pain to end, as it raced closer and closer. The life of parenthood I had always looked forward to, I had worked so hard for, had now been smashed to pieces and I didn't want to be here anymore. I couldn't imagine going on, I was exhausted, a failure for losing my marriage. The train burst out of the tunnel and along the platform hurtling towards me. Suddenly, thoughts of Liana needing me to be there for her as a father, if nothing else, flooded my head. It wasn't me that mattered, it was her. At the very last second I stepped back. The carriages whizzed past just inches from my face in a blast of wind, and at that point in time I committed my life to just being there as a father for Liana. As much as I wanted to return to England before all this had happened, and now could, as much as I wanted to run away from all the hurt, I would stay there for Liana. I would be there just for her, to be as much a father for her as I could be. Regardless of what I wanted to do with my life, she came first. I made a commitment to myself that I would be there for her until she was at least 16, maybe 18, until she was ready to lead her own life and able to look after herself. And I did.

Months later, one weekend I returned Liana back to her mom and she dropped a bombshell on me. She, very unusually, asked me in and to sit down and announced she wanted to try and work it out and save our marriage. I was shocked. I agreed to try, in the faint hope we could save it even just for Liana. Soon we were back to having a full relationship, staying over with each other every weekend and most nights in between, going out together, sleeping together. Wherever Liana was, the three of us would be, and we were seriously talking about me giving up my flat and moving back into our home, which was still in my name and I was still paying for.

One day on the phone, Liana said "I'll be good for the baby sitter on Thursday Daddy", which was very out of the ordinary. I mentioned it to her mother and she said she was just going out with the girls from work for a meal and then on to the movies, so I didn't think any more of it until the night came. Things had been going really good between us, so why should I?

I got home from work on the Thursday night and sat in my flat and a horrible oppressive feeling came over me. It felt like a dark black cloud had descended inside the room and I felt a crushing, utterly depressive feeling. I tried to ignore it, but it just got worse and worse throughout the evening. I started to feel sick in the stomach and that something wasn't right. The less I tried to think about it, the stronger it became. It was demanding my attention. You have to listen to your instincts, that inner voice inside you when it talks to you, for it's usually telling you something very important. I decided to go over and have some time with Liana, and see my wife when she got home from the movies, just to check everything was alright with us.

I pulled into our drive and there was a strange, small grey, four wheel drive I'd never seen before parked there. I assumed one of her girlfriends must have left it there while they went to the movies. As I walked up the drive, I could see our bedroom over on the other side of the front door, there were candles lit, and my heart began to pound. There was only ever one reason why she lit candles in the bedroom. As I walked past the lounge window to the front door, I glanced through the gap that had always been there at the edge of the curtains and noticed her in the lounge with a guy, his shirt off, her arms around him, champagne on the table, candles burning and seductive music playing. I stopped and stood there in utter disbelief frozen to the spot. My heart jumped up into my mouth and started pounding harder and faster. I was in utter disbelief, confused and dismayed. She was all over him like a rash. My heart was racing so hard I started to feel dizzy. She started to unbutton his trousers and I decided that was enough, it was clear what I was looking at. Of all occasions, it was the only time I'd ever forgotten my house keys and had to knock, instead of just letting myself in like I usually did. I knocked on the door and waited ages, lots of moving of things around and mumbling was going on inside. She eventually opened the door and I received the most disgusting torrent of abuse and swearing I had ever heard her say to anyone in all the time I had known her, and then she closed it and called the police.

I went home when the two female police officers threatened to arrest her for being so aggressive, and I sat up all night in total shock. I hadn't seen it coming. I had always trusted her without question. I had never checked up on what she told me, or did, or where she was, or ever doubted her word in any way. Never. I never thought she was capable of doing what I had just stumbled into, particularly in view of us trying to save our marriage, and that was her request. How could I have missed it? Was that dark cloud that made me go around there at that exact time the angels doing their magic, to keep us apart and help guide our lives off in different directions? From that night onwards, she became a totally different person, someone I had never known. I discovered I was told lie after lie from then on, and could never believe anything she said anymore.

I was in no state to go in to work the next day, and after endless begging phone calls, she reluctantly agreed to come around to where I was living at lunchtime on her way home from work. She walked in dressed as if she had just come from a nightclub instead of work, with a superior air about her, and wouldn't tell me anything about what had been, or was going on, or who this guy was. She only stayed for about five minutes to tell me, all very matter of fact and bluntly that: yes, she had met someone else, yes, it was over for us for good, but also incredibly she "didn't want it to change things between us financially", and as I sat there in tears, she just got up, turned her back on me and coldly walked out like I was nothing.

I was destroyed. After dealing with our marriage break up, my hopes of getting back together had been soaring sky high, that we were going to make it, and now they had been ripped from under me in the cruelest of ways. I sat in that chair for three days and three nights. I didn't go to work, I didn't eat, I didn't drink and I didn't sleep, as my mind raced and I agonised over what had happened. I replayed all sorts of things from the past, words, actions, agreements, favours, whereabouts, events, wondering if I had misread them. Had any of those been lies too? Had this been going on a long time? How could I have missed seeing it coming?

On the third day it finally hit me and I was freed. I realised if she walked in right now and apologised and asked me to try again, I wouldn't be able to do it, not ever. I would always be wondering if she was lying to me again, if she really was where she said she was, or doing what she said she was doing, or with who she said she was with. It would be a major head fuck I could not live with. The trust had been broken irreversibly and there was now no going back now, ever.

I went straight to see a specialist family law solicitor and was laughingly dismissed and told I had no chance of shared parenting 50/50 with Liana's mother. She told me the courts always sided with the mother and ruled against fathers. Unless a father could prove that the mother was an alcoholic, or drug user, or mentally unstable, and prove it in a court of law, the courts always ruled in favour of mothers. If a father fought it they would just end up paying out tens of thousands of dollars to solicitors for nothing. So I had formal court orders drawn up to protect seeing my daughter as much as I could, and permanently terminated the marriage financially. I cancelled all the joint bank accounts and joint credit cards, and she was furious when she found out. She took most of what we had, the paid off the car, all the furniture and most of everything else, and left me with the debts, but I didn't care. I realised money, assets, property and career all meant nothing at all, absolutely nothing. It is at times like these, you realise what is really important in life and it's not material or ego based things so many people desperately crave and relentlessly pursue through life. You suddenly realise money is not important, or what you own. All that really matters is love.

Things changed for the worse overnight. I was no longer allowed to ring up to talk to Liana and I would be accused of 'harassment' if I tried. I would be told my time with her was every other weekend, and abruptly hung up on, or the phone would be switched to the answering machine until after 7:30PM, when I knew she would be in bed. When Liana came to me, her mom wouldn't give me any of all the nice clothes I had bought for her. Instead, she would cunningly send her to me in old dirty clothes, knowing I couldn't let her stay in them all weekend, which forced me to buy her new ones. I couldn't send her back in the filthy clothes she arrived in, so she would often go back in some of the new clothes I had bought, and that would be the last I would ever see of them, she would never return them.

Her mom became obsessed with draining every dollar possible out of me, as if imposing some form of endless fine on me for the marriage failing, and used Liana as the pawn to achieve it. "Mommy said I can only go on the school excursion if you pay because she is broke", was a common one, even though I paid her $400 every week in maintenance, on time, without fail, by direct bank transfer. She still came up with an endless list of excuses to try and extract more money out of me. If I didn't pay extra she would simply punish Liana by preventing her from going on her school trips or whatever it was. Liana was the one missing out, so in the end, I decided what really mattered was Liana, so I would do what was best for her and just pay her mother so Liana didn't miss out. Without fail, just after paying I would hear how her mother had gone out and bought herself a new plasma television, or a new lounge suite, or new kitchen setting. So much for her constant sob stories of being broke. It was utterly parasitic the way she used Liana to drain more and more money out of me.

On one occasion when she dropped Liana off Liana said,

"Mommy parks down the road and around the corner now so you don't see her new car".

I didn't let on that I knew, but she continued the charade for over three months, craftily keeping her new car hidden from me. Yet she still constantly carried on phoning me and complaining of being broke and having no money. I couldn't believe a word she said anymore, so I would just ignore her pleas and restrict the conversation to be only about Liana's welfare.

I could never understand why she was so angry towards me, or why she tried to systematically punish me in every way she could for the next 11 years. I had tried everything I could when we were together to make it work. When she wanted to separate, I did. When she wanted to try again, I did. I went to counselling with her, but all she did was read out a list of demands and storm out shouting, refusing to discuss anything else. Each attempt at salvaging our relationship would end up with me catching her out telling me more lies. Even though I wanted to return to England, I stayed for another 11 years just to be a father to Liana. I always paid her maintenance, and a lot more than I should have been, without fail, unlike all her friends' ex-husbands who were using every trick they could to avoid paying anything. Nothing was ever enough when it came to money. There were occasions when I had no money at all and would have to draw cash off a credit card to make sure she still got paid each week. I found it sad that even to this day, I never received a single "Thank You" at least for always paying her maintenance, or for being there as a father for our daughter. When Liana reached 18 and she no longer could get any money out of me, it finally stopped, and I never heard from her again.

12 - THE MUSIC THIEF

Claire:

I had just settled Jensen into bed, when the phone rang and a strange male voice said, "Hello is that Claire"?

"Yes. How can I help you"? I replied thinking it maybe another student enquiring about lessons.

"I'm actually a guitarist and I work with a musician you used to buy piano music from".

I suddenly felt sick, as he started to chuckle and I thought it was just a prank to tease me. I wanted to melt into nothingness, for somehow that mysterious man was back connecting with my head all over again.

"Yes" Is all that I could mouth, because my heart was thumping so hard, I thought I was going to faint.

"I'm looking for a keyboard player for my band, and he said you were really good. Are you interested at all?"

"Oh sure. What sort of music do you play?" I enquired, drawing long and hard on my cigarette before letting the smoke waft out of my mouth without exhaling.

"Pretty much original. You could come over and audition on the weekend if you like? Got a pen? This is my address ok?"

"Ok Great. See you then. Bye".

I scribbled down the address to his flat and hung up the phone.

"Fuck" is all that I could whisper, wondering who the bass player would be when I rocked up with my synth tucked under my arm and a two year old squeezing my hand? I couldn't wait to audition. I couldn't wait to see if that mysterious man was there too.

That pretty much sums up how I met my second husband and no, the mysterious man, remained mysterious to me and married a mysterious blonde lady instead, but he was responsible for introducing my second husband to me, which takes the mystery about him away I suppose to a certain degree.

The romance between my husband and I did not develop for at least a year after we met and we spent a great deal of time together rehearsing for the band. When he heard me play some of my original classical pieces, he offered to record them for me, as he was also technically proficient as well with professional audio recording equipment. One afternoon, he invited me over to his place to hear the final mix of some of my original classical compositions and I was mortified to hear that he had added drums and a screaming guitar over the top as well, which violently drowned out the delicate movements I had created, without even consulting me about it first. The drummer told me later that he had also approached a record company presenting my material as his own work and I was utterly livid to think that someone I trusted could have no respect for my original work at all. I kissed him on the forehead and said that was the last time I would ever see him again and slammed the door behind me and if not for the lives of my children, I wish it had of been.

A year later, he rang me to tell me that his mum had just given birth to a new baby girl and could we get together again. Instead of saying no, I gave in to my religious conditioning to turn the other cheek and to simply forgive and forget. He was back in my life and I was too weak to stop his hooks from slowly making their way inside me all over again, where they would twist and gouge away at me for another twenty years.

He got a new job closer to my home in a Hi Fi shop and coincidentally, his boss was the mysterious man from the music shop again, who had moved jobs some months earlier from the city also. We still shared an uncanny connection, for one day I was sitting in the bath trying to come up with a name for our new band, and a word just came into my head like a light being switched on. When my husband came home, he said, "Oh guess what? My boss came up with a great name for the band today. What do you think?" I turned away as my face drained of colour in complete shock, for my husband repeated the obscure name I thought that I had come up with all on my own in the bath. These so called coincidences happened to me every day and I wondered if the mysterious man was equally aware of it happening invisibly between us too?

One of my old friends from school was going out with the sound designer from Mad Max, an Australian movie made back in the 1980s and when he heard some music I was writing said that it lent itself perfectly to the film industry as well. I went into Eaton's and recorded a collection of short pieces, reflecting different moods just on the piano and he loved them so much that he arranged for me to meet with the editor of another film he was working on. I was absolutely amazed with how much the editor liked my work and he offered to introduce me to his good friend Bruce Smeaton, who had composed music for lots of iconic Australian films. I was gob smacked by such belief and support by a complete stranger and I felt so shy about meeting him on my own that I invited my guitarist friend to come along as well.

Bruce Smeaton changed my life forever. He shared many stories about the film industry and how his amazing success as a composer hadn't started until middle age, when he had got cancer of the lip and could not play the horn anymore, so he took up orchestration instead and became a successful screen composer. "Something good always came out of something really bad", he said and I admired Bruce's attitude towards making something wonderful out of such a difficult time in his life. Perhaps one day, something wonderful like that could happen to me, I paused to dare the universe, just in case anyone was listening.

I thought Bruce Smeaton was utterly brilliant! His kindness blew me away as well when he listened to my Eaton's tape and gave me the thumbs up about the content of my compositions. Within a week, he rang me to offer me my first jingle, which was a 30 second national television commercial for Le Specs sunglasses.

I wish that I had been strong enough to develop my musical career on my own, but as fate would have it, one jingle after another came along and my husband and I worked together at producing them. We just evolved as a working couple really and that is why we ended up just getting married.

Unfortunately it wasn't long before I started finding it difficult knowing how to cope with his flash anger. After one particular day of enduring his abuse, I ran to my car and locked him out, because he was screaming violently at me. He kicked the passenger door in and left such a huge dent, that it was a wreck and I never drove it again. He never paid to get it fixed and he never apologized for doing it, blaming me instead for making him so angry in the first place.

I eventually threw him out, but I was too weak to keep him out. I was pregnant and getting back together seemed like the right thing to do. I was so enthralled to discover that I was carrying twins and had a strong sensation that they were going to be very special. My father gave us the main house and moved into Daisy's flat to give us more space for the babies. I had a nightmare that I actually had twin boys, but both of them were born dead. I was really uneasy about giving birth and at thirty seven weeks, went into labour and gave birth to two beautiful little baby boys. The oldest we called Rick and the second one Christopher.

Chris tragically died of cot death ten weeks later. Apparently most mothers who lose a baby to cot death have had a premonition similar to my dream, almost to warn them that something was not quite right to prepare them. So my dream was half true and I found it extremely difficult with just having one twin to look after, because Rick's baby face reminded me of his twin. The grief was unbearable.

My sister Jana and her little ones came down to come to the funeral. I wondered why my father had suddenly taken off in the car and gone away for a few days at a time when I needed his support most of all. Later when he finally returned home, he told me that he had gone to Albury to bail Jana's husband out of the watch house for indecent exposure as a paedophile and made me promise to keep it a secret from her as well.

This was the brother in law who used to buy me chocolate every time he came to visit my sister and my father found it more important to bail him out of jail, than to attend his own grandson's funeral. It always struck me as being a bit sick really protecting such a disgusting crime instead of being there for his daughters. It struck me that to be that way, one would have to have been abused also and I started to wonder if my father had been molested somewhere in his early life. It was like he and my brother law shared the same offence in wanting to keep it a secret, as I could not imagine anyone decent ever protecting a paedophile unless they too were guilty of the same crime.

As if reading my mind, my father then told me to be very careful that I made it into heaven one day, so that my baby had a mother when I died. Those words gagged my thoughts in an instant. I was being mind controlled all over again into submission, just as I had been throughout my childhood and so much so in fact that I never said a word about it to him for the next twenty years.

13 – RICK

Claire:

Rick did not reach the normal milestones that I expected and he soon showed signs of being different to other babies the same age. He would stare right through me without seeming to recognize me, as if in his own world. He would only eat tinned food and would choke and spit the food out when I offered him my own home cooking. He was also obsessed with spinning things to the point where he became expert at balancing anything round as it span on the edge of the coffee table, without falling off. If he needed a drink, he would simply grab my hand and point to the orange juice in the fridge, without looking into my eyes and he would not speak at all. My husband and I would become really angry and lose our tempers with him by screaming and smacking him to try and change the behaviour, but nothing ever changed. Rick seemed to get worse in fact. When I tried to cuddle him, he would pull away. He started to hit himself and sit on the floor staring into nothing, whilst flapping his hands at the same time and rocking backwards and forwards nonstop. I was afraid that he was deaf, because he seemed to ignore me and so I reached out to the doctor to get some answers.

I wondered if the tragic death of his twin brother had shut him down emotionally somehow, but the doctors all denied that this was the problem. Instead Rick passed the hearing test and was seen by one of only two doctors in Melbourne, who were qualified to diagnose his condition. When they told me that he had a 50/50 chance of ever speaking, I realised how special this little boy was after all. That feeling I had when he was growing inside of me was absolutely right. This little boy indeed was special. Rick was autistic.

My husband was never involved with any of Rick's care or behaviour management. The only time he seemed to get involved, was when he had enough of Rick's difficult behaviour and became violent with him, which I believe only shut Rick down even more and I do not think that his father to this day understands just how special Rick is. It was my friend Kerrie, who was by my side throughout these difficult times and she was so inspired by Rick, that she eventually took a course in Special Education to work with other autistic adults some years later.

Of course, I was relieved on one hand to understand what was happening with Rick and terrified on the other, because there was no cure. Yet something wonderful was happening to me on the inside. My inner landscape of belief systems was being rocked and shaken again. Rick was calling something magical and mysterious out of me. Just being able to communicate with him required a whole new way of thinking and I had to be creative about it, because nothing my mother or father had taught me about parenting worked with him and nothing the way I raised Jensen worked either. I had to come up with another way to communicate and so I started to listen and trust my own inner voice again and not monitor myself on what other people thought or told me what to do anymore. I started noticing how Rick was also drawing out the lightness and the darkness in other people as well. I suppose I expected people to make fun of him because of his disability, but Rick was drawing something patient and kind out of people instead. My husband's step dad, who seemed to me to be very quiet and distant, suddenly became warm and compassionate around Rick and I was mesmerized.

I would spend my time sitting on the floor mimicking him, rocking and flapping my hands for hours and gazing into space. Rick would never look me in the eye, or encourage me in any way, but deep down I just wanted him to accept me and doing whatever he did seemed to be a good place to start for him to let me into his world. I instinctively felt that he was shut down, because of intense fear, even though the doctors had all denied this theory. Sometimes when I just wanted to run away from everyone and hide away somewhere, I imagined that Rick had done just that and was hiding somewhere in his mind, where it was safe and peaceful to play all on his own.

I had this notion that since Rick loved repetition so much, then perhaps I could show him how to talk by teaching him first how to sing. Wherever we were together, I would sing a simple little melody that I made up over and over just changing the words to the place we were, at that particular time.

"In the garden, in the garden, in the garden with me. In the garden, in the garden in the garden with me".

Over and over I would sing this little song and Rick would continue staring into space blankly, without acknowledging that I was even there beside him at all. Sometimes it would be in the bath. Sometimes we would be in the car. I think the same old melody drove the rest of the family crazy, but something inspired me to just keep on going. Every night I would tuck him into bed and kiss him tenderly on the cheek.

"Nigh' nigh' Ricky". I would whisper, but there was nothing – just the silence and the blank stare, as if the person inside had simply gone away, where nobody could reach him anymore.

"Love is simply the name for the desire and pursuit of the whole".

— Plato, The Symposium

14 - SPIRITUAL AWAKENINGS

Mark:

I breathed in the fresh air of a long forgotten freedom I hadn't even realised I had lost. If I needed to work back late, I could. I no longer had to phone home and suffer all the usual huffing and puffing, being told off and made to feel like I was being selfish, as if enjoying some form of masochistic fun needing to work late, and then inevitably hung up on. I could even just go out for a drink after work and not have to ask, nor be on a time limit. I loved slowly coming home from work, putting on some incense, lighting a candle and lying on the couch and meditate. It was so peaceful. I would try and relax and think of nothing, absolutely nothing, it's actually a lot harder than it sounds. Thoughts just keep sneaking back into your conscious mind and you suddenly realise you're thinking about something again and have to banish them away and focus back on nothingness, absolute nothingness. It wasn't easy at first, but as time went on I became better and very therapeutic and relaxing. I loved the serenity it brought to life.

The months flew by and I was still struggling with processing the implosion of my marriage. I wanted to understand why? It was that 'why?' gene in me rearing its head again, demanding I delve in to it further. It would have been so much easier if I could have just told myself 'whatever', let go, and moved on, but I'm just not wired like that. If you don't understand what you did wrong, or why something didn't work, you are destined to repeat it.

One day Liana and I were walking through a department store and she insisted on going over into the children's book section. As I followed her in, weaving around the kiddies couches and play pits, my attention was immediately drawn to a very out of place looking book sitting there at face height, staring right at me. It clearly was not a child's book. For some reason it seemed to call to me like the hypnotic notes floating out across a lake from a siren, compelling me to come forth. I went over and picked it up, turned it over and read the synopsis on the back. It was called 'Five Stages of the Soul' and about why we go through major crises in mid-life, such as marriage breakups, serious illnesses or other major life changing events. Co-incidence? It was pure synchronicity. The book sounded like it was written exactly for where I was at that point in time, and had been positioned there by the mystical forces of synchronicity to be sure it found its way to me. A door had opened, so I bought it and stepped through to see where it would take me.

As soon as I got home, I started reading, page after page, as fast as I could. I couldn't put it down. It felt as though I was receiving a mentoring talk from a divine presence, explaining this is where you have been, and this is where you are at right now with your life. This is why you're here, and these are your choices to go forward. Some of it resonated so profoundly with my experiences that I found myself reaching for a pencil and underlining passages so I could find them again later, to contemplate on a deeper level. It talked about how many of us are sent major crises in mid-life to awaken us spiritually. Sometimes things have to get much worse before they can get better. It reminded me of the terrible bushfires I lived through in Sydney. Bushfires that completely destroyed entire forests leaving them a black barren landscape of charred stumps and seemingly totally devoid of any life. Only weeks later there were new tiny bright green shoots sprouting everywhere from the charred blackness, allowing it to regenerate and grow back bigger and stronger, and more beautiful than ever before. It's not always a negative event, sometimes we also need to have a bushfire rage through our lives, to clear out the bad and stagnant things and regenerate us to start afresh at a new higher level, and it can be very traumatic. It is up to us how we look at it.

We aren't forced to evolve spiritually, but we are presented with the opportunity to choose whether we want to go through our own personal metamorphosis, to look inward at ourselves and grow, or not. The door swings open and the choice is ours as to whether we step through it and embark on that inward journey. It's a scary journey, as it requires complete honesty about yourself, and you need to be brave. Some choose to see the light and embrace it, whilst others turn away and reject it, blindly carrying on living their same old detrimental life patterns, angrily wondering why the same issues keep re-occurring in their lives.

I had always been interested in space, the cosmos, science, life, death, the soul, astrology, the supernatural, paranormal and psychology. I had always wondered how, or even if, somehow these all fitted together as pieces of some giant unified cosmic jigsaw puzzle. It had been simmering away in me all my life and I never had the chance to delve into it deeper. My ex-wife really wasn't interested at all, so I hadn't pursued it while married, but it had never gone away. This was the catalyst for me to reconnect with my soul's journey and begin to start to try and connect some of those cosmic jigsaw pieces together. The biggest bushfire of my life had burnt right through it and I was now standing in the barren black landscape left behind, with the first buds of new growth now appearing. With an open mind, I chose to be brave and begin my journey inwards, one step at a time.

Being truly honest with yourself is about being honest regarding both the good and the bad things you have done, and about how you have treated other people. It is about having empathy, the awareness of the consequences your words and actions have on other peoples' lives. I had always worried if I had upset someone, somehow, or that I might. I have never done anything purposely to hurt anyone, ever, but inevitably we all do, even if unintentionally. If I did, I would beat myself up and agonise over it for ages afterwards. It had always felt a burden to carry, but no, empathy was actually a precious gift I already had, without even realising it. If everyone had empathy for others the Earth would be such a kinder planet to live on for all of us.

I always have, and still do, wonder why so many people seem so at ease and don't care if they upset someone else to get what they want. They don't consider, think, or seem to care at all about how their own actions affect other people's lives, or who they tread on to get what they want. To me they are a different species I just don't understand. We see it in our ordinary day to day lives, colleagues at work who walk up to you while you are in a conversation with someone else and just talk right over you, because they think what they want is more important. People, 'friends', relatives, who will lie to cover up their own bad behaviour, often by pointing a finger at someone else to deflect it. The companies and banks of this world who are only interested in what profit they can make for themselves with no thought for what misery and hardship their actions might bring to lives. How can people treat other human beings like this?

They justify it by lying to themselves that they 'had to do it', it was 'just business', they 'had no choice', it 'wasn't their fault', or some other cliché to appease their own inner guilt. They did have a choice, they selfishly chose what was best for them. The fact they have to make excuses is at least a start in the right direction, an implicit admission what they did wasn't a good thing, but many just don't care at all. One day they too will have their own bushfire and doors will open for them to choose to look inwards, or not. If they don't, one day when they eventually start to think about their own mortality they will just have to hope there is nothing after death, no life review, no reckoning of how they treated others during their time here.

I had heard about astrology and birth charts many times, so it felt a good place to go next. I found an astrologer that felt right, made a booking and went along. I approached it sceptically, but with an open mind, and watched and listened as she did my birth chart. She explained many things to me, such as having a lot of Libra in my chart, the 'scales of justice', meant I liked things to be fair. It was true, I could never stand seeing anyone being treated unfairly, being bullied, taken advantage of, lied to, deceived, cheated. I had always believed everyone should be treated fairly in life, even though the reality is far from it. Integrity had always meant so much to me, even before I realised what it was, it felt like it should be the cornerstone of being kind and respectful to others - it was in olden times, honour, honesty, trust, commitment, and yet I could never understand why it seemed to mean so little to so many people nowadays. It has largely been replaced by lying, deceit and spin – the art of deflecting and talking your way around something to avoid it altogether - cancers that pervade our society today and that sadly force the rest of us to be constantly on our guard and suspicious as to the true motives of others.

A few months later, a friend just happened to recommend a Tarot reader she knew, just as I was thinking about it. Synchronicity. Another door opens and an invitation arrives to step through. I had no idea how it worked at all, but I accepted and went with an open mind to experience where it might take me and draw my own conclusions. I had heard all the usual accusations of cold reading and fraudsters and was careful not to give any information out via body language, or reinforce what she said in any way. It actually felt quite rude to be with someone and not give them anything back at all, you don't realise how much you give out in a normal conversation until you try not to. She did lots of things with her cards which all seemed eerily spot on for me, and at the end finished off with a card reading where she laid out a card for each of the next twelve months and explained each one. January's said I was going to move home, and August's that I would meet a red headed Aries woman with whom I would have a serious relationship. She recorded it on an audio tape which she gave me to take home. I was impressed she had the confidence to give me a record of her reading to check back against.

For the next year, at the end of each month, I would pull out the tape and play it back to see what she had said for that month and if it had happened, being very careful not to just make things fit. I soon forgot what she had said, so each month when I played it back they often came as a surprise. Month after month they turned out to be eerily spot on. When I played the tape at the end of January, not long after having moved home, I remembered she had said I would move home, and I had.

As I wondered what next, another new friend recommended someone she knew who was a really good medium. Another door opened and another invite to step through. It was a two hour drive up into the country to where she lived. When I arrived she was overrunning with her previous person so I sat and waited.

She made us a cup of tea and we sat down ready to get started and straight away told me one of my grandfathers was my spirit guide watching over me, and he was right there now, and she was passing on messages from him. I noticed she seemed to be using phrases I remember he used to use. She knew nothing about me, nor that he had been a farmworker around Wolverhampton most of his life and often used many old English Black Country sayings, and now she was also using them on the other side of the planet. Coincidence? Maybe. She said I had been born two weeks late, I should have been a November Sagittarian, not a December one, something I had no idea whether it was true or not, but something I could check. My hour with her turned into two and a half, telling me many things, including that something big was going to happen in my 50s. When I left I tried to pay her for the time she had given me, but she refused and would only accept payment for the single hour I had originally booked. She wasn't on a money making exercise.

On the long drive back home I rang my mother who lived in another state, and had no idea where I had been, and simply asked if I had been born on time? She said no, I was born late, two weeks late actually. I should have been born in November, exactly as the medium had said and which just made me wonder all the more about the other things she had said.

15 - OVER 40s DATING UGGHH

Mark:

Long over my first marriage's demise I was ready to move on to a new relationship, the question was, how do you go about that when you are in your 40s?

I discovered dating is an absolute minefield for the middle aged and totally different to anything you ever knew before. You can't just go into a bar, or to a party and assume most people around your age are available as you can when you're a teenager, or in your 20s. Most 40 something's just don't go to bars or parties alone, or hang around in single sex groups anymore. You just can't tell who is unattached, available and looking and who isn't.

At this stage in life the best solution seemed to be internet dating websites. They at least start with those unattached and actively seeking a new relationship. You can also pick out those of a similar age, who live nearby, who have similar interests, and desires from life and a relationship. It's a great way to start, browse and see who takes your fancy before any contact has even been made at all. Instead of being based merely on lustful eye contact across a bar or dancefloor, or an alcohol induced lustful spur of the moment one night stand only to discover the next day they really aren't the sort of person you would ever otherwise get involved with. They do come with their own dangers though, not so much the 'online axe murderers' cliché adult children always seem to insist on bringing up (yawn), but more those who lie about their age, or height, or with 10 year old photos, or obscurely angled ones hiding something, or professional studio produced photos all made up, dressed, and posed to look like someone you will never actually see.

At that age most people have been through one or more long term serious relationships, marriages and divorces, and often already have children and all the responsibilities that come with them. They have exe's, and all the scars that usually come with them too. A lot have been hurt, badly; physically, mentally, financially, emotionally, often all of the above, making dating sites an absolute minefield of personal insecurities and fears to navigate. People are so terrified of repeating the same issues they had with a previous partner they have little or no tolerance, and can be very blunt about it. Innocently say one word or phrase that triggers a past issue for someone, and that's the last you will ever hear from them, and often won't even know why.

I noticed we all seemed to have three 'shopping lists': the 'must have' list, the 'would like' list, and the 'must not have' list. The 'must not have' list is the new and most revealing one, revealing the scars of previous relationships. The more relationships people had experienced, the more their shopping lists grew. That in turn actually made the odds of meeting someone else, whose both 'must have' and 'must not have' shopping lists matched your 'must have' and 'must not have' shopping lists, shrink smaller and smaller. Like I said, it's an absolute minefield.

I decided to try and carefully constructed a profile. I included all the good points from my past relationships and added others, such as honest and spiritual. Someone on the same inward journey was now a 'must have' and at the top of my list. I posted it on a couple of the more popular local dating websites to see what responses it might bring and waited.

I would open messages with nervous curiosity to see who it was from. Some I would chat with online, or on the phone. One of the first three questions I would nearly always be asked was ... "What did I do for a living"? I soon realised it was just a way of estimating my income, it was about money. It was fear based insecurity. I would never ask that question, and never did. I didn't care if the right woman for me was a multi-millionairess, or a toilet cleaner. For me a relationship was not about a person's income, money or security. I was looking for love and happiness. There are plenty of very rich couples out there dreadfully unhappy in their relationships, and plenty of very poor couples blissfully happily in love. It just said to me they weren't looking for true love - they were looking for someone to support them financially.

Others made it clear their priority was their children, their families, their girlfriends, their job, their hobbies, their sports, and it left me wondering just where they would fit in time for a close relationship if the love of their life walked through their door? Others made it bluntly clear that they now had their own 'security', usually property from their divorce settlement, and would not be risking it by sharing it in any new relationship. It was clearly a blunt message of 'what is hers is hers', but would expect your income to be ours. I remember one profile which I thought was a joke at first, but was actually serious, saying she was looking for a gym fit guy, model looks, very financially secure with a successful career and high income, intelligent, masculine, a stud in the bedroom and who would supply her with a house in her own name, a luxury car, regular holidays in five star accommodation and an annual four week trip to Europe, which must also be five star. In return she promised great sex. It just sounded to me like a cold business agreement with no interest in finding love or romance. I mused if there actually was a man who fitted all that criteria, then surely he would be in so much demand why would he even need to be advertising himself on a dating website at all? Fortunately, not everyone is so obsessed with the materialistic.

Nothing really seemed to be happening and I noticed the dating website also organised singles functions for the over 30s. So I decided to go along and see what they were like. It was an eye opening experience. A lot of the events seemed to be flooded with a large proportion of young males, who hardly even seemed 30, and who would smoothly zero straight in on any attractive older women who were present. Talking to women later, I found out that a lot of these young males weren't even 30, and admitted they were actually attached or married, and not happy sexually in their relationships at home. Sex can so often be turned into a reward system by immature women to control and manipulate. The young guys thought the much older and mature women were 'desperate' and would easily go for no strings attached sexual flings with a much younger guy. Sadly their trusting wives and girlfriends were sitting at home under the impression her guy was working late, or out having drinks with his mates after work, not realising he was actually at over 30s singles dances trying to pick up older women for the sex.

The functions always seemed to be in obscure out of the way locations such as retired servicemen's clubs, golf clubs or country clubs, so I would be forced to drive to them, which meant I couldn't really drink much alcohol with all the breath testing traps around. I soon devised my own rating system, based on how many cokes I would stay there long enough to very slowly sip my way through. A two coke event was quite good, I was encouraged enough to stay and buy another drink, but some were just one coke, or even less, a half coke event if really bad and I didn't even stay long enough to finish my first drink.

At one venue I went to, the room was full of big round tables with all the women sitting in groups at tables furthest from the bar. All the men were standing scattered in a line along the bar, drink in hand, eyeing off the women across a big empty no-man's land. As the evening progressed, a guy would brew up enough courage to suddenly break away and head off across the no-man's land, weaving his way to the left and to the right through the maze of empty tables and chairs, and zero in on his target, bend over, and say something whilst pointing towards the dance floor. More often than not, you'd see her shake her head side to side and all the guys at the bar would look at each other with a grimace of 'ouch'. Then you would see him smile and try to convince her, another shake of her head, sometimes with her pointing towards her friends. He would then accept defeat and give up, retreating back along his approach, weaving right and left through the sea of empty tables and chairs, flames and smoke billowing out behind him as he crashed and burned. All the guys watching along the bar would stand there horrified, looking at each other raising their eyebrows or rolling eyes in an unspoken agreement of fear, reluctant to be the next one. It was harrowing. As the night wore on the venue slowly filled with more and more smoke from guys crashing and burning, so I left. I think I only stayed as long as I did, as I was mesmerised watching the antics across the no-man's land as guys plucked up the courage to make contact and nearly all were rejected. It wasn't a good way for males and females to casually mingle and connect, risking humiliation in front of everyone if rejected it felt more like an emotional battle field. I decided that was it for these events, and resigned myself to not going to anymore.

Just as I gave up I received an email about another event at an upmarket hotel, and easy to get to in the city centre, which was rare. I decided to go just one more time to see if the location changed the atmosphere and dynamics, or attracted different people than those I had regularly seen at the other functions. I went along and it was actually quite impressive, a three coke event. After standing around by myself for well over an hour though, sipping on my third coke I decided it was really just more of the same, only in an upmarket setting, and decided to leave. Just as I was finishing off my drink and about to walk out, a very exotic and voluptuous looking woman with heavy makeup suddenly appeared out of nowhere and came straight towards me and started talking to me, yes me, recounting my online profile in detail, word for word. It was a bit spooky and I looked around to see if I was being setup by someone, somehow, as she seemed to know all about me and I had never seen her before. She said she had been studying my profile for ages, but didn't have the courage to contact me, even though she had really wanted to, and that she couldn't believe I was actually there and had to come over and say hello. She told me she was an astrologer, an Aries, and only dated Sagittarians. So I knew instantly she was spiritual, and from our conversation she clearly had a brain and made it very clear she was interested in me. We spent the night talking and left together and I made sure she got home safely.

16 - THE ASTROLOGER

Mark:

The astrologer and I got on so well we started seeing each other every night. The second time I met her she turned up dressed entirely in black, black feminine clothes, black stockings, high heels and heavy makeup, and I suddenly had a flashback to that woman all in black who I had fantasised about so much back when I was just a pubescent teenager. Was it her?

I realised each of my previous relationships had been slowly evolving in a specific direction. Strong, feminine, sensual and now spiritual, each one adding another layer on top of the previous one, each new partner adding another new dimension to a relationship. Is that what we all do? Was I simply following and developing my taste in women, or was I being slowly drawn towards a specific woman? I rationalised it couldn't be the latter, as they had all been chance encounters, where they had in fact approached me. But who says logic is enough to describe events we experience? Our lives might work in synchronicity much more than any of us ever realise, with people and events coming into, and leaving, our lives at the perfect time for who or what we need right then, even if we didn't realise it at the time. Maybe we all know subconsciously there is someone specific out there for us, 'the one', and in each relationship we are subconsciously selecting more and more facets that define who they are, each slowly subconsciously guiding us closer to one day finding them.

A few days later September arrived, as usual at the end of every month, I pulled out the tape from the tarot reader last year, and played it to see what she had said for August. I had completely forgotten it was the one where for August I would start a serious relationship with a red headed Aries woman. I had met her the week before, the last week of August, so that was one out of three, and she had already told me she was Aries as well, two out of three. But she didn't have red hair, it was dark brown and I wasn't going to allow myself into making that fit. The next time I saw her I told her about the tarot reading from the year before and the tape, and what I had been told for August. She just burst out laughing and I wondered what was funny? She said her hair actually wasn't really dark brown at all, she dyed it dark brown, pulling out some photos at the same time and showing me it was really red. Three out of three.

She worked as a shop assistant in a new age shop and did the odd astrology reading there. She only dated Sagittarians and specifically sought them out, half man, half animal, always shooting an arrow upwards towards the stars, always striving to greater heights and pushing the boundaries, she would say with a wicked giggle. That's what she wanted. We connected immediately on a spiritual level and she had integrity, morals, was passionate, feminine and was very sensual and we got on fabulously.

I thought I'd finally got it right this time, I mean, what could go wrong here? Our shopping lists matched perfectly, and we both had a teenage daughter, but the thing about shopping lists is, they mainly focus on the past and what you have already experienced, which can leave you blind to new situations you've not encountered, or ever considered before, or personal things people would never put up in a public forum.

She wouldn't allow me to go around to her place, and would always turn up late to mine, by hours, sometimes so late I had given up and gone to bed. Three months passed before I was finally invited over to her place and I started to find out why. She saw me looking at her cooker, which was thick with dust, and told me it hadn't been lit for seven years. She couldn't bring herself to use it, or any appliance in the kitchen, not even a kettle to boil water for a cup of tea or coffee. Her daughter had been raised for the last seven years on take-away, or pre-packaged food that didn't need cooking, heating or any form of preparation.

Not long after she sat me down and explained that seven years ago she had discovered the man she lived with, a well known television celebrity, was cheating on her with young men, and from that day on she had suffered with Obsessive Compulsive Disorder (OCD) from the revulsion of it all. Every night she was left alone to close up the new age shop she worked in, with its vast buffet of lit candles, lights, doors to lock and alarms to set, it gave her panic attacks every night. Sometimes it could take her up to two hours of returning back and forth, before she actually drove all the way home.

A lot of guys would have been off like a shot, but I still believed it was about compromise, and other than that we got on perfectly in every way. She was definitely a soul mate, and I went into compromise mode and focussed on working with her and her OCD, by being loving and supportive to try and fight it. She insisted we hire the movie 'As Good as It Gets' with Jack Nicholson and watch it to get an idea of how her world was.

She was always broke and every week was a struggle for her just to scrape enough money together to feed herself and her daughter, never mind pay any rent. Her ex-husband had just taken off to Queensland and completely abandoned her and their child. He didn't take any interest or show any responsibility towards their daughter, or pay anything towards making sure she was clothed and fed, or had a roof over her head - nothing, yet they could see online how he spent plenty of money on himself and his expensive photography equipment. I will never understand how grown adult men can do that to their children.

The flat she was living in was one of her parent's many investment properties and she hadn't been able to pay them any rent in years. Straight away they started pressuring her to move out, calculating I would step in and take on looking after her and her daughter, and of course I did. We rented a flat and moved in together and I took on being responsible for the two of them, as well as Liana, paying the bills, sorting out issues and everything else that came along for all three of us, as well as dealing with her OCD.

I insisted it was time we at least have a microwave oven in the kitchen and decided to make a stand. It was important her daughter had the chance to at least cook herself a hot meal at home when she wanted one, and not have to live off takeaways which had made her overweight and caused self-esteem issues. I bought some microwave meals and showed her daughter how to cook herself a hot meal at home. She was absolutely elated. She was fifteen and couldn't remember ever having a hot meal at home.

I could see she was not just a good astrologer, but a very good one. She had that knack of making people feel so at ease and had that sexy mystical gypsy look too, which all added to the mystique. She was missing her calling as a shop assistant, so I encouraged her to do astrology professionally. I said that I would support her in every way I could through the transition, while she built up a client base of her own that she could then live off and become independent doing what she loved. She started doing readings in various shops and soon had all sorts of clients coming to her, from the usual married mums in tracksuit pants with their best friends, pathetically wanting to know if they were going to have an affair while their husbands were out at work, through to high court judges wanting to know the names of which men at work fancied them, to rich women with nothing better to do than agonise over what colour to paint their kitchen. Eventually she was earning enough money to stop being a shop assistant and able to focus on being a full time astrologer, her dream. I was so happy for her.

At home OCD slowly started to dominate my life too. I was being asked, forced, to wash my hands every time I touched things that she considered 'unclean', and that was nearly everything. If she washed her hands in the bathroom, she wouldn't want to turn the tap back off, because she had touched it with 'unclean' hands to turn it on, so now the tap was 'unclean' too, and she would become stuck in a loop. If I washed my hands then she still considered them 'unclean' afterwards because I had touched the tap again to turn it off after washing them, and so then I wasn't allowed to touch her, or any food or drink. If the bathroom door closed behind her while she was in there, she wouldn't open it as she believed the handle was unclean from others opening it on their way out after touching the unclean taps to turn them off. I would find her standing in there calling, or just silently waiting for someone to come along and open the door for her. She considered that germs somehow jumped from person to surface, surface to surface and surface to person, and they lived on the surfaces forever waiting to infect someone.

I started to notice that all the doors in the house had red lines appearing along the white paint at the bottom of them on both sides, just a few inches from the floor. I eventually found out it was from the red nail polish on her toes where she would open the doors by hooking her foot around them to avoid touching the unclean door handles. After it became open knowledge, we were then asked to leave all doors ajar so she could always hook them open with her foot and never have to touch the unclean handles. Her portable solution was to always carry antiseptic moisture wipes with her to open doors, car doors, turn taps or touch anything she considered unclean, immediately throwing them away. I constantly had one thrust at me when out somewhere because I had touched something 'unclean' and was asked to wipe my hands. I usually couldn't even work out what is was that I had touched, I would just take it and wipe them to keep her happy.

Each issue that came up I tried to help her, and work on it together, to make her life more normal, but after a few years with no progress it was becoming exhausting. She said she hated her OCD and wanted to rid herself of it, but just couldn't. I tried everything I could think of, but being loving and supportive just wasn't enough. I discovered you can't reason using logic, it just doesn't work with people suffering from OCD. Even she could see and agree with what was logical, but she still felt compelled to do the rituals she did.

I researched OCD online and read all I could about it, the causes, the variations, the treatments, the effect it has on people, both those with it, and those who live with it. I took her to the best OCD specialist I could find, and afford, for regression therapy. We went together but it didn't change anything. I had to think of something else. I found a local OCD self-help group and we went together to try that. I sat in the meeting with her and the others, listening to people's experiences with OCD and the burdens it was putting on each of their lives. One man spent a large part of the meeting showing the plans to a flat he was considering buying and fussing and obsessing over every little tiny detail. One afternoon he had stood across the road from the flat for hours, wanting to see who the neighbours were, how busy the road was, how noisy it was, and so on. He didn't pay any attention to the fact he was actually leaning against a primary school fence, until the police turned up after being called by the school headmaster about a middle-aged man acting funny and who had been suspiciously hanging around by the school gates for nearly four hours.

Life was becoming unbearable and the relationship was imploding. Things eventually began to cross that line in the sand for me when it all becomes too much, and you start to question would you be happier alone? Gradually each aspect she struggled with was starting to be turned around into an attack on me: that I wasn't being understanding enough, I wasn't being thoughtful enough, or considerate enough. I was living nearly all of her rituals with her and yet somehow now being told I was the problem, not her OCD.

After four years of living like this I was drained, and realised she was probably never going to change, at least not for a very long time. The good aspects of the relationship that had once made the bad ones bearable, were now being outweighed. The attacks on me escalated and the final straw came when she started attacking Liana for no reason and it got out of hand and we had to involve the police. I only saw Liana every other weekend and it wasn't fair she should be attacked, or afraid to be with me, because of my partner's problem.

I had allowed myself to be slowly ground down and made to feel that I was a really selfish and bad person, and the stress of it all was taking its toll on me. I developed a tick above one eye where the nerve just kept twitching uncontrollably day and night and never stopped, and then another twitch on my lip began. I had constant pains in my abdomen and ever increasing mind numbing headaches from the stress. With my health clearly deteriorating and feeling emotionally drained, I had no choice but to look after myself, and took the decision we needed to separate and I needed to move out. She was absolutely furious.

You know it's definitely time to get out of a relationship when you reach the point of realising you would be better off alone than continuing in a bad relationship. It was something I had always realised far too late. Some people cut and run from a bad relationship prematurely, without giving it a real chance, without really trying at all, whilst many others, like me, stay there far too long, the eternal optimist, believing issues can still be 'fixed' by compromising, when in reality they can't, and losing myself in the process. Some things just can't be 'fixed'.

I moved out and immediately started receiving a barrage of emails, every day, pages and pages describing in graphic detail what a bad person I was, how ugly I was, how fat, how selfish, and how I would be worse off without her and all sorts of other derogatory things. The voicemail on my mobile phone would be filled up with her multi-part voice messages. She would send so many text messages that my message bank would be full, and then I would get home from work to find my landline answering machine completely filled with yet more long abusive multi-part voice messages as well. In all the messages, after the torrent of abuse she would end by saying she wanted to get back together. How do you process being told what a horrid, awful, selfish, ugly person you are by someone, and then being told that they want to be back with you in a relationship? She was angry, and I didn't know what else I could do.

When it eventually stopped it was such a relief. There was no need to punish me, I was quite capable of doing that myself. Another failed relationship. What was wrong with me? Why couldn't I get it right? She was a soul mate and felt sorry for her suffering with OCD. She opened me up in many ways spirituality and was the perfect person to be with at that time in my life. She had the same ambitions and desires that I had, and wanted to do all the same sorts of things I wanted to do, in every way imaginable(!), but she couldn't, or wouldn't, because of her OCD. It was utterly debilitating. I was glad I had helped her become independent and self-sufficient doing what she loved, and quietly hoped she would overcome her problem one day and meet a nice guy to make her really happy. She deserved it, but it wasn't going to be me.

17 - COMPROMISE DOES NOT WORK

Mark:

I went back to a simple single life routine: gym, work, eat and sleep, as I slowly healed and started putting my life back together. Being able to cook at home, meditate, and not having to wash my hands all the time was such a relief. Within a few weeks the ticks and pains and headaches started receding. It really sinks in how much the stress of a bad relationship can affect you both physically and emotionally. I felt lighter, at peace, and there was a serenity re-appearing I had been missing. I was glad I had the conviction to end the relationship when I did, and not stay in it any longer, as I had with my marriage. It's always easier when you don't have children together to consider. We all need to learn to love and nurture ourselves enough to not stay in relationships that just aren't happy anymore.

I started to question my long held belief in compromising. Was it a strength? Or was it actually a weakness? I had learnt there are times when it doesn't matter how much you compromise, how much you give, how supporting or how loving you are, there are some situations, some relationships, when it will just never be enough and compromising does not work.

We should all expect to be happy in a relationship, blissfully happy. If we aren't, then we are with the wrong person and should get out. We shouldn't just be suffering our way through it, compromising and missing out on the pleasures in life, the adrenalin rushes, the peace, the happiness, we each seek. We should be brave enough to free ourselves to be available to meet someone new, it may even be 'the one', and to also free our partner so they too might meet 'the one' for them.

My life now was about having Liana every other weekend. When she arrived on a Friday night we would go grocery shopping together and she loved it. We would cook and I would teach her little things that would help her later in life. I would get up to find she had washed up, cleaned the kitchen sides and be hoovering, not that it needed it, as I would have done all those things before she arrived, but she just loved doing it herself. We would have a wonderful time, sailing around Sydney Harbour on the ferries, going to the movies, a drive to the beach, or just being silly and having fun at home. Come Sunday she would want to stay longer and ask if she could phone her mom to see if she could stay an extra night, which I would always happily agree to.

In contrast, her mom refused to take her anywhere on holiday, saying it was my 'job' to take her. To me it was a pleasure, I never understood why her mother wouldn't want to take her too. I wanted her to have a good relationship with her mom as well as with me. When I did have to talk to her mom, she still insisted on always going on about being broke, and I would still hear how she would go away on holiday herself while Liana was with me, or buy a new car, or furniture, or clothes, I just didn't believe her anymore. It was clear she spent money on herself first, whereas I would always make sure Liana was looked after before me. I didn't really care about me, I had an aging wardrobe of just a few clothes, a beat up car and owned nothing of any value. I always spent what money I had on my partners and their children, and Liana first, and me last.

18 - IN THE PRESENCE OF A LIGHT BEING

Claire:

Whilst others seemed so carefree and focused on just having fun, I felt that life was so difficult, so talking to God through reading the Bible seemed the most obvious way to connect with Him.

One afternoon, as I was reading a passage out of Revelation, I started to feel very strange. I did not do drugs, and I had not partaken of any alcohol for some days. I cannot remember exactly the chapter or verse that I was reading, but time seemed to warp out and stretch into slow motion. At the same time the words on the page began to get bigger and bolder, floating up off the page letter by letter, very slowly towards my face, before dissolving like specks of dust particles into nothing before my eyes. This was not a hallucination by any means. Every hair on my body was charged and standing up on end, as if an electromagnetic current was beaming straight through me. My heart was thumping like crazy and I had this intense feeling that I was in the presence of someone or something divine. When I had the courage to look up, my breath was paralyzed, as I gazed in awe upon a Golden Light Being about eight feet tall standing in the doorway. I wanted to scream and throw up at the same time, but I was just frozen with terror instead. It seemed to enter me, yet it was still standing in the doorway, faceless and ethereal with just the golden glow of celestial radiance. I felt it take control of my mind, which resonated with the words, "Will you write down prophecy for the children"?

I was trembling with awe and terror at the same time. It was absolutely the most terrifying encounter imaginable.

"I am not good enough", I thought back with all of my being without making a sound, only using my mind instead. "No. No, I could never prophecy for children. I am so weak. I would be too scared!"

"Faith", came back in another wave of telepathy.

"If you only had enough faith Claire".

I felt so stricken with hopelessness and failure, as the being vanished like an electric light being switched off, that I thought I was going to die. Really. It was not a joyous and peaceful experience as one would expect, like when I had previously been surrounded by the host of angels singing, but rather this encounter had left me feeling like I was disgustingly impure. I was so struck dumb that I could not even scream. I was afraid to look at myself in the mirror, because I had an eerie glow shining through my face, which really freaked me out and Kerrie and my husband thought that I was somehow changed and both wished I would just be normal again. I couldn't drink coffee, or smoke cigarettes, or drink alcohol for two days, I couldn't even wear an ounce of makeup either, which for me is unheard of.

I did not pick up the Bible again, because I was terrified of what would happen to me. It had left me completely traumatized, knowing for certain that there are many other types of beings amongst us. I was left wondering who in fact had made their presence known to me and why? Was it an angel, or was it in fact a being from another world? One thing was for certain, I hoped that I would never find out for sure…

19 – SOUL MATES

A few months later, I gave birth to my gorgeous little daughter Emma, having my hands full with taking care of the family, as well as writing music and recording in the lounge room with my husband.

Jensen was so clever and doing really well at school. He also had a gentle way about him, even though his father was still giving us all grief by not showing up for access, or paying any maintenance and still sending me death threats. Sometimes I would come home and his father would be sitting in a chair under the carport and laughing just to frighten me in a warped kind of way. I was terrified of him, because I think he was just nuts and so unpredictable, and he knew I was intimidated by him and rather lavished it I think. He had remarried and divorced for the second time, because he had been violent with the second wife as well, so I consciously made the mental note that it wasn't just me who made him into such a monster.

My second husband was so stubborn and short tempered and he would bully both the children and I so much, that I felt it was just to keep us all under control. I would threaten to leave if he ever touched me and he would threaten to leave if I did not shut up about it. This power play went on until we recorded another new song and became best friends all over again. If his ego was stroked, we got on famously, if not, there was hell to pay. I was constantly telling him how good his writing was, because I thought he really was brilliant, but he insisted that we shared the composition rights to everything, even if I had composed something entirely on my own. I on the other hand, insisted that he retain all of his royalties if he wrote something without me, because I simply wanted to make a stand about it. I just could not stop him from taking from me what was rightfully mine. I was being raped of my identity.

My husband controlled the money that came through the door as well and I felt barefoot and pregnant without any self-power at all. Work seemed to slow down to a trickle and when we enquired at one of the top advertising agencies if anything was wrong, the creative director informed us that he was not going to use us anymore. My husband had committed the cardinal sin and not used virgin tape on the last master he had delivered. Word had got around that we were unprofessional and our jingle work just dried up.

Everything seemed to close down for us in Melbourne after that, and the autistic school which we had enrolled Rick in to attend the following year had lost his file as well, so he had nowhere to go to school the following year. I continued to work with Rick by singing my little song to him and one day out of the blue I decided to stop singing half way through, just for something different. He suddenly stopped rocking and flapping his hands, looked straight into my eyes and mouthed the missing word! I had goose bumps all over my body and I kept missing words out on purpose, whilst he kept filling them in for me by mouthing each word without making a sound. There wasn't even the trace of a smile from him, but I hugged him tightly and smothered him in kisses anyway. I tucked him into bed and caressed his forehead whispering, "Nigh' nigh' Ricky", and a beautiful little voice replied, "Nigh' nigh' mummy", before his eyes closed shut to go off to sleep. It was as if what had just happened was perfectly normal for him.

I ran out of his bedroom and burst into tears, because I was the happiest mum in the world. My autistic son had learned to talk and I was so moved to hear the sound of his voice for the very first time. He never mumbled single first words like little babies do with 'mum', 'dad' or 'bub'. No. Rick was using perfect sentences right from the beginning at four years old!

I had followed the wisdom of my inner knowing and I had done what I felt was the right way to be with him, regardless of what the doctors and child psychologists had told me to do. They had all encouraged me to get used to the fact that he was different and would probably never truly connect with me emotionally, even when he was an adult. They seemed to believe that my work with him was pointless, preferring me to adhere to their own behaviour modification methods, but there was no way I was ever going to give up on my little boy.

I was finally beginning to have some real faith in myself as well now and the reason for the light being's visit started to prickle deep inside of me. It felt like the sacred phoenix within was taking her first deep breath, before rising high above the ashes and into the great sky. Yet it would be many years until I finally learnt how to use my wings like that.

Rick was helping me to discover my own self power, by pulling out my own instinctive mothering skills. I realised that nobody actually takes our self-power away from us in the first place unless we allow them to take it, and that is what I had done with both of my husbands. It was just that I had never known that I was even entitled to having my own authority before, because my parents had programmed me to be completely submissive. Up until now, I was just a doormat for anyone and everyone to wipe their dirty boots over and to take whatever they wanted from me. Yet experiencing this domination from both of my husbands, helped me to recognise how inadequate and helpless I felt about myself, and how intrinsically wrong that was for me. Even though I was not able to change that aspect overnight, at least I was suddenly aware of why I was feeling so unhappy and not just accepting that feeling as being normal for me. Rick was certainly working with me on that level and I was deeply grateful to him.

20 - DESTINATION HELL

Claire:

My husband's mother and husband had moved to the Gold Coast in Queensland and inspired us to move up as well. The beaches were covered in soft white sand and washed in never ending waves of azure blue. It was paradise. Even the tourism slogan was, 'Beautiful one day. Perfect the next'. It sounded too good to be true and the feeling of Melbourne's weather had come to reflect how I was feeling in my marriage. We thought the change to the sunshine would do us all good, so we decided to give our marriage one more chance to make it work.

My husband's flash anger continued to make it difficult for me to maintain my dignity and self-esteem regardless of the change in our environment. I felt it was my fault that he lost control and would either hit out at the children or myself. It was like being a little girl all over again, living with parents who thrashed me for reasons sometimes I could never understand. He would yell at me and say it was my fault that he lost control and I believed him, because that is just the way I had allowed my mind to be programmed for so, so long. Whenever the phone rang, I would have to deal with debt collectors and there was never enough to pay them whatever he had promised. When he gave his word that they would receive the funds, my stomach would turn, knowing that there was no way he could ever meet that commitment because there was never any money in the bank. I never knew where it went or what he spent it on, he would just spend it without telling me.

Sometimes we were so desperate for food, that he would take me to the supermarket and pay by cheque, knowing that there were no funds in the bank to cover it. When the cheque bounced, the bank and the supermarket would be on the phone drilling me for the payment, plus fees for overdrawing the account. I was a stressed out mess, because I couldn't tell them when they would receive their money.

We would hire session musicians and he would promise to pay them and never did. I did not know how I could stop it or change it. I could not leave, because all my own money had run out, yet there was always alcohol and cigarettes and a big recording studio with the latest gear and a swimming pool with a Mercedes Benz in the driveway. Sometimes the stress would be too much, because there was no food left in the fridge and I didn't even have enough money to buy a loaf of bread or a carton of milk and I never knew when there would be enough money to go shopping again so that I could feed my children. We lived the high life without the money to back it up. He wanted to be a rock star and we lived as if we were. It was another gigantic lie and I was miserable.

Deep down, I felt that my way of nurturing the children patiently was being undermined by his inability to understand what I was doing with them. Perhaps he was still a child also and I wondered when he would ever grow up. I had decided long ago not to bring my children up the way I had been, but to treat them with love and respect, patience and understanding. Yet in reality, here I was with someone who controlled me like my mother did and my children were being hit and yelled at just like I had been. Yet I still stayed. He even told me in the middle of an argument, that six years prior, when I first joined the band with him, the bass player who introduced us, (the mysterious man from the music shop) talked about me all the time, so my husband lied to him saying that we were lovers just to scare him off. I was so angry that I wanted to scream, for my husband and I were not romantically involved for some years after that. He lied just to get what he wanted and what he wanted then was me. Unbelievably still, I stayed.

My husband would go out all night and not even call me to say that he wasn't coming home. I would breakdown and cry out in agony throughout the night, feeling heartbroken and wondered if he had been in a car accident or was lying in a hospital somewhere. I could not get to sleep, because I was so worried where he could be. It never occurred to me that he was having an affair, because I just trusted him. It was torture. Then in the morning, he would walk in the door still drunk from the night before and I would be so relieved that he was alive, that I would just feel like an idiot for worrying about him so much.

His violence was unstoppable, even throwing me across the room for something, which I do not even recall as to why, he smashed my wrist in nine places and I physically could not play the piano any more. I was devastated, because I could no longer use my gift to express my most inner emotions and my only income was effectively compromised as well. I cried and cried and could not stop. About the same time we were evicted out of the house for not paying the rent. I did not know how I was going to live with him any longer. The roller coaster was a nightmare and I just wanted to get off and probably should have then and there.

Yet I was pregnant again. My husband was actually very supportive about it, which seemed like another great lie actually, but that was the end of my live performance days and my husband stayed out most nights after that.

Three months after our youngest son Kai was born, one of our clients decided to build an audio visual studio, where he wanted to make movies and record television commercials. The deal was that he wanted us to supply the audio suite and for my husband to work full time there as a producer and for us both to write original music for his products and films whenever he wanted us to. It all sounded really good. All we had to do was sign over our recording equipment to him. I was adamant that my grand piano was not to be included in the deal, because it was a personal item I had owned long before I knew my husband and not part of the business, which our business partner verbally agreed to. When we went into his office to sign the contract, the children and I had to wait in the car for two hours because the papers were still being drawn up. I was so anxious because Kai had been screaming the whole time and I could not seem to settle him. Eventually when we were called in to sign the document, I quickly scribbled my name instead of reading all of the items to be signed over first. I was more concerned about settling my baby and distressed not being able to calm him. I trusted that my piano was not included in the deal, as was discussed and agreed to in the meetings prior. However, when the truck arrived to transport the studio, I was mortified when they took my piano apart and loaded it onto the truck as well. There was nothing I could do to stop them. My beloved grand piano was indeed listed as one of the items to be handed over. Now it was gone and there was nothing I could do about it.

I had lost the strength in my left hand to even play, because my husband had smashed my wrist and now to actually lose my beloved piano on top of that was utterly dreadful. I felt like I had lost my best friend that had seen me through all of the ups and downs of my life. I did not know what I would do anymore, because I felt so sad and helpless. My husband on the other hand, walked away with all of his precious guitars and PA and speakers, because they were not on the contract.

All of the studio equipment was in both our names, yet it was my father who lent my husband the money in the first place to buy each component, one piece of equipment at a time over several years, and which was never paid back to him. Not a cent. In fact my husband has never acknowledged to this day that he ever owed my father any money at all. I also find it remarkable that my father would lend my husband more than $100,000 over the years behind my back without even discussing it with me first. The only reason I found out about it, was years later when my father told me he was broke. He had sold his house in Melbourne and moved into a unit on the Gold Coast to be closer to me and told me he had to sell it to have enough money to live. I was flabbergasted! My father always had plenty of money. When I asked him why he was broke, he told me that all of his savings had been lent to my husband, because he thought it would save our marriage. I was furious. Can you believe the audacity of someone thinking they had so much power over another? Power over me that is, or my marriage? Why didn't he ever discuss it with me before handing over any money? I was beyond angry. My father did not even have the formal papers drawn up to arrange a repayment plan, so there was never any proof of the loan in the first place. I shook with horror as to the sheer weakness of two males whom I so dearly wanted to love and respect as men, but was simply left disliking both of them fervently instead. Yet somehow in the process of this shocking news, my father had successfully manipulated me to think the reason he had no money left was my entire fault.

Without my piano, my creativity still buzzed and sparkled without an outlet, so I turned to writing and voicing children's stories instead. Into each story, I interwove a little moral of honour such as honesty and integrity, which I called, 'The Once Upon A Time Collection'. I had learned what the power of music had done for Rick in teaching him to talk and so I wanted to create something special for other children as well, based around stories and songs. Instead of nagging at children to do the right thing, I wanted to inspire them in a fun and entertaining way. I had written a collection of three CD's, which were all produced to stimulate a child's imagination of up to about seven years of age. Each story was fully produced with sound effects and music, so that all children had to do, was close their eyes and imagine the story unfolding and sing along with the song at the end of the story. The package also included illustrated books, so that they could even learn to read along as well.

Our partner had decided to run a series of interviews with me on television, promoting the package to sell as one of his home shopping products and cut my husband and me both into the profits after expenses. As it turned out, the new business partner and my husband did not see eye to eye on many issues and we ended up walking away from the business altogether. Our equipment including the piano remained the property of the other partner, because we had broken the contract and we were broke again without any savings in the bank or means to pay the rent anymore.

Other than my husband performing live music a couple of nights a week, we had no other regular earnings and our financial commitments were horrendous. We were living in a huge house on the top of a hill overlooking the ocean and we couldn't afford to stay there anymore. Miraculously, when another business opportunity arose to move to Sydney to put another studio together for an events company, we felt it was our life boat out of the financial mess we were in and had no choice but to go. This time the other partners would pay for the new equipment and my husband would run the studio. One of our new Sydney clients was the CEO of George Pattison Bates Advertising Agency and my husband gave him one of my children's story CD's to see what he thought.

It was not long before he rang us to arrange a meeting with his creative director as well and had us both sign a partnership agreement with "The Once Upon A Time Collection" that very day. There were lots of meetings about it and we unanimously decided that the concept of little morals for children be woven into a complete television series, instead of simply marketing them on CD. I called it, 'Kid Zoo' and wrote the entire synopsis for thirteen episodes as well as writing and recording the theme music, which I had my own kids to sing. Fox Studios even agreed to shoot the trailer as a test, but other priorities became the focus of our attention and we never pursued the opportunity further much to my dismay.

Today, my ex-husband, the music thief, has re-named the collection and is selling it on the internet as his own material, even after I denied him permission to do so. When I denied him, he promised me that he would never do that.

Marc Hunter out of Dragon, a very famous Australian rock band, became ill with cancer and my husband and I were asked to write a song in his benefit, to perform at the Good Vibrations concert together with other iconic Australian artists. Marc unfortunately died later in the year and our song "We Come Together", which was a 50/50 co-write made it into the charts and was included on a double CD. Some years later, I discovered that my husband had re-registered the song as another title altogether and was claiming 100% royalties for it without my name being included as co-author. I wondered why the ego needs to steal someone else's magic. Surely my husband knew he had more than enough of his own.

In Sydney we ended up living beyond our means all over again and decided to move back to the Gold Coast and start all over again. I do not know how my husband presented me with a white grand piano, but he did and we rented yet another luxurious house we couldn't afford on millionaire's row high up on the panorama overlooking the entire Gold Coast. Half the house was a wall of folding glass doors covered in shutters, which opened up onto the vista of the ocean and the twinkling lights of the city. Our lounge room became yet another recording studio, where we produced more music and film clips. The driveway was a mile long, high up on a steep and winding road, where wallabies grazed and the odd python slid under the shrubbery. I remember entertaining every night, cooking for clients and drinking to run away from the stress of living so far out of control. Yet the drinking never made the slightest difference to the way I felt about myself, for I was still only half human and the other a programmed zombie.

21 - THE FINAL CUT

Claire:

My husband was still singing live in the evenings and one night a gentleman introduced himself as one of the producers for the Sydney 2000 Olympics. Thinking this was a great opportunity, my husband gave him a copy of a song I wrote and arranged called, 'Spirit of Australia', which my husband sang on as well. The next day we were both invited into his office and were asked to write a song for the 'Team Welcome' for the Sydney 2000 Olympics, where two hundred children's choirs would welcome each country into the Olympic Village. Part of the brief was to use the word 'G'day'. My husband had to go to Sydney for another client and so while he was away, I wrote and arranged the entire song and sequenced it onto the computer, whilst Emma helped me to pitch it into the right key for children, and she also came up with a line in one of the verses.

The following Sunday I picked my husband up from the airport and we went to record the children's choir over the top of the backing at a different studio. There was never a question as to who wrote the song. All parties were fully aware of the truth. Yet they wanted the royalties to be dispersed three ways. I refused, as it was totally my song, but was coerced against my will via threats into agreeing. This was the last straw for me. I did not mind sharing the royalties, but I wanted full credit for the actual composition, which was subsequently also used as the first song at the opening ceremony at the Sydney 2000 Olympic Games.

The headlines on the front page of the local Gold Coast Bulletin read, "They're Playing My Song". The producer for the games had taken the full credit of it himself. Once again greed and ego overtook the joy of being involved in the actual magic and I was devastated. My lawyers told me to sign the APRA card 33% and that we would fight in court about ownership later, otherwise the Olympics producer would just pull it from the games and use another composition in its place. I signed under duress only because I believed it would be resolved later. When later came, it turned out it would all come down to having to put Emma onto the stand to testify that she had witnessed me writing it alone. I would never put her on the stand to testify against her father, because I had too much respect for my little girl. To this day he sells my song online and has interviews published where he talks about how 'he' wrote it, and has even tried to sell it to big national companies for large sums of money, and I was forced to have to take legal action through copyright solicitors to stop him.

The realisation that my husband was never going to stop robbing my identity inspired me to make the final cut. The opportunity to learn the lesson had presented itself to me when we first met, yet I still had not learnt it well enough to move on. I had also come to the end of my patience with his lack of respect for me, and I was over allowing him to control me and abuse me whilst his hooks had torn into every part of who I was and seemed to have ripped me apart until there was nothing left of me that was sacred anymore. It was whilst we were all watching the movie Titanic, a flood of tears uncontrollably welled up and ran down my face, as if I was washing myself clean from him finally. My Jack, 'the one' I knew was out there somewhere still, and it was time to be free so that he could finally find me too.

It was my birthday, and my husband was still in Sydney performing my song at the Olympic Games and taking all the credit for it, whilst I had returned home after attending the rehearsal for the opening ceremony, which was packed with one hundred and ten thousand people at the stadium. Over the next few days I searched for a place of my own and I found a unit, which was so small it reminded me of a little dolls house. I took just a few things along with my gorgeous children, leaving most of my possessions behind. Jensen had already bought his own place and was studying to become a microbiologist, whilst Rick, Emma and Kai came to live with me. When my husband returned home, I had already left.

I soon had a job with a major promoter as a marketing manager, which gave me enough financial independence to finally move on from my husband of sixteen years and to begin the long journey of putting myself back together all over again. Yet I still felt so small and powerless, like a baby bird trying to look after three other baby birds all on her own.

22 - LIES, LIES AND MORE LIES

Mark:

I was always low on the Sunday nights Liana went back to her mom's, the twelve days in between would feel like an eternity. I would keep myself busy, reading, enjoying the peace and solitude, or finding a bit of excitement to occupy myself until the time came around again to see Liana. Like a huge wheel turning, the feeling of something unfinished would come around again, and I would realise it was calling me not give up on finding 'the one'.

Nothing happens unless you actively put it out there and call it forth. You have to help fate along, by opening a door for someone else to step through, or being out there looking for an open door to step through yourself. So eventually I constructed another profile and put it up on a dating website, and let it simmer away on the back burner.

One particular woman seemed very interested and kept pursuing me, but I wasn't sure as her photos were clearly professionally posed glamour shots. She was slim, blonde and looked stunning all made up for the photo shoot, but for all I knew she might not look anything like that in real life, even occasionally. Her profile said she was spiritual and a property developer, which seemed in conflict with one other to me. She kept contacting me and we started to talk regularly on the phone. She had a brain and was witty, romantic, and made it very clear she was very sexual as part of her seduction.

We eventually met up and started to see each other and none of the warning signs from the past seemed present, but they were only based on my previous experiences. It was romantic, affectionate and exciting from the outset. She lived in a huge house, so big one 'wing' had once been rented out to a family of four. She had four grown children, three of which had already left home, and her ex-husband had hung himself.

The first sign I encountered that things weren't going to go smoothly was one night when just as I was leaving, her two daughters drove up her driveway and she tried to introduce me to them, saying "come and meet Mark". One walked right past me with tightly clenched lips and gave me an angry looking glare and said nothing, and the other I clearly heard say "no thanks", and quickly jumped back in her car and drive off before I could get any closer. She told me to ignore them, as they 'had issues', so I just let it go.

I soon found out she wasn't really a property developer, she had been sitting at home for the last three years, living off the equity in her mortgage, drawing money off the mortgage to pay the next mortgage payment, in a downward spiral. After that had ran out, she had moved on to living off the 'interest' repayments from a very dodgy sounding 'loan' she had made to a 'friend'.

Her previous late husband, was trashed at absolutely every opportunity by every member of the family, safely knowing he wasn't there to defend himself. She loved to joke about how when his family demanded his ashes back after his cremation to give him a burial at sea he had always wanted, and had started to threaten legal action when she refused to hand them over, she had given him his 'burial at sea' by emptying them into the local creek amongst the floating garbage, so his family couldn't ever get them.

Before long I was staying at her house, and she wanted me to give up my flat and move in permanently. I didn't want to so soon, so instead I moved in the things I needed on a daily basis. I had a key and started paying towards all the bills and so we were living together full time, and things seemed to be going along very passionately.

A few months later she asked me to setup up email on her laptop computer, so she could download her emails. I had problems configuring it and made a number of attempts over the following weeks to try and sort them out. One evening I was trying out yet another setting, when an email popped up in her inbox. It had failed delivery and been bounced back. There sitting open in front of me I couldn't help but notice it was to someone on a dating website, thanking him for his email and asking questions about him, his children, and included photos of herself. I thought at first it must be old, but it wasn't, the timestamp on it was that morning whilst I was out at work.

Over the next week I checked a couple of times, hoping it had been an isolated incident, but each time I found she had sent more emails to other men. I could have just exploded and stormed out, but I wanted to know why first? It didn't make any sense as there wasn't any issues between us. I joined the website she was using so I could see what her profile on there said, and soon found it, saying she was 'single and looking'. Each time I checked while I was out at work, there she would be, green and 'online available to chat'. When I looked just before getting home she would always be red and 'offline', and when I walked in she would greet me with a strained voice about what a hard day doing housework she'd had.

The following weekend during a long conversion, the subject of fidelity came up and we got into a discussion about it. She insisted on making the point that she was totally committed to our relationship, was trustworthy, wasn't the sort to fool around behind my back, and hadn't had any contact with any other men since we met. Soon a worrying dark shadow emerged from her, as she started to become angry and attack me, saying that I must be lacking self-confidence if I didn't trust her, that I was clearly 'paranoid' and I had issues I needed to work on. Here we go again I thought, she was in denial. She was twisting things around and back onto me as the one with issues, when I knew she was the one who needed to look at herself.

The next day I decided to confront her and asked about the first email. I warned her before she replied that the only way we might be able to salvage things was if she was completely honest with me about what had been going on. She lied and completely denied it, until she realised I really had seen an email. She thought it was just the one, so admitted it saying it "was just the one email and that was all". Then I revealed I knew of more than one, and she said "it might have been two". Then it was "maybe three". Then she "didn't know how many". She was in damage limitation control, trying to keep whatever else had gone on from me. I knew then that she wasn't going to tell me the full story. She displayed no remorse at all about it. Finally I brought up the dating website, her 'single' profile and being online chat every day. She insisted she was only on there to "chat about the weather". On a dating website? Who was this person? And how stupid did she think I was?

I was so glad I had held onto my flat. I spent until 3AM calmly filling my car and shuttling all my things back to my flat. When I left with the final carload I told her we were finished, and that clearly she still had serious issues to work out on with herself, and left.

23 - THE HYPOCRACY OF GENETICS

Mark:

I accepted the relationship was over and slipped back into my single life routine again. I was sick in the stomach whenever I thought about it. It didn't make sense, how can someone treat you like that? Was she just looking for someone to pay her bills? Had she just grabbed who she could at the time and secretly carried on looking for someone better? I recalled there were other strange occasions early on when she would suddenly refuse to answer her phone to me, and I would drive over and even though I could see her sitting in the lounge, she would bizarrely just ignore me and refuse to answer the door. Only she knew what was going on in her head and she hadn't told me. I went back to my own single life and tried not to think about it anymore.

Three weeks later the downstairs door buzzer sounded and it was her, begging me to let her in. I knew if I let her in she would worm her way back around me and I would eventually cave in, but I couldn't send her away when she sounded so remorseful. She was all apologetic, saying how stupid she had been and how she didn't know why she did what she did. Her friends had since told her she was mad, considering she had been telling them all how happy she was with me. She insisted she had now worked out her issues and really wanted to be with me and begged me to give her another chance. There was still no explanation as to why she did it, but I'm a sucker for remorse if it's genuine, and it seemed like it was. That's how people truly grow spiritually and they deserve a chance.

We restarted the relationship again, slowly from my point of view. One thing that horrified me was she later confessed that when we had split up she had told her daughters some intimate aspects of our sex life, very selective bits, carefully enhanced to make me look the bad guy and get sympathy. I was appalled. To me what you do sexually with someone, in the privacy of the bedroom (or wherever), should stay private, forever, even after the relationship has finished. I never talk about such things on principle. How can anyone ever feel relaxed and free in a relationship with someone, to enjoy and experiment sexually, if they had to worry about whatever they may like doing, or try, might one day be told to others to try and embarrass or humiliate them? To compensate, she was very eager to make up and made sure the evenings were action packed and full of excitement and adrenalin, and I'm not talking about going parachuting.

She spent her days sitting in her massive home doing basically nothing. She had no money, and her only income, besides me, was from the dodgy loan she had made to this 'friend'. In fact she had got all her friends and even her children to lend him money as well, and each month they would get their interest payments and be all smiles, until one month he disappeared and that was the last anyone saw of him, or their money. He was a thief, running a Ponzi scam stealing from these people. She drew me into it as well, and I lost some, but others had given him their entire life savings, 6 digit amounts, and lost it all.

There was a really dark energy about her house, and it never really felt warm enough or comfortable. I discovered when I lay down in the bedroom with a light on and closed my eyes, a large dark shape seemed to be flying around the room. I would open my eyes and there would be nothing there, but when I closed them it would be there again, flying around. It was the same effect as closing your eyes with a light on and moving your hand around in front of your face. Whatever it was, it felt very dark and oppressive.

Eventually, her daughters started talking to me, but it always seemed to be about running someone down behind their back. Their favourite was about what a "witch" their brother's fiancé was, how she was "fat" and had made their brother "fat" as well, and they both hated her. It was brutal. In all the time I knew the 'witch' she was always a kind and pleasant person, so I couldn't understand their outright hatred of her.

The sisters completely ran the family. They had keys to our home and would just let themselves in whenever they wanted to. We had no privacy, even when alone at home. Then they would inform us there was going to be a dinner at our house, for everyone, on a certain date, and expect us to buy all the food, cook, and clean up after they left. If we went to a restaurant instead, when the bill was presented they would all look the other way, or walk off, leaving me to have to pay it. I was warned by their own brothers never to get on their bad side, as they could get really vicious and they never gave in. How right that was going to prove to be.

I eventually discovered every member of her family lied. They were so casual and convincing I hadn't noticed it at all. It was only when they pointed it out, about each other, that I started to notice. Then I saw it all the time, and they all did it. Whenever it made life easier for one of them, or helped them get what they wanted, or their own way, they would just lie. It was so casual it was utterly convincing. If I ever dared point it out, no-one wanted to know and they would run for cover, and I would be accused of causing trouble.

I started to notice strange things happening at home. They were just little things at first, but over time they started to add up. She would always disappear Friday lunchtimes around 11:30AM, for two or three hours, and turn her phone off, which she never did any other time. I would notice straight black hairs on the floor of our ensuite, which didn't match either of us, or any of her family, knowing they were all ginger. I found new books under our bed about 'how to tell if a man fancies you' and she had turned the PIN lock on her mobile on. Why? So the question becomes, should you leave someone purely based on a suspicion? Without any real proof? Or just trust them? I agonised over it for months.

Christmas arrived and we put a tree up and at the end her daughters bought out a 'special' box of baubles to hang on it. Each one had an individual family name custom painted on it in gold glitter, but not everyone. Something about it irritated me, and a few days later I realised what it was. All the names were only of genetically related family members. Anyone who wasn't related through blood, such as husbands, partners, step children, didn't have one. When I pointed it out, my partner said she had never thought of it that way, and actually I was quite right. She raised it with her daughters and suggested everyone in the family be included, but the daughters were outraged and objected angrily, they were even against having ones for their own husbands. So in defiance my partner went out and had extra baubles made up, one for each member of left out, which utterly infuriated her domineering daughters.

We had somehow become engaged, but inside I was having more and more reservations about how things were going and feeling less and less happy, particularly about whether I wanted to risk marrying again. It was clear to me I wasn't welcomed by her adult children and if I tried to talk about my reservations they were each trivialised and dismissed. I had such a low opinion of myself, I talked myself into believing this was the best relationship I could ever achieve, considering what a bad person I was, and if I gave up on it, I probably wouldn't ever find another one and end up alone for the rest of my life. She picked up on my growing doubts and started making a very big effort to keep me interested, being extra nice and agreeable on everything and anything. Absolutely everything, and wanted to push all our boundaries. It must have worked, as I eventually found myself being carried along with making the arrangements to get married.

My ex-wife heard I was marrying again and was furious and rang me up to tell me I was making a big mistake. I didn't understand how she could make such a judgement? It was nothing to do with her anyway. The two of them had never met, and openly despised each other. The former because she seemed to think she still owned part of me, and the latter because she had witnessed at close hand how hard I tried to be a good father and how difficult my ex-wife purposely tried to make my life. On numerous occasions when Liana was being picked up, or dropped off, I had to stop her going out and telling my ex-wife what she thought of her.

We eventually got married and she hoped it might finally win over her bullying daughters, but I later found out they had always been totally against her marrying anyone again, not just me, and had regularly told her so. Even on the morning of her wedding day they selfishly reminded her they were totally against it, instead of at least letting her have one special day.

I finally let go of my flat and she changed her mortgage into joint names, all based on my income, and finally told me the truth about her mortgage and the fraud she had committed to get it. It had been with a major bank and had been based on falsified documents she had brought from the same 'friend' running the Ponzi scam. For a fee he had fabricated a completely false employment and income history for her, and she had been living in constant fear of being caught committing fraud. When I asked how she got past the bank verifying the documents, she said her Ponzi 'friend' also had another 'friend' at the bank who worked in the mortgage approvals team and who did him 'favours for a fee' to get the mortgage applications of his clients with falsified documents approved.

About the same time, I had a large tax bill come in, and although I could pay it off myself in a few months, she insisted we pay it from the new mortgage. When I suggested we track when it had been repaid separately, she insisted repayment would just be me paying half the mortgage, an agreement I would later live to regret and end up costing me 100 times as much. It wasn't long before she stopped making any payments towards the mortgage at all, saying she had no money to pay her share, and so that was the end of her side of the agreement. I soon found myself paying 100% of the massive mortgage, as well as all the household bills and everything else that came up for her and her son. What a mess I had got myself into.

24 - THE SHAME OF UNLOVING PARENTS

Mark:

One evening I was quietly sitting watching television when the phone rang. I picked it up and it was Liana sobbing hysterically.

"Daddy please don't let mommy send me to a boarding school", she said, sounding absolutely terrified.

As I was trying to find out what was going on, her mother came on the line from another handset, screaming down the phone about how she couldn't stand Liana anymore. Liana screamed back at her, and then she screamed back at Liana, and I sat there as a remote audience while the two of them continued their screaming tennis match. It was so loud everyone in the room where I was could hear it, but they didn't need to ask who it was, it wasn't the first time it had happened, and they hastily cleared the room.

In the end Liana asked if she could come and live with me and I had no hesitation. I had always known the day would eventually come when her mother's obsession with control was broken by a normal teenager's non-compliance. It had taken five years. Discipline needs to be so very carefully rationed, and timed, and only used on what really matters, not devalued by being repeatedly dished out on little things that aren't really that important.

I picked up all of Liana's things and joked to her mother that after paying her maintenance for the last five years, I assumed that would be getting reversed as well. The horrified look on her face said it all, as she spat back at me she could only afford $20 per week, and 'that was it', she didn't care what the correct rate was, the rate she had insisted and threatened I had to pay her 'or else'.

We gave her a spare bedroom and she changed schools. All my wife's daughters could say was to complain how that they had now lost 'their' spare bedroom, which they used at most one or two nights a year. The way her mother had treated her hurt Liana a lot and I would often find her on the bed sobbing. I couldn't understand it, I mean what loving mother does that? She had Liana for the easy childhood years, when a child is unquestioning and compliant and just happy and always full of love, and when the troublesome teenage years arrived, she had just given up and shipped her off to me, in the most selfish and unloving of ways.

From then on I bought Liana up. I was so happy to come home and have tea together, and see her everyday now, and be able to help her with things like schooling. Her previous school had complained for years that she hadn't been doing her homework or assignments and I soon found out why. She told me her mom never made her do any homework or assignments, never mind help her. Her evening regime had been: have tea, watch Home and Away, watch Neighbours, and then go to bed. Whenever I asked her mom about it I was told "mind your own business". For years, she constantly insisted Liana was "not academic" and didn't bother to try and help her. She had left school herself without achieving anything and it was as though she didn't want Liana to achieve any more than she had. Liana's grades at school were abysmally low, averaging around 23% when she came to live with me, so I contacted her new school, and made sure they informed me what homework and assignments she was given and I would make sure she did them.

I spent many hours sitting at the dinner table helping Liana with her homework and assignments. Some days she wouldn't be in the mood and I would have to just leave it, and some days she would race through her Maths or English and I would sit there in complete astonishment. I discovered she did know a lot, and could learn, she just needed some help and encouragement. A year later her average grade was up to 52%, and one subject even scored a whopping 83%. Pretty good for "not academic".

The weekends became reversed and now it was every other weekend off to her mom's. Many weekends Liana would outright refuse to go. I would frequently have to sit her down and talk to her, explaining that it was important she had a relationship with her mom as well, and maybe it would be better between them now, not seeing each other every day, and that it was also a break for me. On that she would agree to go. I could never understand why her mom treated her own daughter so badly.

The previous year it had been agreed to go to my family in Adelaide for Christmas, but my wife's daughters had overruled it, telling us in October that they had made plans around us being in Sydney and they couldn't be changed, even in October. My wife was too afraid to tell them we had already agreed otherwise, and as usual it was easier for her to get me to change than them, so as usual, I gave in again and we had to stay in Sydney. So this year was with my family in Adelaide.

We flew into Adelaide and stayed at my parents. As soon as my sister came over, she walked straight in and took me into another room and said to watch out for our youngest brother, as he was "just itching to start a row" with me. When our other brother came over, as soon as he walked in he did the same. I realised I had walked into a powder keg just waiting for a spark to explode it, a really nice way to start off a family Christmas week together.

Our youngest brother had a big chip on his shoulder. In his mid-40s, had never had a job, nor a serious relationship, and was still living with mommy and daddy. He thought he knew better than everyone else how the world worked and how to bring up children. He and our father lives consisted mainly of watching the hundreds of hours of television programs, mainly sport, they had recorded. It was a far cry from when I was screamed at to go out and "get a job and bring some money home". Numerous times over the years my parents had come to stay with me, telling me of his latest drama, and how they'd had enough of him and would be telling him to move out when they got back home, but it was all talk, they never did. A suicide attempt when he was a teenager had given him a blank cheque to get away with causing all sorts of trouble ever since without anyone standing up to him.

Two years earlier he had been arrested. Our retired parents were greeted at the crack of dawn with police banging on the door with a warrant and storming in, arresting him, searching their home and taking bags full of his things away, including his clothes, mobile phones and computer. Being elderly retired pensioners it upset them a lot. He refused to tell anyone what it was all about and he instructed all of us not go to the public court to hear the charges against him. We told him he had no right to tell us not to go to a public court, but in response we were the ones under attack and berated by our father to do as he said. The police kept him on an all night curfew for two years, along with all of his belongings they had taken. He used to ring me up and ask what sort of data is left behind on a computer when you done certain things, run certain applications, or been to certain websites. I dared to question why all the secrecy if he was innocent? And why hadn't they dropped the charges and given him his belongings back for two years? Both he and my father turned on me and launched an all-out vicious scathing attack, as if I was the one who had done something wrong, rather than look at what the real issue was. There was that twenty first century disease again, point the finger at someone else, so you don't have to look at yourself.

So with these simmering under currents of the last two years, I made doubly sure I gave both of them absolutely no reason to have a go at me during the week and spoil Christmas for everyone. On the very last day at the airport, right at the terminal gate as we waited to board our plane, my dad suddenly turned on me, launching an all-out attack how my sister, my other brother and I were "three little shits, who should show Kefan more respect". He went absolutely berserk, ranting and raving and shouting at me, with hundreds of people in the terminal turning around wondering what was going on. Liana was in tears, her cousin was in tears, whilst my mother and wife sat there in utter shock and embarrassment. I sat down and told him to just go away. Three times he went, and each time he came back to launch another barrage of abuse.

"I've hated you since you were a child", he shouted. What sort of parent says that about their own child, any child? And what had I done to deserve being attacked? I had no criminal record, hadn't been arrested for drunk driving, or accused of assaulting an underage girl, like my brother had. I'd never been violent, done drugs, or anything bad to anyone.

I told my father how he didn't do anything for anyone else, he always did just what he wanted for himself which just made him even angrier.

He told me he was "sick of hearing about my relationships", which was kind of funny as you couldn't talk to him about anything like that, nor had I ever been able to about anything personal. So I don't know where that came from. I had relationships with women and experienced much life has to offer, both good and bad, experienced highs and lows, and learnt many things and grown from them. I had loved partners' children as my own when their dads had abandoned them, often without any gratitude, but hopefully given them some good experiences and memories to aid in their growing up, even if they might not have appreciated it. I did it out of kindness to them, and for me, as that is who I am. I had spent all I earned on them first, before me, usually instead of me. My father was so self-righteous. He had no idea I had heard all the stories of him blowing his top at our elderly mom and then driving off leaving her abandoned at the beach, or the shops, anywhere, and the countless calls I had from her saying she had enough of him and wanted to leave him. I would always tell her she should, but he had her trapped with no money or contacts and she had no choice but to stay.

Eventually he selfishly stormed off and drove away, leaving mom and his two young grandchildren stranded at the airport with no way of getting home, and me about to board a plane. It was revolting the way he had gutlessly waited all week until literally a few minutes before boarding my plane to ambush me, knowing I could hardly say much back right there and then. He had no concern for leaving his elderly wife, and grandchildren marooned at the airport with no way of getting home. I think it was one of the most selfish and spineless acts I had ever seen.

When I told my sister and brother what had been said about the three of us, I expected they would be upset too and have the integrity to stand up against such a violent outburst against all three of us. But sadly it turned out they were only worried about the impact it would have on themselves. My sister said she knew if she stood up to our father she wouldn't be able to go around to their house and see our mom anymore, and my brother was only concerned about anything upsetting his plans for his upcoming wedding reception at our parents. So at that point instead of facing up to our father's behaviour together, they chose to put their own priorities first, and pretend it didn't happen and swept it under the carpet, alienating me, and the family was split forever.

Over the following months my father's words started to make sense about so many things that had happened during my childhood and teenage years and right through into adulthood. Even with just the few examples I've included in this book (there are many more I left out), always being the first accused as a child, the After Eight mints, the slap in Tahiti, being screamed at to "get a job and bring some money home", going to university to "avoid getting a real job", there was never a good word or praise spoken, or anything loving said to me. Even when I achieved an honours degree he had nothing good to say. They all started to make sense and fall into place.

I had already reached a point many years earlier where I realised he never had anything nice to say about me, so I just stopped trying, but I hadn't realised he had that much hatred in him for his own child. Whenever he came to stay, it wasn't to see me, it would always be because he wanted to go to a test match or research something in a bigger library, and I was just a free hotel for him to stay at. He would always be up and out early in the morning, and go to bed early in the evening.

Often the most horrific and hurtful things come into our lives to teach us something. He taught me you should never let genetics impair your judgement. If a family member treats you badly, it should not exempt them from being treated the same as if they weren't a family member. Similarly, people who are not family members, and who are kind and loving towards you, should be welcomed into your life and embraced as 'family'. We refer to people like this as our 'soul family' and are vastly more important than genetic family. Genetics forces us to have to deal with them, and maybe that's why they come as family. The problem with genetics is when it allows people to treat us badly and get away with it. They expect to always be forgiven for whatever sin they commit against us, and that eventually you will forgive, just because you have the same blood in you. The challenge is for us to learn to love ourselves enough to stand up to them and say 'no more', even if it is a father, a mother, a brother, or a sister. That is the principle both Claire and I live by today and so I no longer have anything to do with my father or brother. The issues are theirs alone, and they will have to face them and resolve them on their own journeys, and in their own time, when they are ready. If they don't well from all the stories I have heard from people who have died and been revived, they will have to face the pain they inflicted on others in their post life reviews when their turn comes. All we have the power to do, is to remove them from our lives, and I have. It is something we all need to learn, to disempower those family members who try to abuse us in any way.

25 - DROWNING

Mark:

One day I came home from work early and walked in unexpectedly. My wife didn't like me coming home from work early, and would always seem irritated if I did. If I gave her warning so we could do something nice, like go out, or have a romantic time, by the time I got home she would always be doing something really dirty like cleaning the oven, or gardening, as if to prevent it.

This day I decided to try something different and didn't tell her I was coming home early. As I walked through the house I could hear her on the phone saying, "he shouldn't complain about spending three hours a day travelling to and from work", or working long hours as "that's what men are supposed to do", as she took another drag and flicked her head back, blowing the smoke out. She went on about how I complained the bills were spiralling upwards out of control, as she flicked her cigarette and took another drag, about how I complained about her son sitting around doing nothing all day, and how he never did any chores and always left a big mess everywhere he had been.

I stood there for nearly ten minutes listening to her reel off the insult after insult about me until she happened to glance over and notice me standing in the doorway. She slammed the phone down instantly without even saying goodbye, and then tried to convince me she didn't really mean any of it, it was, "just girls talk, as we do", she said with a lying smile. Then she began to tell me off for coming home early, for not telling her I was on my way, for coming into the house quietly. Suddenly it was all my fault. That twenty first century disease again.

Not long after I had a nightmare. I was trying to get along a thin strip of land between two back to back beaches as the water was slowly rising on both sides. I fought to get through the water as the strip was submerging. The water was up around my knees and rising, as I waded my way through and onto dry land, to be met by my wife. We walked over to another beach that sloped down to the water. The next thing I knew I was looking up from beneath the water, and being held under. I could see her above the surface looking down at me, her hands around my neck holding me under. As I fought for air she just pushed me down harder and harder, and I was drowning as I fought harder to free myself. I suddenly woke up in a cold sweat, shaking, and thought, I have to get out of this relationship, it's killing me.

I didn't want the relationship anymore, her bullying domineering daughters, her son who just sat around watching cable television or playing computer games all day, the huge house with the crippling mortgage and bills. I had become a 9-5 zombie again, serving her and her family, with little or no thanks or appreciation, and not doing anything I wanted to with my life.

She decided to start working again as a nurse, and picked night shifts so would usually be asleep during the day. She had a draw crammed with all sorts of illegal drugs she had taken from work, drugs to knock herself out, drugs to sleep, drugs to stay wake, and all sorts of others. She would go to bed in the daytime leaving explicit instructions not to be woken up, and I would spend my evenings and weekends pretty much alone.

Drowning 195

At this point I'm sure the angels stepped in again and gently helped move things along, and us off in separate directions.

One Saturday, the more bullying of her daughters rang during the daytime and wanted me to wake her mother up. She was drugged out and had given me clear instructions she was not to be disturbed, and probably couldn't be, even if anyone tried. The daughter demanded I wake her up immediately, or she would come around and do it herself. When I calmly and quietly repeated I had been told not to, she blew her top and screamed and shouted and swore all sorts of abuse at me down the phone and hung up.

The next I heard she had lied to everyone in the family and told them I had screamed and swore at her down the phone, and like lemmings, they all believed her. No-one ever bothered to ask me what happened, but then, they knew it didn't matter, they daren't cross her as then she would then turn on them too. The two sisters got together and delivered their mother an ultimatum: she couldn't see either of them again while she was still married to me. She had to choose: it was her marriage, or her daughters.

We went to see a very good psychologist, who went through the whole family history and dynamics, and within minutes she was correctly predicting how each person would react to others in different situations, and was telling us what would happen next before we could even tell her. She came to the conclusion that everyone in the family, for varying reasons, had unresolved issues, from as far back as childhood because of what happened with their father and previous step-father, and my wife had them going all the way back to her childhood with her own father. She turned to me and said she thought I was actually the only 'normal' one there and I was expecting normal behaviour in return, which I wasn't going to get, so I was wasting my time even trying to reason with any of them.

Soon things that had been kept from me all along started to come out, including how the same daughter had disliked every man my wife had ever dated, had verbally attacked a number of them as soon as she brought them home, cunningly scaring them off to keep her mom single. It reminded me of when she tried to introduce me to them on the driveway. It came out that before I was even around the daughters had told their mom she should stop dating guys, stay single, should stop dying her hair, should dress more conservatively, should stay at home and just be a grandmother for their children, and be there for whenever they called on her. She had not told me any of this, it had been kept from me all along. The psychologist said they were bullies and should be the ones seeking counselling.

She revealed how there had been many battles with her daughters before, and they had always won. Every time my wife, or anyone else, had tried to stand up to them, the daughters would hold out however long it took, years if necessary, until they won. They never gave in and got their own way. I was shocked at what I was discovering. I told her if she was ever going to choose them to just tell me now and we could finish it right away, and I would just go, and we could both just get on with our lives without wasting any more of each other's time. In a way I was hoping she would, but she totally agreed that they were bullies, and said even their family GP has commented about it once, and said she had been bullied by them for many years before I was around, and had always given in to them, but didn't want to anymore. This time she wanted to stand up to them, but was also terrified and didn't have the strength to fight alone, so could only do it with me and the counselling.

The stalemate continued for two years, her bullying daughters regularly taunted her sending photos of newly arriving grandchildren, saying if she ever wanted to meet them she would have to leave me first. We carried on seeing the psychologist and I thought we were making progress, until one day she left her mobile phone bill out on the desk in the office. I noticed calls to the daughter who had lied and caused all the trouble, a lot of calls, and who she had said she had not had any contact with. When I asked her about the calls it turned out she had been meeting her secretly for months and immediately announced she wanted a divorce. When I asked why, all she could say was "but they are my daughters", as though their genetics gave them the immunity to get away with any despicable act they should choose to, even if it meant destroying their mothers marriage to have her exclusively for themselves. It was the power of genetics and she had given in again to them, yet again. I had wasted two years of my life fighting beside her, supporting her, and helping her try and stand up to them, along with all the stress it brought, for nothing.

The next six months were spent preparing the house for sale and it went on the market in one of the worst property markets in decades. Divorce settlements were common place, with properties being sold at discount prices to enable settlements to be completed quickly against deadlines, and property investors circled like vultures waiting to make money out of others misery. Everyone was shocked when the house sold to the very first buyer, and at market price. Thank you angels.

She began furiously packing boxes everyday while I was out at work, and sealing them up with layers and layers of tape, saying nicely and with a smile, that she had shared things fairly and packed old and new things for both of us and to trust her. I asked her to wait until when we were both there, but she just ignored me and took full advantage of me being out at work earning the money to pay all the mortgage and bills, and said she was saving me having to do it.

Then she demanded I pay her back the money we had paid my tax bill with from the mortgage three years earlier. The agreement had been for me to 'just pay half of the mortgage in return', and I had been paying the whole of it for three years, not just the half we had agreed, while she had not paid her half towards it at all, she had paid nothing.

All year she had been regularly claiming her pay had been so low that she couldn't afford to pay anything towards the mortgage or household bills, and I had paid instead. I stumbled across bank accounts she had kept secret, and discovered her pay had in fact increased and she had been depositing large parts of it into her secret accounts for herself. Her deceit was sickening. I discovered she had drawn thousands of dollars off the mortgage without telling me, just as I came onto it three years earlier, and lent it to her daughter who had then refused to pay it back. I had unwittingly been paying the interest on it for three years without even knowing about it. The list just grew and grew. After all the money I had put into our relationship, home and her family I was now looking at walking away with practically nothing. I would be nearly fifty years old and completely broke, whilst she would walk away with enough money for a deposit to buy another home. She had financially broken me without me even realising it. But her lies, her deceit, and the bullying antics of her daughters would still be there in her life, and at least no longer in mine. In that respect, I was really the lucky one.

". . . every psychic advance of man arises from the suffering of the soul"…

- Carl Jung

26 – RISING FROM THE ASHES

Claire:

I never had that sad period of mourning, as many newly single people seem to have after a serious relationship dies. My grief had already passed long ago, during the many years prior to leaving my husband. I could finally take charge of paying the rent and I could buy enough food to make proper meals for the kids for the first time since I was single in my early twenties. It was now time to be the sort of person I always wanted to be again, without someone else taking control and sabotaging me with a flash of anger and the aggressive swing of a hand across my face.

Why were my relationships so impossible I wondered? Was there something intrinsically wrong with me? Why had I always walked on egg shells every day, unable to fully trust, side-tracking head games and feeling grossly misunderstood, manipulated, controlled, sexually and spiritually depraved and profoundly alone within each partnership? Deep in my heart, I still believed there was someone out there who complimented me, but he seemed so elusive and so impossible to imagine. Not that I was looking for him actually, because on some level I suspected that I actually was not ready to meet the man of my dreams, even if I tripped over him in the middle of the street somewhere.

One thing was clear at least by being single, the feeling that something dreadful was about to happen to me at any moment, completely left me. I could even fall asleep at night without worrying like hell about the safety and whereabouts of someone who did not care about me anyway. I could actually breathe without that feeling of a giant boa constrictor squeezing at my chest and crushing down my spirit relentlessly day in and day out. I could confidently answer the telephone with a smile in my voice, knowing with all of my heart that it was someone I wanted to actually speak to and not some debt collector chasing money that was never in the bank. I could even buy my kids presents for no apparent reason, if I so desired, because life was just too damn short now for me not to celebrate the fact that I loved them so. Even if there was hardly any money left over to spare, after the all bills were paid for.

I started to chuckle whole heartedly from that deep involuntary place in the belly, which sounded just like a witch, as she gleefully bursts into a spontaneous cackle. The thought crossed my mind that the sheer magic of laughter itself is the very alchemy, which has the power strong enough to transform even the handsomest prince into a humble old frog. Suddenly I realized that the witch was me and I also had the power to transform myself into a much happier, positive and stronger version of myself.

At forty two I was beginning to realise that I had my own self power and that all of my negative experiences had somehow awoken the real me to emerge. I yearned to find a way to use it in a way that didn't harm anyone else and somewhere deep within, the voice of my inner child called me to venture inside and remember a secret that was all but forgotten about.

That little girl who used to sit in the back seat of the yellow Rolls Royce was still hiding from being further tortured from her parents and subsequently both of her husbands as well. Somewhere in a faraway castle of the mind, she had built a dungeon where she had hid from everyone, including herself.

She was still trapped in a time when she was eight years old, needing healing and saving and setting free, so that she could finally grow up and have a life of her own. She had been gagged for so long, waiting for me to return to rescue her, but I had simply forgotten all about her all of this time. I wanted her to come outside into the world with me and play, just as my autistic son Rick had done, when he was so small and too frightened to talk. I would always be there now to hold her hand step by baby step, until she was ready to let go and stand tall all by herself. I just wanted to protect her and let her be herself. Finally a voice seemed to echo in my head and a penny dropped with a very loud clunk. "My relationships were childish and could never work out until I was the one to finally grow up".

I knew that I could not rewrite history, but that I could rewrite the way I looked at it. For me, the process to healing those painful memories, still happens as a step by step process of viewing the situation from a higher perspective. Each wound and hook in retrospect, is a reminder to look within, until I find the precious gem inside the pothole of the bumpy road of my life. From that perspective, it is about the continual journey of that road and no matter how difficult or stupid I sometimes feel about myself for staying in an abusive relationship longer than would normally be deemed ridiculous, the message for me is to always try and remain calm and learn something new about love in the process. That is the jewel which is more precious to me than silver or gold and what I continue to discover every time a challenging situation crops up.

I have come to realize that sometimes even our parents are still on the journey into the soul, learning to become more of love, and that they too are stuck in the dungeon of their own painful childhoods waiting to be rescued also, by their Higher Selves.

Some make the journey and reach the destination, while others never do, staying trapped in the ego. In the meantime, they project their fears onto their children, creating even more fear and subsequently a family of 'programmed zombies'. Each of our journeys is about becoming more of ourselves whilst gently releasing the fear based belief systems programmed into us by them. As a parent, I am very conscious of allowing my children to be exactly who they are regardless of whether I like it or not. My gift to them is freedom and I want them to understand what love really is, so that they never have to do the work I have had to do in reprogramming myself. They can simply just be.

I have come to know that this is the voice of my Higher Self, actually teaching me how to heal, by spending time alone and listening from the inside out. I found that my fears were gently transforming into something beautiful for myself, until inner Claire and outer Claire were intrinsically becoming one. I started to look at the story of my life through new eyes of unconditional love and instead of cowering from the space of being the victim, I found power in a precious new story I had created out of the pain I had suffered throughout my life. Ultimately I was still alive and was able to remain just a like a little white daisy, bobbing about in the storm and that was a really beautiful thing to me. I had not become 'the storm' or an even greater destruction and yet all my life I had been carefully brainwashed by my parents and my ex-husbands to think that I was and everything was my fault. I came to see that I was love and I was not afraid any more to face the truth about it.

I discovered that whenever I could find something wonderful about those difficult times, I had started the healing and found the power to love my way through them. I was able to separate myself from the anger that my parents and my ex-husbands dumped onto me and realised that the bad feeling was just the way they were feeling about themselves. It was merely their expression of feeling out of control. They were not unhappy with me. They were unhappy within themselves.

Jealousy, sexual abuse, domestic violence, envy, manipulation, control, insecurity, greed, dishonesty, denial, unfaithfulness and all the other negative traits that I had encountered could now all be healed by understanding the fear behind them all, which I came to recognise as the ego.

This process in my life seemed to resemble that of the caterpillar, as it out grows its skin over and over until becoming the mysterious chrysalis, shutting out the world and transforming into a butterfly from within. The chrysalis must die before the butterfly can emerge, just as my ego had protected the little girl in the dungeon, as she slowly grew up to transform into her Highest Self.

I started to think about my father and wondered again if he too had been abused as a child. I decided to question him about it the very next time I saw him and his response did not really surprise me.

"How did you know that Claire? I've never even told a soul that it had happened to me in my life when I was a little boy. Nobody knows that now except for you".

Oh my God! I just wanted to hug him and forgive him right there. I forgot feeling sorry for myself, because I felt so sorry for him. If only my father had been brave enough as a little boy to tell someone about his abuse, the power of honesty would have diluted that fear. Instead he was hushed and the fear grew and grew until he became the perpetrator of the actual fear itself, allowing the sickness to re-infect itself over and over with his children and grandchildren.

I told him that nobody would do that to someone, unless it had happened to them first. Then I asked him if he ever abused me, to which he replied "Of course not. Naturally, when you were asleep though, I had to make sure that you were menstruating properly"

I was absolutely revolted and livid and as my stomach turned, I shouted at him in disgust, "Get out of my life. Never come back. This is where history must stop repeating itself now Dad and I never want to see you again".

Just as I was feeling that I could forgive him, I was thrown off the cliff and back into feeling revolted and violently enraged about it all over again. My relationship with him still posed too many unexplained contradictions. The journey to forgiveness seemed impossible for me. He did not have the normal boundaries most people are able to live by, thinking it was normal to check if I was menstruating properly, when in fact he was being highly inappropriate instead.

If he only had loved himself enough by not being ashamed when he was abused as a child and had the courage to tell someone the truth, it would never have kept growing and manifesting over and over again. He thought it was completely normal that he touched me like that when I was young and all the stories my sisters told me, suddenly hit me with a thud. I was no longer in denial about it. I felt so horrible that at the time I never trusted them enough to support them through such atrocious times. Two of my nieces were molested by him and my nephew said he became gay, because apparently my father sexually abused him also when he was very young. The growing pains of this knowledge stung my face, as tears shot down my cheeks. My earlier denial was the mind-set of a little child, just as my mother's must have been also.

The only way to let go and move forward, was to be brave enough to confront the truth and let him go out of my life altogether. All the silence in the world did the victims no good at all. That is where I discovered the demon had its power. We were all afraid and from that fear, more fear and pain and shame were created, until now that is, as I write this book and connect with all of my heart with you. If you have been abused in some way, talk about it. If you have abused someone in some way, be brave enough to talk about it also. Share the truth. The demon loses its power when it steps into the light and when everyone can see it and know about it, no matter how disgusting or shameful you believe it is. By confronting the truth, we can heal. By hiding it, the fear simply perpetuates over and over again, surviving and growing even after the perpetrator dies.

My friend Kerrie in Melbourne came up to stay, shortly after my final altercation with my father. I was dismayed that she still had not moved on from her sexual abuse as a child and she had even tried to commit suicide, because her mother still refused to believe that her own father (Kerrie's grandfather) was the perpetrator of her suffering. She told me that she did not want to be here anymore, because of the way she felt about herself being abused and that her family did not believe her either. They were in denial, just like I had been about my own father for all of those years. Denial is fear. I believe the ego is protecting us from facing the truth, because it is just too painful to confront. These horrendous atrocities happen to give us all the opportunity to move out of the ego and into the soul of our

Highest Sovereign Selves, if only we are brave enough to respond and listen to that oh so quiet little voice within.

Kerrie was also diagnosed with schizophrenia in her forties. No wonder. I believe her personality had split into many aspects of herself as a final spiritual cry out for help to finally go deep inside, where she could have healed her sadness and pain. When I took her to the airport to return her home again, I cried and I cried with poignant tears of loss, as though I knew on an intuitive level that it would be the very last time I would ever see my dearest friend again.

Three months later, Kerrie was found dead in a Melbourne hotel room with an empty bottle of French champagne and a cocktail of sleeping pills by her bedside. She had taken her own life, because her fear of not being heard and believed, was too much to bear and she had surrendered herself to the perpetrator and died the victim. It was all written down in a note beside her pillow as well. I cried until I thought I was bleeding from my eyes. She and Lesta were the only ones who had ever understood me to the core and now I had lost her before she had been able to heal. She even prepaid her funeral and chose the music and clothes she would be cremated in. It was all intricately planned two weeks prior.

Then one week after her funeral, I received a beautiful card from her that she had written and addressed to me before she died, thanking me for being her best friend and true soul sister in this life like we had promised we would be to each other, so many years prior. Her mother posted it up to me when she found it amongst things in the top drawer beside her bed at home. Kerrie was speaking to me even beyond her death. When I read the card, I realised that genetics for me had nothing to do with what family blood lines meant anymore. Those who resonated with my soul were my true family and with that knowingness appeared a simple truth. Kerrie was indeed my beloved soul sister and whilst she was in my soul, she could never truly be separated from me in this life.

About a year later, I felt the time had come to have a bit of romance in my life again – one which was to be a spiritual relationship, so that I could learn more about myself by confronting any negative tendencies that arose. It just so happened that I attracted some pretty massive negative tendencies in myself, because this person did not want to make a commitment to me at all, but rather just wanted to be 'friends with benefits', whilst he also had other lovers.

It's amazing how the universe provides Angels in the form of human beings just when we need them, because my prayer for the spiritual came in the arrival of my beautiful friend, Craig about the same time as my 'friends with benefits' lover. I would share with Craig how painful it was to be with someone so noncommittal. Craig's understanding of unconditional love and the human psyche taught me how to trust my own inner wisdom again, allowing my insecurities to rise up and confront them without blaming the other person for any negative feelings. He taught me how to journey into more of my own core with the wisdom of an androgynous soul, and to remember who I really was.

I was not the sort of girl to have more than one boyfriend at a time and so in my mind, I was absolutely committed to my 'friends with benefits', whilst he was free to sleep around, which happened regularly, especially at gigs, where he was the lead singer in a cover rock band nearly every weekend. I actually believed that he would fall helplessly in love with me one day and make the commitment down the track. Nearly five years later, however, this still did not happen. In the meantime, I learnt to transform so much of my own negative tendencies into becoming more gracious within the relationship, than I had ever conducted myself before. I even had the grace to stop manipulating emotionally and just allowed him to be whoever he wanted to be instead, without any consequences from me.

In past relationships, I would simply dump my stuff onto whoever I was with at the time and nag my partner about anything I was unhappy about, as if he was responsible for my happiness and I was responsible for his. So in this relationship I learnt to be independent emotionally and looked at my own faults instead of focusing on his.

Whenever my feelings of jealousy and possessiveness arose, I got to experience them in such a potent way that I tried to get right inside them to understand where they actually came from. I would suddenly wake up in the middle of the night wondering who the hell he was sleeping with at that moment and made myself so sick, that I would spend the rest of the night in the toilet throwing up or having a nervous bout of diarrhoea. Eventually in the early hours of the morning, I would dry away the tears and make a pot of herbal tea to try and analyse my feelings of jealousy and insecurity, which always came back to fear by the way. Fear of not being pretty enough, or skinny enough, or sexy enough or just plain cool enough. I soon realised that it was up to me to change how I felt about myself and not what he thought about me anymore.

Some of my inner transformation occurred by allowing my partner to be whoever he wanted to be, without trying to change him in any way, but rather looking in at myself, whenever I felt awful about him to change something about 'me' instead.

Imagine paying to go out to dinner with your partner on their birthday, only to discover that they are sitting at another table ignoring you with someone else and then going home to your place in separate cars so that he could partake of the so called 'benefits' part of the relationship. It was a nightmare learning to keep my mouth closed, but I succeeded and for that I am really proud of myself.

I believe my inner personal growth in those years with him was preparing me for someone more special to come into my life someday. It was as if to me the little girl in the dungeon had bravely uncurled herself from foetal position and finally grew up, rising like the phoenix from the ashes in transforming her Dark Shadow Feminine aspect into the wisdom of her more gracious Higher Self and boy, was it hard work!

27 - RICKS MIRACLE

Claire:

Rick was in his last year of special school and just eighteen years old. He would bash himself up a lot physically, until his face bled, which was very upsetting for all of us. He would also yell at the top of his voice and talk his thoughts out aloud all of the time, which used to drive us crazy too. He developed a bit of a sore throat and a cold sore, which did not want to heal up as well, so when we had been to the doctor about three times, because he just did not seem to get better, no matter what antibiotics the doctor prescribed, I asked if we could run some blood tests. The doctor agreed, although he told me not to worry so much and that I was just being an overly protective mother. Well, I believe that all mothers sense when something is not quite right with their children. It is a psychic intelligence that is razor sharp, which should never be underestimated by anyone. That same afternoon, I received an urgent telephone call, telling me to rush Rick urgently to the Gold Coast hospital.

There appeared to be a blood disorder of some type, which the doctors were not prepared to name without a lumber puncture and further blood tests. However, as soon as we got there, Rick and I were rushed to a larger hospital in Brisbane an hour away in an ambulance, so I suspected it was pretty serious like meningitis or something, considering that there was no hospital on the Gold Coast suitable to care for him. I rang Jensen, who followed us up to Brisbane in my car and his friend also followed in his car as well, whilst a beautiful friend of mine named Vera, went and stayed with my other two children indefinitely like a Guardian Angel.

My heart felt like it had suffered a knife wound and was pumping out pure adrenalin, but I just had to be strong for my boy. He was going to need me more than ever to keep his spirits stable as well, no matter what the outcome would be. I knew in my heart that my own strength is what Rick would need from me most. When we arrived at the hospital, I noticed that we were taken straight into an oncology ward, but my head was spinning so much that I did not take in the meaning of what those words implied. Rick was put into his own room with a wash basin outside and every time the nurse entered, she washed her hands and every time she left, she would do the same. The night sister set me up on a reclining chair next to Rick with a cup of tea and a biscuit, which I did not even have the stomach to touch and as she squeezed my hand, whispered softly into my ear,

"Just take this journey one step at a time and try not to deal with everything all tonight".

I cannot tell you how much my head was spinning and how much I prayed that God would look after my son. I even prayed aloud so that Rick could also hear me and at the end, I heard him say, "Amen" with me. His voice was very weak and then he sighed and softly spoke,

"I think I'm going to die tonight mum".

"Just have faith darling", I whispered. "Everything is exactly how it is meant to be right now. You are in the best place possible and I will never leave you, no matter what happens to you Rick, I promise. Now please, just be very gentle with yourself darling and try to get some sleep".

I was shocked that Rick had bravely spoken the words that I was silently thinking as well and my response of maternal comfort was as much for myself as for him.

"We are love mum", Rick's trembling voice affirmed and I felt that he too, was trying to comfort me as much as himself.

"I know love. Whatever is happening is meant to be happening. Don't be afraid. I love you so much".

"I love you too mum", he whispered.

The night seemed endless and I was aware of his every breath, as he drifted in and out of sleep. My mind knew that something very serious was happening to my son and every time the nurse came in to prod him this way and that with her thermometer and bump around the bed with a noisy blood pressure trolley, my heart would race more rapidly and then my voiceless prayers would calm it down again, until finally I drifted off to sleep for an hour or so.

In the morning, another nurse brought in a jug of water and nineteen tiny pills for Rick to take. Well Rick had never swallowed a single pill in his life, let alone a whole handful all at once. People do not realize how difficult some basic things are for someone like Rick who has Autism. I had always crushed his medication up with a little jam or honey on a teaspoon to make it easier for him to swallow, whenever he was sick. After all, he already had enough difficulties to overcome by just learning to be appropriate in an alien world, without gagging on little pills as well.

He was utterly terrified, which triggered a panic attack whilst he tried to swallow the first pill. He scratched his face until it bled red raw, gagging so violently that the whole jug of water ended up on the floor, much to the nurse's annoyance because she did not have any idea why he was making such a fuss. I started to try and calmly tell him how the pills would make him feel better, but the nurse's face reddened as she abruptly warned that all of the pills had to be taken immediately and that there was plenty more where they had come from and Rick better get used to it anyhow. No matter how trivial the exercise sounds, it was one of Rick's most difficult challenges and the routine of pill popping was to be repeated on mass daily and subsequently, for the rest of his life.

Following the lumber puncture and blood tests, the head sister of the ward called me into a private meeting room, where she asked me if I knew what was actually happening. When I shook my head, sitting anxiously on a little two seated sofa, she quietly said that Rick had tested positive for Lymphoblastic Leukaemia and that he would need to start chemotherapy immediately. I burst into tears and bawled uncontrollably, to which the sister put her arms around me and handed me a bunch of tissues from the box on the coffee table.

"Everyone I have ever known with cancer died", I sobbed.

"It's ok, she said. Nowadays, there is a very good chance of beating cancer and we have a high success rate here in Brisbane Claire".

"Oh really?" I implored, blowing my nose loudly and taking a huge breath at the same time.

"Oh yes. Cancer is no longer a death sentence anymore", she claimed.

I immediately stopped crying and felt an overwhelming calmness fall upon me like a comforting blanket of peace. It was so tangible, that I felt that I had the feeling of how to pick it up and cover Rick with it as well. I remembered my mother on the morning that I had knelt at her bed, praying for a miracle to heal her breast cancer and how she had refused to believe it could happen to her all those years ago. Yet I believed in the miracle and now was my chance to keep on believing with all of my being for Rick. At the same moment, I also remembered the Angel who came to visit me after Rick's twin brother died. The message I received when I declined to write prophecy for the children was to have faith. Right now, I wondered if the prophecy was actually about Rick's illness and that my faith was needed to help open up Rick's mind also for the miracles to happen in his life.

I thought about the many miracles that Jesus performed in the Bible and in particular the one with the lame man. Jesus had simply said, "Pick up your bed and walk".

Can you imagine being crippled and curled up in pain, lying on the ground and someone saying to you to get up and walk? Doesn't that sound absolutely crazy? It was not just Jesus who manifested that miracle, but the lame man, who had to be courageous enough to believe that he could actually get up without falling down in that very moment as well. Even though the miracle was granted, it took the lame man to act upon it to manifest. So what if the lame man did not act upon his faith? The miracle could not be realised and he would have died there, being understandably just too afraid to move. I held that thought like a precious stone, turning it over and over gently in my mind.

Rick took the news of his diagnosis as calmly as if he were told he had the common flu; after all he had not come across the word 'cancer' before in his life, so typical fears associated with it did not exist. "We'll do whatever we have to do to get rid of it then, won't we mum?"

"You will have to stop bashing yourself up now Rick", I stressed, as I patted his hand to emphasize the point from the chair beside his bed. "From now on you have to start really loving yourself and being patient with yourself, if you want that medicine to work and you have to really believe that the medicine is going to be successful as well". I noted how all of the doctors and nurses seemed to stare at me dubiously, as if they were watching me addressing a small child and not the handsome young man nervously twirling a stray piece of hair with his index finger and right thumb, until it was just a messy matted dreadlock hanging over his forehead instead.

"Yes, that's right Rick", began the oncologist as his eyes briefly smiled at me in acknowledgment of my method to communicate the obvious before shifting back to the innocent wide eyes on the bed, "Those who do well with the outcome of their cancer, keep a very positive attitude compared to those who don't do so well. However, we must commence the chemotherapy immediately, if you are to have the best chance of knocking it on the head. Unfortunately you will lose all of your hair and become very sick before you will start to feel better again and it will take many months of staying here in hospital before you can go home again".

A dam of tears rose up in a flash flood, burning the backs of my eyes, as I fought to keep them from bursting onto my face. I imagined with horror the loss Rick would feel without his full head of hair. He already seemed to be processing the doctor's words and all I knew he would be distressed about, was the fact that he was not going home for a very long time to see all of his model ships and books and to be able to lock himself away in his room and to sleep in his own bed, but the full impact of his illness was yet to be known.

I knew on an invisible level, Rick would have to do some difficult inner work on himself to deal with what the doctor was saying to him. It was not just going to take drugs and the right medical treatment to bring about his recovery; this much I knew on a very deep level. I believed that if I could influence Rick to work with me in staying positive, that together we would not be afraid to face whatever happened next, even facing the shock of watching all of his beautiful hair fall out.

As it turned out, losing his hair was not quite the horrific ordeal I imagined it would be, because my beautiful children decided to turn it into an awesome shave party instead. Emma and I sat in wonder, as Jensen and Kai thought nothing of having their own heads shaven at the same time as Rick. In the process they stopped to crack hilarious jokes about their radical new hair styles, with shining tufts of curls falling down amongst the bald bits resembling the undead from a Stephen King horror movie and not even showing the slightest sign of terror at watching all of their blonde strands being stripped off from the scalp as they tumbled onto the bathroom floor.

Observing all of this filled me with an enormous pride for my children, as they paused at the mirror giggling, taking photos of each other and proudly rubbing each other's soft pink heads which were now completely naked and shaven clean. By the time it was Rick's turn to go under the razor, he was so busy chuckling and having a party with us that the nurse had to keep stopping the razor as well, because her heaving of irrepressible laughter was potentially becoming dangerous over Rick's head. Thanks to my boys being so brave and to Emma outrageously egging them on like a high school cheer leader, Rick thought being bald was pretty cool and from then on actually, I did too.

Over the next months, Rick really did work on himself. He seemed to leave some aspects of his autism in a past life, as if he could actually separate himself from them. By consciously fighting for his life, he had found a passionate reason to live, even if that meant losing it in the end one day. There was something very mysterious about watching my son transform in that instant, when he chose to focus his mind on staying positive and being gentle with himself, instead of merely hiding alone and bashing himself up all of the time in that lonely place I call 'Autistic land'. Those most difficult and negative aspects of the autism ceased for a while and I never found him inflicting self bodily harm, whilst he stayed at the hospital. He also stopped making strange, obsessive noises and he ceased talking to himself out aloud, which was in itself a magical thing.

If I was not with Rick most of the time to check that everything the doctors and nurses were doing was on track though, something would go amiss. I was furious with the nurse who applied the wrong tape to his wound when I was not there one day and especially when she came into his room to change the dressing the next morning. She ripped all of the skin off in one rapid sweep of her wrist, which literally took months to heal properly and if she had taken more care by reading his chart, would plainly see that he was allergic to it in the first place. Part of the problem, was with Rick's comprehension of what was being said to him and without me interpreting it to him in a way that he could understand it. He would openly consent to things, without knowing what was really being implied, because he did not want to upset anyone with saying the wrong thing, so he simply said yes to everything he was asked to do.

More than once, I heard him agree to undergoing some procedure, which was highly inappropriate, before I was able to intervene and stop it from happening.

Another time, after bringing some clean washing back to his room, I discovered a student nurse poking around in his arm with a needle, as if his skin was just a pin cushion. I know that she needed to obtain the bloods and that the chemo had made his veins shrink so much that they were severely withdrawn, but I was heartbroken that she was inflicting even more pain to him. If I had not protested to the haematologist right away about it, I do not know how long Rick would have suffered unnecessarily, for he did not want to speak up for himself and complain to anyone. That very afternoon a central line was inserted into his body, so that the bloods were accessed directly from it and the needles were no longer required. Rick had not complained once and I found myself admiring his strength and was equally humbled by his grace, yet I was also determined to stay by his side and to fight for his dignity to be kept protected at all costs as well. No one else was.

Every day I would wonder how much more pain he would need to endure, yet he never once complained about it. He was so busy being positive and grateful for his life every day, that whenever friends and other family members would weep and feel sorry for him in his company, I would escort them away, because they were already grieving for his potential loss of life and not seeing the magic that was happening to him invisibly. It may sound cruel, but I did not want Rick to start believing that he had anything to be sad about. For that miracle to happen, it had to be believed it was already occurring. And it was, because he quickly went into remission.

It was during this period that I also had to let our home go at the Gold Coast, because I could not afford to keep it anymore. I was not earning any money and was just living on a pension to get by. We were physically homeless, yet I did not worry about it. My home was a bed next to Rick at the hospital now and so I gave away all of the furniture to friends and also let go of all the shackles I had surrounded myself with over the years, which I realised were no longer important to me. There were antiques and things that I once treasured, but I felt that the only thing that was important actually were people and love and nothing else was really worth worrying about in life anymore. Not even money. No problem was worth stressing about to the point of losing yourself over. Things were just things, no matter how beautiful they were and I knew for sure that nothing was as beautiful and as precious to me as all of my children and our life and our love.

The Leukaemia Foundation graciously offered me one of their temporary care homes, so that as Rick was allowed to come out of hospital for a few days at a time, we had somewhere to stay. Jensen was in his own unit on the Gold Coast and Emma and Kai were both staying with their father and coming to stay with us from time to time. I missed my kids desperately and loved it when they came to visit. Little by little during times such as this, Rick would return back to his old negative habits and started to bash himself up again, locking himself in his bedroom. Then to all of our horror and as a matter of coincidence you may say, the cancer would return. This battle into remission happened three times and finally there was no other option, but to undergo a bone marrow transplant.

Rick begged me to let my father come to see him and I was deeply grieved, as I could not bear to see him again, but I also could hardly deny my son a simple wish, so under the circumstances I allowed my father to visit Rick in hospital, but only if the door was left wide open and the nurses kept an eye out for both of them. I simply could not stomach seeing him again and reluctantly, left them to their visits.

I was still seeing my 'friends with benefits' lover, although he was never there when I would have appreciated some support with Rick, or with moving my things out of the house. He only called me when he wanted to partake of the 'benefits' element of the relationship, which was only perhaps once every two weeks or so and sometimes just once a month, which kept me in an intense state of longing for him, though not in need. It was a bit like the old adage of, 'Treat 'em mean, keep 'em keen', if you know what I mean.

Whenever I did see him however, I found myself emphatically energized and charged up to work with Rick all over again, so I continued to see him, as much as he wished to see me. I never once made the initial contact with him to get together and I never told him what I would have really treasured from him deep down where my soul knew how it felt to be with 'the one'. Although he had opened up my kundalini and I was passionately on fire all of the time sexually, I found myself becoming more of love and just wanted to accept him for who he was, without trying to change him in any way. Most of my friends could not understand why I continued to have him in my life and I was never able to explain it, because it was such a spiritually profound experience for me. They never saw my secret inner transformation, through the longing and disappointments that were mirrored inside of me, or the relationship I was developing with my Higher Self because of him.

I was on my own so to speak, realizing that every little trial I was experiencing with him and with the rest of my life, was actually a powerful strengthening process for me. My inner wisdom and self-reliance was sculpting me into becoming more of a whole woman, with more inner balance between the masculine and feminine aspects of myself. If he was not offering me the commitment of love that I so passionately yearned for, I would simply commit to finding that love within myself. And I did. I am not saying that it was an easy process though by any means, because there were times when my private torrents of tears would melt an iceberg the size of Gibraltar, crying myself clean from all of the pain and disappointment.

In juxtaposition with all of this, Craig noted that my work with Rick to manifest the miracle and his ultimate healing was also having a powerful effect on my own spirituality and healing as well. So whatever work I was doing with Rick, I was also doing with myself at the same level and in the places where my wounds were the oldest and the deepest. I discovered that both my son and my 'friends with benefits' lover were helping me with my own spiritual development, where I was seeing much more from the eyes of love and beauty and not from all of my deepest fears anymore.

Rick eventually had his bone marrow transplant and his mouth was covered in ulcers, whilst his body tried to reject the bone marrow as well, yet he never gave up believing that his miracle was happening. When he could not eat for six weeks and was fed by a tube, he still did not complain about it. To make the journey even more challenging, the medication that Rick was taking to keep the bone marrow stable was actually killing his bones. As a consequence, Rick was suffering from another degenerative disease called Avascular Necrosis and the pain in his ankles was unbearable, whilst the balls in his hips were silently disintegrating.

I was desperate to find other natural ways to assist Rick's pain and discovered a lady who practiced master Reiki healing in the phone book. When I researched the word Reiki, I discovered that it was made up of two Japanese words. 'Rei', which means God's wisdom and 'Ki', which means life force energy. I liked the concept that with the laying of hands, the divine life energy could flow through and promote healing. When I finally met this healer, I was overwhelmed by her sense of serenity and compassion. She initiated me into the first level of Reiki, so that I could perform it on Rick's ankles myself and when I asked her how much money she was going to charge me, she simply asked me how much I could afford. When I told her of my circumstances, she just smiled and told me not to worry about it. She said that she loved the way I used makeup and could I show her how to make the best of her features, to which I was delighted to show her how beautiful she was with a bit of war paint enhancing the angle of her cheek bones and the colour of her eyes. She was so pleased, that she had her teeth whitened as well and a whole new wardrobe to match the new look.

The reiki healer also became friends with Rick, introducing him to different types of Angel cards, which were not only beautiful to look at, but an energetic means to help him focus pure light on a specific problem he may have been working through. The cards had an uncanny way of bringing a subconscious negative mind-set into the awareness of the conscious mind. An energetic healing could then happen by focusing on an appropriate affirmation by releasing the negative thought into a higher frequency of thinking. Rick seemed to be very sensitive in pulling out the correct cards not just for himself, but with other people as well and it was not long before friends would come over to ask Rick for an Angel reading. The power of this light work was such a beautiful experience for him and for others. I continued to encourage him to use the Angel cards, whenever he was having a particularly bad day or his energy was in need of a bit of a positive lift.

I was spending half an hour doing Reiki on Rick's ankles two to three times a day and he was starting to feel much better. Whilst we were attending a follow up appointment with the orthopaedic surgeon at the hospital, the x-rays proved that Rick's bones in the ankle had miraculously healed, when previously we had been told that they had actually died and nothing could be done. We were so happy. Reiki had created a miracle, which caused a bit of controversy as to whether they got the diagnosis right in the first place.

Although he had to quit his last year of special school before the end of his year, he was invited to attend the graduation concert. Rick had recorded himself singing his very own version of Frank Sinatra's, "My Way" as a tribute to his miracle in overcoming cancer and they asked me to supply a copy to be played as the finale. There wasn't a dry eye in the house and Rick got a standing ovation too which was very moving.

He was also honoured with the Queensland High Achievers Award, which gave him more belief in continuing the journey of his miracle as well.

By now Jensen and his beautiful future wife had decided to move to Melbourne and I moved the few belongings that I had kept into their flat together with Rick's ship books and things, which was about an hour's drive away from the hospital.

Each night, before I went to sleep, I would notice a large oval light on the wall next to the doorway, yet there was not a light source that could have created it, because my bedroom was at the back of the flat away from traffic and all other people. I know that we were being looked after by the Angels and I always felt protected somehow, wondering if it was actually my Guardian Angel letting me know that he was taking care of us.

Shortly after we settled in, without any warning my ex-husband dropped Emma and Kai over to the flat with all of their belongings, telling me that they had to live with me from now on, as he had met someone and could not have the kids anymore. I didn't have any beds or extra blankets, so we all slept on the floor for a couple of nights until I found a four bedroom house for us to rent. What sort of man just dumps the kids on you to live, without even asking if it is ok or organising it with you first?

Out of nowhere my gall bladder erupted and had to come out. Whilst I was in hospital, my father came over to visit Rick without telling me. Apparently, Kai walked in and caught my father with his shirt off holding Rick's hand and was making him feel the bare skin on his chest. Kai freaked out screaming, "What the fuck do you think you are doing Pa? Get the fuck out of this house right now and never come back".

I sensed that forgiveness is only made possible if the perpetrator stops repeating the transgression, because they have had a true inner recovery about it and stop doing it. When my father asked for my forgiveness on his deathbed, I refused. I was not being cruel. I was not trying to be vindictive and I was not reacting to the horror of it all. My heart just could not physically forgive him. I told him that too many peoples' lives had been damaged by him. I told him that I loved him and wished him all the best on his journey to transformation into spirit and that was all that I could give him. I never went to his funeral and I never went through his personal belongings to try to take anything from the past either. I did not need his things to be a constant reminder of all the heartache. It was time to put all of that pain to rest at last.

My father's crimes with children are still the most difficult subject for me to pour love over, simply because innocent children are involved and are often damaged forever by it. I know that I loved my father. I just hated what he did to wreck so many young lives over a lifetime of secrets. After he died, one of his old friends contacted me to say that she had not heard from him in a long time and was everything ok? I decided not to keep the demon in the darkness anymore and told her bluntly that he was a paedophile, to which she told me that she already knew, because she had a secret all of her own that she had been keeping for sixty odd years. She told me that something had happened when she was just a little girl living at my father's farm with her parents, who had come out from Holland and worked as farm hands for him. He had done something inappropriate to her then and she had kept it a secret all of this time.

"Why didn't you tell me before? Why didn't you tell my mother? Why didn't you tell *your* mother? Why? And why do you still care about what happens to him? You could have stopped so much trauma just by bringing it out into the open and stopping him from doing it to his children and grandchildren".

"I was afraid in those days Claire", she whispered.

I was beyond livid now. Even more victims than I was aware of had protected him from the consequences, so that he never had to suffer them for himself. All of his victims had done that for him instead, just by keeping the secret and in doing so had also owned his crimes for him. All of us had carried them, as if they were our own. How could I allow my father to continue inflicting the most intense horror over me, even though he was no longer here anymore? He was dead for God's sake, so how could I continue to let him hurt me like this? How could I stop it?

Strange how it suddenly came to me as I sat to write this book. The answer I had been praying for all of my life came to me quietly and coherently, as if God himself had waited to hand it to me when I was ready to share it by writing it down.

For me to heal, I just had to realise that my demons were my father's crimes and not my own, which needed to be possessed by him alone and returned to him. I mentally and very deliberately decided to pass them back to him, where they now rest without power inside the grave. I, with all of his other victims, and I even include my mother here, suffered, by carrying and protecting my father's crimes all of his life, just by staying in denial and keeping his secret. I now know, that this is fear. This is not love.

We never truly know another's suffering, but everyone has their own inner struggles to battle, sometimes not realising when they are unintentionally being projected onto others, as in this case with my sisters and I as young children. For that, I can finally forgive both my mother and my father, for they must have both been suffering unbearably to project so much of their own sorrow and agony onto us.

28 - NEVER AGAIN

Mark:

It was a huge relief to be out of my second marriage. Day to day life had been massively stressful those last two years, and especially the final six months. It was clear it was a decision she had already made but had kept from me, and I wondered if I had not found her mobile bill when I did, just how long she would have continued living a lie and deceiving me? But then, it was probably her way of telling me by leaving it there intentionally for me to find. In those six months, even though I masochistically still wondered if we could save things somehow, I spent a lot of time processing what had happened, so by the time we finally physically separated it was a mere formality.

For the first time in four years I could be at home, relax and not feel under any pressure from domineering adult children or manipulative wives. I had been walking on eggshells and worrying way too much about who I was going to upset next, and what sneaky games were being played out behind my back, for far too long. Liana was so much happier to be out of it as well. Early on in the relationship she thought she had gained new brothers and sisters, was happy and positive, until we eventually realised that they didn't accept her as such as she had the wrong genetics to ever be treated as an equal member of the family.

In the house we rented Liana worked and helped me for days cleaning, unpacking, washing, tidying and had things organised before I could even get to organise them myself. She was incredible, and just when I needed her to be. Before I had even thought of it, she had even written out a shopping list of things we didn't have any more and needed to go out and buy.

As we worked our way through unpacking our boxes I started to realise what a daze I must have been in to have allowed my ex to have taken so many things. She had packed for me everything she didn't want, all the odd cutlery, and cracked crockery, the odd or old saucepans and not much else. I was discovering her 'sharing' was actually packing all the nice or valuable things for herself, the new things, the sets of crystal, and packing what was left for me, making sure she had heavily sealed the boxes so I wouldn't dare open them to check, and so not know until it was too late. She had taken all the complete sets of things, all the new things, all the expensive things, all the electrical appliances, even things I had bought for myself or had owned before I knew her, and she left me the things she didn't like or didn't want, or didn't work. It had the energy of someone so insecure, so angry, that she had to grab everything she could to feed some form of insecurity, or inflict a sadistic punishment.

Fine, I thought. If she had wanted all those things that badly then let her have them. I had learnt from my first marriage breakup they are just things after all, and things really aren't important in life at the end of the day. You just don't realise until you choose to grow spiritually, or eventually and inevitably have to face up to your own mortality. She had been able to walk away with everything from her previous marriage because her husband had hung himself, and this one by taking advantage of being at home while I was out working to pay for everything. I remembered how she had said she was "spiritual" in her profile on the dating website, and it showed up just how abused the term can be. It's a verb and about behaviours, belief, and a lifestyle of caring about others and our world around us, and the actions you take in your life to live that way. Her Karma would come one day. I told Liana we would go out and buy all new things and we wouldn't be surrounded by things that constantly reminded us of those bad memories as she would constantly be. So we laughed and wrote a big list out, and went out and had great fun on an almighty spending spree around the home centres buying everything we needed anew.

Liana was now old enough to get herself up and off to school on the bus in the morning, home again afterwards, and then cook herself tea if I had to work back late. It freed my time up entirely and took the pressure off having to race home after work and be a baby sitter. She loved being independent and organising herself, and she was very good at it. They were good skills to acquire for growing up as well, so I knew she could look after herself, and would not be flapping around all helpless if anything should ever happen to me. I was so proud of the way she had handled the whole transition and risen above it in such a positive and mature way.

The next couple of months I spent most of the evenings, and entire weekends, prostrate horizontally on the sofa after Liana had gone to bed, without any lights on, sombrely digesting what the hell had happened with the previous four years, and how I had let myself marry into such an abusive and manipulative family? How I had let her back in to my life, over and over, in the beginning when I should have ran away. How had I let all these people trample who I was underfoot in their own self-interest for so long? The list went on and on, swirling around in my head like debris picked up in a tornado, flashing across in front of me before being dumped back down with a thud. Now I had 'me' back again, I realised just how badly I had lost who I was under their evil spell and how I had allowed my ex so easily to reel me back in after each blow up and separation.

I had tried so hard in all my relationships, I had genuinely loved my partners with all I am, I had given and shared 100% of me and everything I had, every time. I had taken on and loved step children as my own, when their fathers had abandoned them, I had always tried to help anyone who I could. I had always been responsible and worked and provided a home, given support, and unconditional love, even when I was totally exhausted and falling apart at times. I hadn't been perfect either, but had worked on my issues. My wife had a bad habit of going off at me, and then refusing to let me get a word in to defend myself by immediately putting her fingers in her ears, humming "la-la-la" and telling me repeatedly to "f*** off". Infuriated, I would pursue her to make her listen, but learnt that was wrong and trained myself not to stop doing it. I would just wait until she had calmed down, and then calmly have my say. So what was I doing wrong in relationships? The problem was I was still not loving me. Again I had neglected my very own self. I had not loved myself enough to say "No" and leave a relationship when I was not truly happy. To not say "No" when someone was taking advantage, or being abusive, to me. I hadn't loved and nurtured my own soul first. I had been obsessed with loving their souls, their needs, their wants and giving all I could to them, bending over in their wind to accommodate them to the point of breaking, allowing myself to be crushed in the process and sucked dry of life. I had forgotten to nurture myself by loving me.

We all have to love ourselves, nurture our soul, and allow ourselves to find true happiness. It's not selfish, as I had always thought. Selfishness is about the ego and greed, wanting and taking for the sake of it and never considering others in the process. This was about nurturing our own Soul as well as others, not instead of. If we are unhappy in a relationship, no matter how hard or impossible it might seem, we have to love ourselves enough to leave it. Compromise is not the answer. I would never allow that to happen to me again and if I should ever consider another relationship, it would only be with someone who made me rapturously happy and that I would love myself too, anything less and I would just walk away. Maybe I had finally got it. But I couldn't imagine ever meeting anyone else or wanting to get into another relationship again. It was all too late now for this life. I couldn't do it again. I wouldn't do it again.

One day Liana told me my wife had contacted my first ex-wife, and they had been meeting up for coffees. Considering they had never met and absolutely detested each other throughout my second marriage, constantly threatening to tell the other what bad mothers they were, I found it all quite repulsive. I assumed it was a case of now having a common enemy, even if they didn't really like each other, they could reassure each other that they weren't the problem and I was. Worst of all they were meeting in shopping centres with Liana present. She had to sit there and listen to them both absolutely trash her dad, and told me how they exchanged personal information about me, my new address, where I was working, how much I was getting paid, my finances, my income, tax, even my bank account numbers.

Their dark shadows were out in all their glory, salivating at the opportunity to plot making my life hell. Even after we had parted and no longer had any need to have further contact, they wanted to intentionally inflict more punishment. It was a display of pure evil, each entering into a partnership with someone they despised, for the sole intention of inflicting pain on someone else. The dark shadow of their psyche was on public display, full of hate, when they should have been looking within themselves at their own behaviour, and actions from our failed marriages. I found it absolutely disgusting and devious and it just showed how low they were both capable of stooping.

The final contact I had with my second wife was a nasty and poisonous email she sent me, accusing me of all things - stealing money from her, of being a thief, ruining her life, her family, and what a horrid person I was, finishing off with a long and graphic piece on how fat and ugly I was. It was pure darkness, vicious, and written full of hate. I could clearly see that she had chosen to deal with all that had happened, by manipulating the truths around in her own head, convincing herself she wasn't to blame in any way at all, or her children, no, it was all my fault, totally. It was the same behaviour I had witnessed throughout the time I had known her, instead of looking honestly at herself, she chose to lie to herself and deflect all the blame at others. If that was part of her journey and where she needed to go right now, and it made her feel better and able to deal with her life going forward, well, that was her choice. I didn't give it any dignity by responding. I had moved on and no longer involved with her dysfunctional family. I knew the truth and I had always been honest and come from love. I could walk away with my head held high and a clear conscious, and that was all that mattered to me.

I was fifty and single once again. It's lonely feeling old, reflecting on your mortality and being totally broke. Is my life done now? Will I ever be in love again? Am I going to die alone? I accepted that the answer was probably, yes, no and yes. I would probably never have another relationship, I couldn't allow myself to. Certainly not a serious one, I was now too terrified to risk ever getting into a committed relationship ever again. My choice in women seemed abysmal. So what do I do now? I really wanted to recommence the journey inwards and continue the spiritual development I had been doing earlier, which had all but stalled again during my second marriage. I wanted to try and connect with my Higher Self and explore my soul. I wanted to, needed to, spend some time on Me and I now had the free time I needed for that. So I decided to try and recommence the journey and go exploring and make the most of being single.

One day, I stumbled across Eckhart Tolle and started reading his work. A couple of days later I discovered he was about to be in town giving a presentation on synchronicity. What synchronicity I thought! So I jumped online and bought a ticket and went to see him. It was a great presentation about living in the 'now', and the energy at the presentation felt light and wonderful, although I did notice about 90% of the audience were women. Why don't more men open up to themselves and explore who they really are?

I had been reading about the idea that people can get together and their combined thoughts can create energy, and that energy can manifest significant change in the world around us. The more people who combine their energy for a common idea, the more likely they can manifest it. I wondered how we could actually organise the whole planet to do that together, at exactly the same time, globally, to try and make the world a little bit of a better place. I jumped on the computer and spent a few days furiously coding up a website I called Collective Thoughts …'A meeting place for the Collective Unconsciousness' (www.collective-thoughts.org), where users could post a thought of what they wanted to manifest and invite as many people as possible across the planet, to agree to join in and hold the same thought at that same time, wherever they are on the planet, even if only for a minute. It's probably still out there languishing somewhere on the net, no-one ever really used it, but I thought it was a nice idea.

I realised that having integrity and choosing love over fear was all that is needed for spiritual enlightenment. We don't have to become a Buddhist monk guru in orange robes sitting on a mountain top in silence for ten years. It can be achieved by anyone if they so choose, regardless, or race, sex, nationality, fame, power or financial situation. Each and every one of us is on the journey and it is up to us when we finally get it and begin choosing to be love, there is no discrimination. It is quite easy really, its within reach for every one of us, we just have to make the choice and honour it. We can all be gurus.

As time passed by that big wheel started to come by again, turning another full cycle, and I started to wonder about 'the one' still being out there. Logic told me not to bother. History told me not to bother. But something just kept niggling away at me that there was unfinished business, someone was out there and it was still unfinished. But what could I even do different next time? Was it even possible with all the conflicting extremes that I am, how could I ever hope to meet a true soul mate and get it right this time? And at fifty years of age? No, don't be stupid Mark. Something just kept calling me back, telling me not to give up, and that it is possible. Never give up hope, believe, have faith. I tried to ignore it.

29 - RECLAIMING THE DREAM

Claire:

My heart suddenly ached, whenever I would see lovers huddled together on the street somewhere just holding hands. Even in nature, I noticed that the birds were always paired up in twos and I yearned to be part of that mystery of life as well. I did not even think that the true story of my love life had started to unfold as yet, even after two failed marriages and five kids. "Where are you?" I whispered to the moon. "Are you still there?" It was my birthday and I had just turned fifty years old.

I had not heard anything from my 'friends with benefits' lover for over six weeks and I started to wonder what was going on, so I sent him a text message from my phone asking him to join me for dinner. His reply devastated me to the core, saying that he did not want to see me anymore, as he had met someone. My self-esteem dropped like acid to the pit of my stomach and my heart felt like it was being stabbed over and over again. Why had he not told me sooner? Why did he think so little of me not to say anything? I cried myself to sleep, feeling so wretched and sorry for myself that I thought I was going to die. That feeling that there was something wrong with me had returned and there was nothing I could do to change it, until sleep was my only relief.

The next day, I thought I would take a crack at making myself feel better by pondering on the potential of 'what if?' The heaviness around my solar plexus began to shift and I started to feel lighter, as I asked myself, what if I could attract any man in the whole world? Just for fun, I lit a candle, grabbed a full packet of cigarettes, poured myself a very large glass of chardonnay, got my favourite incense happening and started to make a shopping list of everything I desired in a man, and I mean absolutely everything. I also included what I did not want though. This step was very important, because nearly right was not good enough for me anymore. I would have rather spent the rest of my life alone and just had the odd lover to keep my kundalini smouldering, than to attract another immature mate, where I was constantly losing myself with.

If I would have asked for a passionate, tall, dark and handsome stranger - period, I may have attracted an addict, or a gay version, or one who preferred lots of lovers at the same time, so I was also very specific about being in a committed, monogamous, non-gay relationship with him.

Generally speaking, I had attracted partners, who I felt were much younger than I was, no matter how old they were. It is not that I felt superior to them, or wiser than them, I just felt older. Perhaps I was just an ancient soul and had never met a male with a similar energetic frequency to me before. Consequently, I was never able to feel that I had essentially ever known a real man (who I was interested in romantically) in my entire lifetime and I even wondered if any actually existed at all.

My pen began to frantically scribble, as if it had a life of its own, the essence of things I supposed a real man was made up of to me. He would be kind, yet he would be assertive. He would be honest and yet somehow wicked. I wanted to attract a man who would respond to me with his heart instead of reacting to me with his head. He would walk into the room and I would know that I lusted after him as much as he lusted after me. Yes that's right. I wanted to experience both love and lust in equal measures and I could not see why I could not have my cake and eat it at the same time, so long as neither of us got hurt in any way. Isn't that what cake is for?

In my life, I had experienced lust and I had experienced what I thought was love, but never the two together. It was time to allow myself to have it all. I wanted to be treasured and I wanted to be able to treasure him. I wanted to feel sensual as well as sexual. I wanted to be able to give as well as to be able to receive love in as many intimate and beautiful modes of expression that we could fashion together. I wanted to be feminine, without him trying to strip me of my makeup or my perfumes and my high heels. I wanted him to be comfortable around my creativity and my love of beauty. I wanted to trust and I wanted to respect and be respected. I wanted to grow in love and be supportive of his unique spiritual journey as well.

In essence I was talking about meeting the balance of my own 'Twin' energy here, not whether or not he was strong physically, or how much money he had in the bank for heaven's sake. None of these things mattered to me in the slightest. It was about an overall feeling that his inner strength, or his spirit matched mine exactly on a purely energetic level. I had met males with similar sensitivity and intelligence, coupled with sexual magnetism before, but this is still not what I was talking about. I'd met men with beautiful strong bodies and muscles bulging from their torsos, yet this too was not the strength I was after in a man.

I was aware of my own balance of masculine and feminine energies and realized that my true love would have a fine balance between male and feminine energies also, without seeming at all effeminate.

I had worked so hard at transforming the negative in my life into something beautiful and meaningful, requiring both male and female energies to do so. I realized that this man would be an alchemist too. He would definitely not be afraid to look at himself in the mirror, without dumping his crap onto me and be able to laugh at himself, transforming into a higher version of his essence as well.

I pondered the odds of not just finding this man, but him being available for me on this planet in this lifetime. I threw back my head and roared with laughter. I honestly thought my sides would split wide open, thinking this was all really very silly of me.

I had composed two full pages describing in exact detail what he was like, yet how could this man exist? How could I ever meet this spiritually free – thinking, tall, handsome sex god with long curly hair and eyes that flashed fire and played tango with mine from afar, let alone entice him into my life and live happily ever after with him?

Still, something compelled me to keep writing about him; something tempted me to keep pouring out my heart's desire on paper, describing the most deliciously attractive attributes I imagined possible. I was having so much fun thinking about him, that I actually caught myself in the mirror smirking just like a cheeky school girl does when she flirts with the teacher.

And then like zooming back in a time machine to the past, I remembered the poignant memory of my childhood, when I lay on the floor of my mother's bedroom on the little cot mattress, calling out to my one true love in the darkness. I knew with all of my heart that he was out there somewhere too. I trusted that he could hear my soul whisperings with the glow of the moon shining down on his face, right at that very moment in time so very long ago. I knew he was there and I knew how he felt and the words on my wish list resonated exactly to the feeling of him. He was 'the one'. I had captured his very essence in black and white scrawl so that he was not just part of my imagination any more.

With a flash, I was back to the present, remembering how weak and unattractive I had felt after being dumped by my 'friends with benefits' playboy the day before. How different could two men be I sniggered? How way out of resonance with my soul had I been with all of my previous ex's as well? Perhaps that is what pressed me to keep writing, because on some gut level I knew I was definitely doing some wondrous magic on myself in seriously flirting with the most sacred powers of universal law in the form of synchronicity. Those two most healing words, 'what if?' had gathered me up into a world where anything could happen and where I started reprogramming my old limiting belief systems about myself into ones which resonated with my dreams instead.

Without another thought, I folded up my scribblings and threw them into the bottom drawer and forgot all about them… Not realizing that this carefree gesture activated yet another sacred universal law, expressed by Deepak Chopra as 'non attachment'. My heartfelt dream of dreams was in the process of manifesting out there somewhere in the perfect realm of all possibilities. Yet all I thought I was doing was trying to cheer myself up, after feeling so utterly alone and miserable at being dumped by my ex.

I even began toying with the idea of finding my true love on the internet and the thought had kept entering my mind over and over again, like the record player being stuck on repeat. Friends had previously even suggested online dating to me, and said that other men and women that they knew who were my age, and even older, were having a great time meeting new people on the internet. It was the modern way to connect with everyone nowadays they had said with a wink, and also a discerningly private way to engage a new lover for someone like me. What did they mean - someone like me I wondered? Did they mean someone desperate, or someone old? Did they think I was sexually depraved and unattractive, or was I their idea of that cheap and brazen hussy my mother in law used to love to whisper about when she'd had a few glasses too many of chardy, over a gossip session I wondered? Bloody hell.

Personally, no matter what they thought, I felt it was a dodgy way to meet prospective lovers and speculated that only desperados with weirdo agendas or sleazy characters, like those married men wanting affairs resorted to meeting in this way. Not to mention all of those axe murderers Emma had so responsibly warned me about, who were just lurking in the shadows of social networks, waiting to pounce on and slaughter any unsuspecting victim on the internet meat market these days.

Anyway, didn't all nice girls encounter fresh male blood through work or at social events I mused? Yet, the only men I had been chatted up by in recent times, had all been the drunken strangers at the local pub. So I considered that I had nothing to lose by putting up a profile very discreetly on the most popular dating site in Australia, just to see what happened. I presumed none of my circle would be so brash as to advertise themselves to other potential souls of vulnerability, let alone recognise my old face in the embarrassment of the desperate and the dateless world of lonely hearts.

I decided to market myself, fancying that I was doing an advertising campaign for someone, except that someone was me. I wanted the page to echo with mystery, even reflecting my personality somehow in provocative layers that only my true love could recognise, if he was even reading about me by any chance. I did not want to be sounding mediocre and lifeless, because I had decided that mediocre did not reflect who I was anymore and that is exactly how most of the other profiles on this particular website sounded to me. There were just so many other thousands of single females out there obviously desperate to meet someone and I wanted to stand out from them somehow. I on the other hand, was not desperate, but I knew I was different, just like feeling as if I was the little piece of jigsaw puzzle being muddled up and lost in the wrong box when I was born, so I thought I would be proud of that fact from now on instead of being ashamed of it and maybe my true love would recognize me, if he so happened to be out there looking at the profiles as well.

My work had been all about marketing other people, really famous people, but being able to pitch myself out there as a desirable, attractive, single, middle aged woman was a really painful test to my self-esteem, which did not come very naturally at all. Especially when there were so many beautiful, young females profiled there on this site along side of me. Anyhow, I created my profile and posted it on the internet, together with a selfie, which like a teenager, took all afternoon and a million poses in front of the bathroom mirror to capture successfully on my mobile phone.

Jumping into the deep end so to speak, was now just a matter of sinking or swimming amongst all of the other fish in the sea, but this time I vowed, there would be no hooks, for he had to be 'the one'.

Claire2909

"In every moment, we make choices to create the future.. Live the dream...

I'm an independent person with a passion for seeing the beauty in everything I put my mind to, whether that be cooking up a storm for my family and friends, decorating the house or sitting on top of a mountain and catching a rainbow after the rain. I believe that life is filled with opportunities to experience more of who we are and sometimes it takes a little extra courage to find the jewel in a challenging pothole, which we sometimes encounter on the road, but we can all choose to be happy and that's why I guess I love to make as many people smile every day as is possible. :-))) Yeah I know I'm 50, but it's all about energy and my kids reckon I'm younger than them most of the time... Well - life's too short to get old anyway!

I'd love to meet a real man who is ready for a real woman. LMAO!!! Is there just one of you out there? Someone who is actually ready to love and be loved? If you're captivated by a sultry tango that our eyes could perform together and think you could handle some passionate intensity.... RSVP MOI".

The next morning, my inbox was filled with a hundred and sixty five responses. I was so surprised and overwhelmed, that I spent the entire day answering every single email with my heart on my sleeve and with my mind focused on the reality that with this many men available and interested in me, my true love could actually be out there somewhere. I was also sure to mention Rick, because I realised that not all men would accept my autistic son, especially since he was in a wheel chair as well, and still fighting cancer to boot. I wanted to know who was genuine and who simply was not. I figured if I could manage to scare ninety nine percent of them away from the outset, I would be left with only the true potentials with muscles resembling my description of what a real man could be for me, without being afraid to stand by my side. I was only looking for one real man after all and surely he would not be too hard to recognize out there. All I had to do was to make my way through the list of emails and subsequent profiles, discerning who was not suitable, who was worth a look at and who was definitely worth getting to know and welcome into my life for some serious interviewing.

I was aware of how my instincts honed in on someone, without even speaking to them, discovering that my sensitivity to reading a face was sharpening. Their eyes would tell me if they were kind and intelligent, or if they were just looking for a bit of a fling and not worth pondering over. I wasn't worried about whether they were good looking or not really, although it was a bonus when they were, but I concentrated my perception on the energy I was feeling with them and whether my heart raced or not when I read a profile.

I looked at the way that men used words to create the deeper aspects of their personalities, as they communicated with me. Those whom I felt a connection with, I gave my phone number to very quickly, so that I could sort out if there was a genuine connection there or not. Those that wrote things like, "Hi babe, I think you're hot". I simply responded with something like, "Thanks but I'm looking for something more serious", to which they would either run a mile or continue to hit on me until I told them I wasn't interested.

The second day, I had another rush of emails and kisses to respond to and by the end of the week found that my new full time job, apart from caring for Rick, was interviewing men day and night and I loved it.

Emma had moved out into a B&B, where she now worked and Kai had moved back with his father for a while, so it was just Rick and I again. We moved out of the four bedroom house where we were living to a small harbour side apartment at Hope Island on the marina, which had wheelchair access for Rick also. The tropical resort lifestyle was the perfect environment to host my interviews for 'the one' without having to invite anyone into the privacy of my own space if I did not want them to know where I lived. We even had a hotel within the complex of the resort and right on the water's edge, which was also situated on part of a boardwalk overlooking the stunning marina surrounding the island.

The alfresco bistro at the hotel had tables and chairs covered in black and white market umbrellas and from this vantage I held my daily interviews surrounding my perspective suitors with sunshine and a plethora of bobbing white boats, whilst sipping on wine or an iced cold tea on warm sultry afternoons. I was intent at looking deeply into them to discerningly recognize their very soul, as if I was but a Celtic druid evoking the power of natural herbs before a sacred healing or initiation into the forbidden realms of magic.

I saw behind the masks of wit and charm to a purity of the white flame flickering behind their eyes. I saw into their lives. They shared painful experiences, as they told me stories of past tragedy and betrayal of love. I was not looking at the face, or the body, or the wallet, or what job they had, or what car they drove. I wasn't even concerned about belief systems, or about religion or politics anymore, or the number of their age, but indeed at something more pure and raw. I was looking at the energy of the soul and no matter how beautiful I saw them all to be in their own way, none of them seemed like the man I was looking for. All of these men just seemed so young to me. I even went out with a much older man for a couple of months, who showered me with gifts and treated me like his special lady, yet he was not the man I yearned for.

I would always ask for the time and date of birth on anyone I saw more than once, so that I could visit my favourite astrology site 'Astrodienst', to cast an astrological romantic compatibility report on us, all in secret of course, for any man would run a mile, if he knew I had done something so deeply personal without being in a relationship first.

"Another busy day then", a friend behind the bar observed.

"Yeah just another day at the office", I replied with a quick roll of the eyes and a smile, as I ordered another glass of Chardonnay. I walked back to my table outside overlooking the marina and the crimson of Bougainvillea cascading down the walls of the exterior part of the bistro reminded me that I could have been in the set of a romantic Italian opera. As the moon cast her silvery shimmers upon the water beside me, I knew that I had not yet found 'the one' and he was still out there … somewhere, mysteriously eluding me, as if I was searching for something so rare, that discovering the perfect black pearl in a Tahitian oyster shell would be an easier mission. He was still waiting to dance the tango with my eyes and I to merge into the flames of his volcano and into the oneness and rapture of true love.

"I am ready for you now, but I wonder if you are ready for me?" I dared the moon with a wink and quaffed the remains of chardonnay in one casual slug. It had been yet another busy day interrogating three new men and high time I went home to bed.

30 – CHERRYBROOK

Mark:

After my second marriage demise I promised myself that was it, I wouldn't ever marry or get into a serious relationship ever again. I would stay single, and maybe just have casual affairs if the opportunity arose. But there was a fire inside that still had a flickering flame burning, drawing me back to not giving up. It felt like I had been searching for fifty years and still hadn't found 'the one' to be truly happy with, so why should I now?

I was driving along the M2 motorway one day, still wrestling with the prospect of whether I should go out there on that thin dried out old creaking limb again. I remember looking to the sky and I drove and calling out to God, "If I try just one last time, please let me find the right woman for me this time. P-l-e-a-s-e. There must be one, just one, 'the one' woman out there just right for me, who is honest and affectionate and feminine and sexy and not into playing games or deception, and isn't sexually repressed nor have any other concealed problems and who I would be perfect for, and who would love me just for being who I really am? Please God!". By the time I had finished I was in tears.

I decided to try the dating site which uses psychometric testing and does saturation advertising on television. I selected that I was separated right at the start, and then spent forty five minutes answering all of their questions, only to be told at the end I was 'ineligible' as I was 'separated' and I needed to be 'divorced' to join. Who were they to dictate to me about my personal situation, and judge when I was ready for a new relationship? And to take all my personal data from me before telling me? It didn't matter though, their questions were all very cold and sedate, there was absolutely nothing about lust, passion, sexuality, things many mature adults value greatly in finding a vibrant and passionate relationship. I wasn't looking for someone to just hold hands with and go for walks on the beach and not much else, or compatibility matches based purely on cold statistical analysis. I was looking for much more than that, someone with whom we could ignite each other with a love that burned with a passion like no other, and decided that wasn't the site to find it on.

So I went back to RSVP, at least there was plenty of opportunity there to write something individual and make it clear who you were, and you could weave a lot of personal and intimate tastes into your profile too. You could also openly peruse other's profiles, read what they had to say and feel out who might be right.

Out of curiosity I did a search on the site for 'single women 10 years either side of my age', and who also 'lived within a ten kilometre radius' of my little part of suburbia, and who had been 'online within the last twenty four hours'. It returned over 800 matches. I was shocked. There were so many, single, mature women actively looking for love in such a small area. I extended the search to 'online within the last forty eight hours', and it jumped to over 1,100 matches. The number of separated and divorced middle aged people out there is unbelievable. And they were only the ones who had actually logged in during the last forty eight hours, in my local area, and on that particular site. When I thought about it I found it very sad. So many women looking for love, aging, their life clocks rapidly ticking away, feeling their time fast running out, as I was, many alone and hurt from prior relationships making it even more difficult for them to try again. I had no doubt a lot of them were being very brave putting themselves back out there, again, like me, still dreaming, hoping, praying they would somehow find 'the one'. I wished I could wave a magic wand and pair them all off with their perfect partner to all live happily ever after, but life seems not designed to be that easy.

I had no intention of wasting my time with people who hadn't yet discovered what they really wanted, needed, yearned for, in a relationship, who they really are, or who were not being one hundred percent open and honest. I had been through this process enough now to realise the huge amount of time you can waste online with people who really aren't just right for you and are never going to be, but hide it all behind a façade delaying the inevitable with carefully crafted conversation.

As women read through it, I am sure many would bail early on, or somewhere along the way flee in horror. Good. That was my intention. I was only interested in the very few who would make it all the way through to the end and still want to contact me. The rest would not be right for me, nor me for them, so the sooner we both knew then it would be the better for both of us. We are all on different stages of our journeys. I just needed someone at the same stage as I was on mine, and if no-one came along, I would stay peaceful and single, and just make the most of that.

Saggie59:

Saggie-ttarian.... seeking an affectionate feminine woman

A kind, considerate and compassionate person who is looking for an affectionate loving woman to have a deep long term relationship with

- someone who will actually want to spend a lot of time together becoming very close.

I place great value on integrity, honesty, transparency, fidelity and commitment, and expect no less from a partner. I won't tolerate lies or deception.

I am a night person. I love the winter. I love it when it rains, when it's windy, with thunder and lightning. Love watching French and old 1950s movies. Life is short and every evening is a chance to have a wonderful time with the one you love.

I'm a good listener, and like to communicate. I need someone who can, and will, communicate also. I have read a lot on spiritual development, and try to put it into practice and lead a spiritual life. We all have our baggage to differing degrees. I believe when your partner's having a hard time, it's time to increase the love, support and understanding.

I am a mixture of extremes. I can be quiet and reserved, but also sociable. I love quiet, cosy romantic evenings at home, but sometimes also doing something spontaneous.

Love a woman who loves to dress and act very feminine, and who loves being a bit daring at times - someone sexually mature and still with energy to burn and life to live.

I work hard, and go to the gym. Like to travel, have worked back in England a couple of times, and would like to live in and see more of Europe. I am a professional software developer, with an honours degree, and live in the Hills District.

I'm looking for a fun uninhibited, sexy, passionate, loving partner to share the enjoyment of all life has to offer and someone to have fun and laugh with. I'm in no rush and happy to just make some friends along the way.

I'm looking for an honest, enthusiastic, loving, romantic, touchy feely, passionate woman, who wants a close relationship. I would love a feminine, classy woman who loves wearing girlie things like makeup, skirts, and high heels and can even be a bit daring in private.

I am looking for someone to adore, and have a best friend to grow old with.

I posted it online and moved on. I kept coming across the term 'spiritual counselling' and my synchronicity alarm went off with the realisation it was demanding my attention for some reason. When something suddenly appears from nowhere in your life, and keeps popping up in different places, you better listen to it, for it's another door opening. I became intrigued about what it really meant and started looking into it. I looked online to see who was around locally and kept coming across the same spiritual counsellor's profile, even after changing my search criteria to try and find completely different matches, the same one came up. That's the sort of 'co-incidence' not to be ignored, so I followed along where I was being guided. Maybe it is the Angel's way of intervening and gently guiding us in the right direction, so after her profile came up for the fourth time, I had to pick up the phone and ring her.

When we spoke she was astounded I had found her profile at all. She said she had actually stopped counselling altogether a number of years earlier and had removed all her profiles online and didn't think there were any left out there, and was surprised I had found any at all. No one else had found any or rung her for some time and she couldn't understand how I had found not just one, but four? We were on the same wavelength, and laughed and agreed it was definitely synchronicity to be acted on, and although she didn't do counselling anymore, she believed the woman who had taught her, Christine, still did and gave me her contact details. At the end of the call she asked if I could show her where I had found her details online so she could be sure to get them removed for good. I rang Christine and made an appointment to see her. As I could only make Saturdays it would be a few weeks before she could fit me in, so I booked for three Saturdays away and put a reminder in my diary.

I made a few local female friends online and went out for the evening a few times. One was nice, affectionate, blonde, feminine and sexy. She told me she would be interviewed by her two adult children after every date when she got home, which after my last marriage experiences with adult children concerned me a lot. A middle aged adult woman who has been through serious relationship breakups and/or divorce(s), would always know a lot more about relationships, and what she likes, than single never-been-married twenty somethings ever would understand. They should leave it to her to pick.

Easter weekend was approaching and I had nothing to do. It was nice that it would be peaceful and serene. My blonde female friend I been out with a few times was off to Melbourne for the weekend with her adult children to see David Icke, so without any other plans I settled down for a long quiet dull weekend home alone.

Well, that was what I thought it was going to be.

To all those not blissfully happy in their relationships…

….out of darkness cometh light

31 - A KISS HELLO

Day 1 - Saturday, 11th April 2009

Mark:

It was Easter long weekend and Liana was at her mom's, so with nothing to do for 4 days I slept in late and dragged myself out of bed long after everyone else. It really was going to be a long weekend. After breakfast I wondered what to do with myself and eventually ended up on my computer and clicking around on the usual websites. I eventually ended up on the dating website I was registered on, but wasn't really interested who was on there. I just clicked around at some of the features I had not seen or used. Being a website developer, I would often do that, just to see how different sites are designed and constructed, and any interesting features they might have.

I eventually stumbled into the 'over fifties' community and was intrigued because it seemed to have a different design to the rest of the site, with a big grid of tiny little profile photographs. I hit F5 a few times to refresh the page and noticed a different set of photos were displayed each time. It was like rolling a dice I mused. I remembered how Einstein once famously said, "God doesn't play dice with the world". Suddenly I stopped. As I stared at this particular set of profile photographs I was immediately drawn to one tiny little photograph of a woman with jet-black hair, buried right in the middle of all the dozens of others. It was as though there was a spotlight shining on her and she was looking right at me, sending a bolt of white light right into my soul. I felt compelled to click on her and read her profile. So I did.

I read it through. Once, twice, and again. The more I read, the more transfixed I became. Was she a siren playing a hypnotic tune putting me into some form of trance? She sounded like she was everything I had been looking for all my life… articulate, intelligent, strong, honest, open, spiritual, fun, sensual, wild, and sexy and clearly had a very wicked side to her. I felt a rush of excitement, felt my pulse increase and a surge of chemicals rushed through the inside of my body. I read her profile again, reading more between the lines this time, feeling who she was inside, and in her soul. I felt incredibly drawn to her.

Then I noticed she lived on the Gold Coast in Queensland. Thump! Sigh. She was over a thousand kilometres away and in a completely different state. My heart sank and I came crashing back down to Earth. Well there is no way that could come to anything, I told myself. Besides, why would a woman as delicious as she sounded be interested in nasty, selfish, angry, ugly old me anyway? I told myself it was probably good she was so far away, as it would make it easier to just move on. Besides, why should I be so selfish as to torture another woman? But I still found myself sitting there day dreaming the morning away and floating through imaginary 'what-if's?

"Ker-thunk, beep, beep, beep, beep, beep". The washer suddenly finished and started beeping away with one of those annoying loud sounds, demanding my immediate attendance. Back to Earth and the mundane. I headed off to sort that out, to hang the washing on the line, put the next load on, and to do the usual detour of other things that I suddenly remembered needed doing like the washing up, tidying the kitchen, and so on.

An hour or so later I wandered back to my computer. I had forgotten all about what I had been doing, until I saw that woman's profile still sitting there open and staring back at me. Hmm. I read it again and thought, "Yes, it would be more than nice to meet someone just like you, but (sigh), I guess I'll just have to wait for someone closer to home to come along". As I went to leave the web page, I don't know how or why, but in a split second a compelling feeling just came over me and without thinking I clicked and sent her a 'kiss'. I thought "What did I do that for? I thought I had just decided not to bother? Nothing can come of it". It was as if some unknown energy possessed me for one second and pressed the mouse button. "That was strange", I thought, as I closed the page and carried on with my day, not expecting to hear any more of it.

> Hi claire2909,
>
> Saggie59 has sent you a Kiss.
>
> He has read your profile and wanted us to pass on this message:
>
> "I'd like to get to know you, would you be interested"?

Claire:

"Hello", I whispered to the photo staring back at me, after clicking on the link to a profile of another new perspective love as it popped into my inbox.

"How very fascinating. There's something so familiar to me about you, but I can't quite put my finger on it".

I touched the photograph of his face with a sweep of my fingers, hoping it would breathe into life and share a deep secret from his soul, whilst explaining to me the reason why I had started to sense that the palms of my hands had unexpectedly become clammy and damp at that very same moment as well.

"You are really gorgeous I must say and if I was the sort of girl who was bold enough to send someone a 'kiss', I would definitely choose to send one to you".

My heart quickened with a rush of pleasure pulsing into my veins, like he had somehow ejaculated his essence into my bloodstream. I gazed deeply at his profile, trying to read the energy of him and what he would really be like, if he was standing just across the room from me. How would I feel about him, if his eyes were penetrating intensely into mine? Would I hold his gaze and merge into the rhythm of the dance, or drop my eyes to the floor, breaking the spell in an unspoken act of unrequited love instead? Or would he for that matter? Would one of us quickly, quietly and like a surgeon's knife cut the magic back into the good old fabric of strangers again, so that we would both know without a doubt that we were not 'the one' for each other after all? It would be just like all of the others then. Oh God. What is happening here?

So, you're from Sydney eh, not that it matters really as far as I'm concerned and oh you're a Saggie? Some of my closest friends are Sagittarians when I come to think about it. I wonder which day you were born on then?

I strained to recall from some ancient memory why he seemed so familiar to me, but I could not think where I could have known him from before. He certainly does not look like a stranger to me. He looks like a musician actually with that long curly hair kissing his shoulders like a god from an ageless Greek myth as well. Hmmm.. It is so strange, but there is also something about the way he looks that reminds me of myself when I was just a schoolgirl dressed up in my college uniform with hat and gloves and all. I do not know why that image keeps going around and around in my head. How strange. I wonder what is going on here. Perhaps it is because he looks like a male me.

I will just respond and see if he is really genuine by offering my friendship first and then see if he comes back. I think you can open up to a friend, saying things you would unlikely share with a lover and that is why I always choose to start off there. I want to unleash as much of myself as possible with him, without hiding behind a carefully erected fortress of mystique just to falsely reel him in, like I used to when I was younger with other men. Let him see me as I am in my nakedness and not wrapped up like a Russian spy in a black trench coat of lies and deceit pretending to be someone I am not. Ok then, here goes…

> Hi Saggie59,
>
> Claire2909 has read your Kiss message and wanted us to pass on this reply:
>
> "I would be very open to a friendship".

Mark:

I went back to my computer and a reply was already in my inbox. She 'would like to be friends'. Wow, that was a quick response. Hmmm. Okay. Then I started to think about it and wondered, why? So typical of someone with their self-confidence crushed to pieces. I had no doubt she would have hundreds of guys hitting on her, no, make that thousands, literally.

I reasoned with myself that those with profiles as seductive and enticing as Claire2909's was, would surely be included in most men's' trawlering nets and get sent thousands of 'kisses'. She would have good looking guys, rich guys, fit guys, local guys, and everyone else, so why bother with me? Especially in another state? I tried to be positive and told myself "well, it's always nice to make a new friend and who knows, she could turn out to be someone I could talk with, confide in, and 'bounce' with from afar, with little risk of ever meeting. Maybe she even just wanted someone to bounce with herself"? So I thought why not? I would not let myself get carried away with any unrealistic expectations and just be an honest friend and see what happens.

So her name was Claire. Lovely. I sent her a short email saying hello.

> Hi Claire,
>
> Thanks for replying. Geographically, I guess a friendship is about the limit, but I don't mind. I have learnt through life to notice when a door opens, and make a conscious decision whether to step through it, as you never know where it might lead you. Typical Saggie some would say...always shooting for the stars, etc. (once lived with a professional astrologer who only dated Saggies!)
>
> So I decided to have a rare ferret around RSVP today...and stumbled into the over 50s section for some reason. Maybe it's because I'll be one myself later this year. Lol. And I was drawn to your profile, and wow, you sound like everything I have ever been looking for. Deep, sensitive, playful, daring, feminine and sexy. So many women seem to have a problem exploring their femininity when it is something I think should be empowering them. All my life I have been attracted to much older women. They are always more sexually mature and in touch with themselves. Nice for those women to be my age now. :-) I'm also a bit over all the women on here who seem so busy with friends and evening classes and family...I honestly wonder where they'd fit in the time for a serious and meaningful relationship with the guy of their dreams, if they met him? Lol.
>
> I've had my profile hidden for a while, as I was a bit over the whole RSVP thing. Made enough contacts in the short time it was up to

follow through on, and aren't into the greed game...you know where some just keep looking for someone better. Only re-enabled it to message you and will be off again soon. You can also email me if you want to contact me directly.

Take care,

Mark

Claire:

My jaw dropped involuntarily. This was not the average generic email from an ego based businessman, or a sex starved twenty something year old hitting on the older woman either, but a genuine heartfelt letter filled with personality and mystique. No shallow chit chat either about his occupation or financial status, wondering what I do for living, or what sort of car I drive for that matter either, which is what normally happens with a chat up. Or God knows another of the endless young bucks on here who have tried hitting on me before with a, "You're so hot babe!" hoping to somehow turn my brain off and magically hypnotize me into one night stand fever. He seems more involved in sharing the intimate aspects of himself, which is what I'm more passionate talking about too. So this is how it feels to finally connect with a real man hey? He must feel really good about himself, which I'm finding enormously sexy I might add. I've got a feeling that seems so old and wise about you Mark, not that I've ever quite had this feeling before...

Hey there Mark,

Thank you so for taking the time to scribble down so much about yourself. A Saggie eh? Hehee my first love was a Saggie, who unfortunately got away. Love your face.

Pity you're so far away...

My website is www.clairebuchholz.com and you can email me.

Let's catch up for a chat sometime.

I hope the choky is most decadent. Happy Easter!

Claire

Mark:

A response arrived almost straight away. Even before opening it, I became more intrigued as that is how quickly I usually respond to someone. Today not many people seem to be as respectful to reply so promptly, or even at all, as if they somehow think themselves above you. I always feel it is just basic courtesy and respect. Now here was this delicious woman, not only replying to me, but replying so quickly. It immediately said there were no power play games going on with her, which was oh so refreshing. So many play those games nowadays, thinking they are so much smarter that the other person and that they won't see through them. Especially the younger ones. I have known numerous women who told me if they are interested at all in a guy they would always make him wait at least a day, or two, or three, before replying to him, no matter how interested they were, just to make him all the more keener and so they would then be the one 'setting the pace' as they called it. It's a manipulative game, an attempt to take control of the relationship and dominate it, and him, right from the outset. For me that would be a dangerous red warning sign with a deafening claxon blaring out of what is to come down the track… control, and it would only get worse. I don't believe in, or play, those power games and clearly Claire didn't either. It was a breath of fresh air.

Straight away we were talking about astrology, something we both knew really does tell us so much about ourselves and others, based on our own experiences. It was telling me she was looking into herself and the cosmos, and had an open mind. Astrology is something we might not be able to scientifically define based on today's 'science', but possibly something we will eventually understand one day, or remember from our past.

I looked at her website. She was a music composer, and offering piano tuition. The most enchanting music started playing on her site, like the music you would hear in a classy French feature film. Her music was wonderful. It was deep and mystical, with layers that wove together and then criss-crossed back across each other, before floating back together again. Music is from the soul and it was giving me a view directly into Claire's.

She had written music for the Australian trailers of very well-known Hollywood movies such as 'Bridges of Madison County' and 'Natural Born Killers'. She had a long list of television and radio commercial jingles for well-known brands and radio stations she had written, played in, arranged and even sung on. She was so talented. She had even written and arranged the official welcome song for the Sydney 2000 Olympics, which was sung by children's choirs to all the different countries' athletes as they flew into Australia, and at the official opening ceremony of the Olympic Games. Most of all I loved 'Vienna', her classical piece she had written and played on her piano, and had won an award for. 'Vienna' made me feel like I was drifting through a cold misty forest at night near Vienna, with a feeling of melancholy, lost, and wondering about a love that might have been?

But that wasn't all, she was a voice over artist, having voiced many television and radio adverts, and she gave voice over coaching as well. It was such a joy to listen to all her many talents, and there was a little picture of her, looking sexy and windswept in bright pink lipstick. But it made me wonder, she must surely have met many well to do men along the way in her travels, in the music business, in studios, in corporate offices, at gigs, and have a long list of friends and contacts. So why did such a gorgeous woman need to be on a dating website?

> Hi Claire,
>
> Wow…what a wonderful and talented person you are! I have to ask the obvious question (to me anyway)…. what do you need to be on RSVP for? Wouldn't you have a string of really great guys queuing up wanting to know you?
>
> Yes, a true Saggie I'm told…by those that know.
>
> Yes, pity about being far away. Love the way you wear makeup in your pictures. And you have black hair. I have a thing about women with black, black hair (is that classed as a fetish? hehe). You can keep your blondes!! Lol. So…do tell me….have you hit a lot of potholes in your search for that jewel? I can offer that I have. I have tried so hard, and will try again when she comes along. My highest value in life is love and affection, and with a spiritual connection I open myself up completely and give everything. It leaves me very vulnerable, and I've been hurt badly in the past, but I'll never give up and will go there again when the time comes. Anyway, I guess a sultry tango of words is second best to one with eyes? ;-) (Hey that's not bad…started off the paragraph with base lustful comments and ended it on a spiritual note!)
>
> I listened to some of your music. It is wonderful. Loved 'Bridges of Madison County' (must get to see that movie sometime). Love music like that (and that's from someone into metal, Lol). And 'Vienna' was lovely as well. I can see why you won an award with that. 'The Child' was nice as well.

Now come on Claire....why is such a lovely, attractive, loving, successful, talented woman like you on RSVP? Huh, huh? Nil comprendo. Does not compute.

I'm 0416 256 xxx.

Take care,

Mark

32 - TOUCHING WITHOUT FINGERS

Day 2 - Sunday, 12th April 2009

Claire:

Nobody has been this articulate, or taken the time to deeply connect with my music without even meeting me before. Oh I am spinning out here. Not even my best friends or colleagues who know and love my work, express themselves with this intensity or passion. In fact, the others I have known before have never even come close to understanding that secret place inside of me, even after knowing me for years and years. What is this feeling I am having? A roar from the soul? It is like I am being pulled back to naked without a body, completely raw without wanting to cover up any bits with him whatsoever.

"Hmmm" is all I could mutter out aloud, as I found myself biting the corner of my bottom lip, whilst spontaneously clicking the keys to write back to him, as if my brain was on auto pilot.

Hi Mark,

Wow, you also seem to have a wicked way of expressing yourself, which I find very sexy. I am on RSVP simply to find 'the one'. I think you can be so discerning here, by looking without touching so to speak and meeting those with whom you feel a connection. Much more exciting don't you feel than falling over someone at the local?

As for astrology, I never start my day without my dose of Jonathon Cainer... am passionate about it actually and have a pretty good understanding. Whenz ya birthday? I'll just quickly throw your chart. Heheee. God I have been known to do that actually! I'm not looking for a Saggie though, I am looking for my reflection. Someone who I can be the best Claire I can be with – in every way. From the erotic to white light spirit and loads of laughter on the way. I guess I've experienced these men Mark, but they have been a journey in themselves and I have learnt much about myself in each relationship.

So here I am hopefully attracting my next set of lessons and having fun on the way.

And errr.... no such thing as fetish - passion perhaps?

Claire x

Mark:

She finds me sexy? Me? I wonder if she is looking at the right profile. Erotic? Fetish is just passion? What a turn on. She must be a very sexually mature woman, uninhibited and not repressed and without the negative controlling hang ups so many others seem to have.

We were completely bypassing those normal 'nice to meet you, what do you do for a living, do you own your own house, and how many children have you got (i.e. how much do you earn , how well off are you financially, will I have to deal with your kids) ?' type of base chit chat that usually goes on. We were going straight to each other's core, our souls, and it felt truly divine. We were asking about who each other really is inside, wanting to connect with the soul, and we were.

Looking for her reflection? Now that's interesting. What would that mean? A male version of herself maybe? It's an interesting way to describe it. I could only dream of meeting a female version of myself. White light spirit is even more intriguing. I can just imagine that brilliant white light that people who have died have said they saw, brilliant, comforting, absolute pure love and inspiring them to become their higher selves.

Morning Claire,

Lovely to hear back from you. I nearly rang you last night (would have texted if it was ok first), but it was getting late and didn't know if it was too late. I'm a late night kinda person, very rarely in bed before midnight (when alone, hehe), and rather zombie-like first thing in the morning. Last night was up till 2AM, and 4AM the night before...long weekend and single I blames it on I do.

Yes, aren't we all looking for 'the one'? And each time don't we think we have found them, only to later discover we hadn't? Looking back with hindsight, I too can see I have learnt a lot from each relationship. I have grown, often painfully, but it has elevated me to seek a higher and more fulfilling relationship each time. I have an uncanny knack of the harder I look, the less success I seem to find. Each time in the past when I have given up looking...the universe suddenly provides ...and someone walks into my life from left of stage somehow. Interestingly my profile has been hidden for weeks, and only re-enabled it to message you and to see if I got a reply. Very happy I did. :-)

I'm a great believer in astrology too. The astrologer I lived with was very, very good and I encouraged her to accept it was her gift and try to do it for a living, and she did and is now making a nice living from doing what she loves. I often go to astro.com and check out a potential relationship. I'll give you my Date, time and location of birth.

I've been mainly looking for my 'best' matches… Leo or Saggie. I've been told another Saggie would be like my own reflection, just egging each other on to push the boundaries and do crazy stuff. Lol. Don't see why that has to be a Saggie though.

Wow, love the way you said from the erotic to the white light spirit. I'm a very sexual guy. Anything goes if it's tasteful and you both enjoy it. I have no limits ;-) But I am also a great believer in the spiritual side of life and there is a greater purpose to our being here. It seems so many people seem to be one or the other, but not able to reconcile both. I have read a couple of books recently that mentioned loving sex in a deep emotional connection being a way for a couple of achieve a higher spiritual connection...which was music to my ears :-))

Mark x

Claire:

Oh God. Kerrie's birthday was the 8th December, Lesta's on the 7th December, my best friend at college who helped introduce me into the music industry was the 4th December and now yours on the 5th. Wow how amazing. I suddenly had goose bumps tingling all over my skin in the realisation that this was not just a coincidence.

I also thought that I would have scared most blokes off with the words 'erotic' or 'white light spirit' by now, yet Mark seemed to be drawing out more of that part of me, which I had suppressed for so long. I am normally very uncomfortable showing my vulnerability, but perhaps my radar had kept me from trusting before, simply because other men had not been trustworthy in the first place and not because I was the one who was incapable of trusting like I have been accused of in past relationships. I felt like I was not just being brave in expressing myself with Mark, but that he actually liked me for it. It also felt as if my whole system was being upgraded to a faster frequency or something. What was going on here? Men had never matched my intensity before and perhaps that is why I used to feel that they were so much younger than me. I was daring myself to be true. Pushing the boundaries of what is normally acceptable for me. How wicked.

Before I could monitor my excitement, I was back at the keys tapping out the contents of my heart, as if I was caught up in the rapture of a romance novel.

Hello again Mark,

Hmm.....

Perhaps then, you are captivated by Tantra...

It is the absolute ultimate dream of mine to experience such, but one must be ready and I believe each relationship brings us a step closer to experiencing the true essence of who we are and that enchanting energy of Tantra.

Love and fear is my belief system and the more we can learn to love ourselves through relationship, the more ready we are to experience the ultimate connection of Tantra... magic... That's been my adventure anyhow!

Love the excitement of reading your soul from my laptop and look forward to more of you, as you feel safe to unveil... Bring it on Mark!

Claire x

Mark:

Hi Claire,

So tell me what you mean by Tantra? I understand it has many different meanings. What do you mean by love and fear being your belief system? Would love to hear more about you.

So did you do an Astro profile? What is your date, time and place of birth?

I better come back down to earth and get on with some domestic chores. Have a house inspection coming up soon I need to clean through for. When my marriage broke up late last year and I rented the first place that came along to get out, until I decided where my life will go next. Was even toying with heading off back to the UK mid-year.

If you want to know anything about me…just ask. I believe in total honesty. I am a very loyal and committed person, especially to a relationship with someone I love. I believe in communication, and working on the bad with the good.

Mark X

Claire:

OMG! How did he know that I was going to do an Astrodienst profile on him? It's best not tell him that I already did that freebie one on our astrological compatibility as well. That would have really scared him off. Hahaha. Wow! He is so honest with me! I can read it in the way he writes to me.

"I really want to trust you Mark with my whole heart". I heard myself thinking aloud.

I decided to give him my birth details as well, since he had been bold enough to give me his. How brazen! How utterly sexy too! I could hardly believe that he is English on top of everything. Oh that has always been my secret fantasy since I was a just a little girl and used to dress up, sitting in the back of Dad's Rolls, pretending I was an English rose sipping French champagne, which all seemed to add to the feeling of mine that I just didn't belong here in this jigsaw. He seemed so perfect for me. I wondered how much more I would read about him in that voice of his. I couldn't wait to talk to him now. If he didn't feel like 'the one', I would just set him free like I have done with everyone else. I was already feeling so involved. Most people would think that I was stark raving crazy. Oh well who cares? I am nothing like most people anyhow.

Hey Mark,

Well by Tantra, I mean the ultimate union of mind, heart, body, soul and spirit. I think that's it really in a little nutshell without going into detail.

As for love and fear, that's a whole six hour conversation... Basically, I do not believe in right and wrong, but that everything is based on love or fear. Fear, being ego based stuff which creates all the shit in the world. Love, being unconditional love. Acceptance of everything... Am I scaring you yet?? Heheheee... I adore the English. Do you have one of those accents that's gonna drive me crazy?

God I hope so...

Claire x.

Mark:

Dear Claire,

Your definition of Tantra sounds divine. What a turn on.

In case you're not aware www.astro.com is where the pro's often generate birth charts. Under the top nav of 'Free Horoscopes' you can do partner matches. I'll leave the rest to you to form your own opinion...interesting reading though from the one I just did.

Here's a link to an idea I had earlier this year for a website, and I knocked together to see how it would come out... www.collective-thoughts.org

I read a book recently called 'An Intelligent Life' by Dr Julian Short. Here's a quote...

"There is not a single human emotional problem that does not stem either from a fear of rejection and loss of love, or a fear of weakness and loss of individual power and dignity."

No, you're not scaring me, quite the opposite.

Hmmmm. Have been told many times I have a sexy phone voice, and it's English as well. You had better run away right now. ;-)

Mark x

Claire:

Hahaha the pros hey? Astro was where I have been going for years as well darling.

I honestly could not believe he was telling me to do what I had already done. Oh he was spirituality so beautiful with that collective thoughts concept as well. What a tease! I was adoring this man and he even wrote like me. It was as if we were the same somehow and on so many delicious layers...

> OMG!!!! Are we 'Twins'?
>
> I use Astro all the time to do composite charts, but never before have I read such a sexy report for two people! You and I are very interesting together to say the least. I'm yet to look at the interactive part, which tends to give more of the negative aspects as well as the positive? Well, I guess this is going to be a very exciting ride!
>
> I absolutely ADORE the concept of your website! If we could only be more of that, I believe 2012 will be the beginning of our higher consciousness and world peace. I love you Mark! xx I honestly do!
>
> Can't wait to hear the voice!
>
> Let the mystery unfold...
>
> Claire x

We were both exploring the deep and it felt so natural. I had just told him that I loved him and I meant it. We were discussing emotive themes, which would have either been laughed at or shut down by from partners of the past. Not just that, but we were in complete unison about whichever topics arose. It was exciting to finally be myself without hiding any bits that would have made me feel very isolated with the others. We were sharing our inner treasures first, the ones usually kept hidden and private from anyone, lest we be laughed at and ultimately rejected for. That is why I knew and not just felt that Mark and I were both in harmony, and it happened right from the very beginning. We were connecting with our electrical bodies and merging into each other, becoming more sensitive, not just within ourselves, but to each other as well.

Mark:

Mwah,

So you haven't run for the hills?

Are we 'Twins'? Isn't that what you called forth? The universe will always provide. ;-)

Which composite report did you generate? I also had a look at your 'Short Report - Love, Flirtation and Sex'. Wow. Where have you been hiding all these years? Lol. If you look at that one for me it is very accurate.

Thanks. I need to decide whether to spend the time trying to get that website known and up the rankings, or start on a new one. Was just an idea I thought worthy of following through on.

If you want to check out my voice just ring my mobile and it'll go through to my voicemail greeting. I won't answer it. When is a good time to ring you later on?

Mark x

We swapped some photos, and Claire said it was as though she knew me straight away. She looked different in each one she sent me. It was so intriguing, she could have been four or five completely different women.

We continued talking via emails going back and forth, each straight after the other. Now it was time to go synchronous. We jumped onto online chat, and opened up a new experience of each other. No composing a few paragraphs, and a brief review before hitting the send button anymore. It was now time to feel each other as we spoke. The connection was clear and deep. I was in awe.

"Btw, I added you to my MSN and sent you another photo."

"Oh God I wish I could meet you tonight"!

"That would be very potent xx ".

"Btw, I adore your hair Mark... You look like a muso too. Do you play"?

"You like my hair??? Lol. I've been asked if I'm a muso many times. Do you want me to email a couple of pics of when I had LONG hair xxxxxxxx?"

"My heart is racing talking to you".

"Wow. Mark, even if this goes no further, I have never felt like this before".

"Me too. But I don't see why it wouldn't go any further. How crazy would that be"?

"Yes I know".

"So do you have any pics you can send me of you? I want to know everything about you Xxxxxxx".

"I want you to know everything about me and I you… This is so amazing. I am going to send some to your mobile".

Mark:

We had only been communicating for just one evening, yet it felt like we knew each other deeply already. This was only the second day we had 'spoken', we had not met, or even heard each other's voices on the phone yet. We were deep into each other's souls, all by just email and online chat, and in less than forty eight hours. It was spinning me out. Was this one of those online infatuations? No. I was too old and experienced to fall into one of those. The fact that I even considered it meant I was wary of the possibility. Was it a rebound? No. I certainly wasn't in any desperate need of another serious relationship, or a repeat of the utterly oppressive darkness that the last one had brought- far from it. This seemed different and real. We were both mature adults, intelligent and perceptive, with decades of emotional experiences in long term 'permanent' relationships. I was dizzy with the rush of a high I had never experienced before. It felt like standing on the edge of a cliff looking out to sea with a refreshing summer breeze blowing in my face lifting me up.

33 – TWINS

"I want to go swimming inside your eyes Mark… As I sip a very long, cold glass of champagne! POP! There she goes".

"Mmmm…Love champagne".

"Me too. God, maybe we are 'Twins'. 'Twin Flames'"?

"'Flames'"?

"Do you know about 'Twin Flames'? Yes. Look it up sometime".

"No".

Mark:

Claire said she had been hunting around on the net about the whole 'Twin' feeling we had both been experiencing and joking around with, and had stumbled across something really quite intriguing. She asked if I had ever heard of 'Twin Flames' or 'Twin Souls'. I hadn't. She sent me some links to websites and asked I take a look as it was spinning her out.

"There's no time like the present".

I looked and couldn't believe what I was reading. 'Twin Flames' were being described as a single soul that splits into two identical souls. Not two halves, but two complete exact duplicates. They spend lifetime after lifetime always together, growing and learning, as one incarnates into a life, while the other remains in spirit, helping and guiding the other. They are also called 'Twin Souls', or even 'Split-Aparts' (as in the movie

'The Butchers Wife' with Demi Moore we came across a couple of years later). They were more than just a 'Soul Mate', which really are separate souls in their own right, and who may come in and out of our life at different times. Soul mates challenge us, or help us, and sometimes that means not necessarily being nice to us, to force us to deal with some unresolved issue.

Some descriptions said everyone has a 'Twin Flame'. Lifetime after lifetime our souls come back, again and again, learning how to conquer fear (greed, selfishness, materialism, ego), and instead to learn to always choose love (affection, kindness, empathy). It culminates with both 'Twin Souls' having their final incarnation together, being born into life at the same time so they may be together in the flesh, and that it will also be the very last time. Everybody has a 'twin flame', but to meet them, you both need to have done the work on yourselves first to be ready. From my experiences, and the venomous attacks I had received at times, I found it hard to believe that in any way it could be referring to me. I was sure I must be somewhere nearer the start of that journey, so how could this 'twins' thing apply to us?

As I read more, the descriptions of 'Twin Flames' started to give me goose-bumps. There were a lot of 'checklists' around to determine if you have met yours or not. Looking through the long lists, it would eerily be 'yes', 'yes', 'yes', for just about every aspect. It was a big co-incidence if that's all it was, but it made sense of so many things we were experiencing in such a short period of time, and we started to wonder? Was it true? Could it be? Could we be? We both searched online and read more and more about 'Twin Flames', and the more we read, the more it seemed to describe what was happening. It was hard to believe. We don't think there is any hard check list to determine if you are 'Twin Flames' or not, but it gave us an idea of what people generally think they are. I'm not even really sure if they are real. How could anyone actually know all this? But then how do we even know that God really exists? But many of us do, in one form or another, and millions, billions, of people around the world believe completely in a God they have never actually seen or can prove in any way exists. Where did all this information come from? As I researched further, it seemed a lot came through mediums or from the 'other side', in various ways, or from others who had experienced it and were sharing what they observed happening. I was reluctant to say it was us, that was a big step, but all the things we were experiencing were there, written down by other people as things that happen to 'Twin Flames'. There was a lot to read, so I thought I would leave reading it in more detail for another time. Right now I just wanted to get back to talking with Claire. We kept our minds open and continued the journey.

"'Twin Flames'. Wow. Yes. You're taking me to new places already. Divine. Love it.

We talked constantly and just couldn't get enough of journeying on into each other's depths. After a while things became a little more intimate and we started exploring each other's sexuality, something very important to both of us, and the conversation began getting a little bit hot.

"Ok. I want to nibble your ear lobe".

"Yumm".

"And let you taste the champagne when I kiss you. Drowning in your eyes"…

"Mmmm... I'd drip it down your body and then lick every drop up".

"…and what would you do, as it slips down the seam of my stocking"?

Mark:

My jaw dropped to the floor. What did she just say? Is she talking about seamed stockings? I nearly choked. Had I misheard? I'd not mentioned anything about how much I had always absolutely adored seamed nylon stockings from the 1950s. How sensual and sexy they are, how classy and feminine I found them and how I had been obsessed with them since childhood, long before I even knew sex even existed. How could she know? Why say something so obscure at all, and so early on? She went to it so quickly. This was still only the second day since we connected and I had never mentioned anything to her about them. I didn't even know this woman yesterday morning.

Wait a minute. Hold on. I had to take a breath and process if I had missed something here?

I started to wonder if this was all a big wind up by someone that knew me, intimately. Some perverted joke or game by an ex to torment me? Or one of their friends, or family? Was it to tease me and lift me up so they could then laughingly drop me from a height? My mind whirred away at a thousand miles an hour for the next thirty seconds, which felt like thirty minutes, as I analysed what was happening. Then I remembered, wait a minute, I had approached Claire, so how could that be? It was as though she just knew me deep inside in every way. Or maybe it was that she was the same as me? With the same tastes? Same desires? Same turn-ons? Same fantasies? It certainly was feeling more and more like that.

"Where did that come from"??

"My imagination".

"It's just that, I've always had a huge fetish for seamed nylon stockings".

"Yes. Yes. Yes. Ha-ha".

"My Achilles' heel".

"Hahaha".

"How did you know"?

"I'm the other bit".

"How"?

"Well I thought we were going somewhere then... probably good that you stopped me. Hehehe"…

Mark:

It was as though it had been planted there as a trigger, a key to help unlock our sacredness. It certainly got my attention and the reverse was soon to happen also.

"Ha-ha.. Ok Mark, I adore this but"…

"But"?

"I so do not want this to be about sex alone".

"I know. Neither do I. Sex is easy to get. Great sex is hard to find. A spiritual connection is near impossible. Both is well"...

"Please let's not fuck this up. I'm sorry... It's just me".

"Just imagine if we lived within driving distance of each other"!!

"If you and I met tonight, I think we would have actually expressed ourselves physically".

Mark:

Music tells a lot about who you are in your soul, so I decided to add another dimension to our conversation and pulled out the odd song I really loved, and sent it to Claire to listen to while we spoke.

"Omg I'm adoring this music. Wow".

"Omg where are you and where have you been hiding for so long? 11:11"

"11:11"?

"It's the time right now, and it's a wake up code".

Mark:

I did a quick search on '11:11' and there was a lot to read. Another one to add to my growing list of topics to follow up on when the time presented itself later. This woman was already taking me places I hadn't been to before. How exciting!

"Hmmm. I'm booked to see a psychic counsellor on Sat. I'll see what she has to say about things, or whatever she does.. ;) Did you like those last couple of songs"?

"Oh yes, I adore them. I wish I was wrapped inside your arms just listening"…

"I feel you".

"Omg! I was about to say, can you feel me? Cos, I can feel your breath on my face".

"This is especially from me to you".

Claire:

The feeling of Mark and I coming home to each other overpowered me, as the Celtic music crept straight into my soul, bypassing my mind and my heart, as if we were reuniting at last where we belonged. The haunting voice of the flute, reminded me of watching the movie Titanic, when I had bawled my eyes out sitting next to my second husband at the time, knowing that I had never loved or had been loved before by anyone like Jack and Rose had loved each other.

The potent sensation of Deja Vu I had initially experienced from Mark's photos suddenly intensified, as the music wafted through me. It summoned me into a vision of Scotland, where a more novice part of myself was surrounded by a small group of people chanting a sacred prayer. We were gathered inside a stone circle at full moon, whilst someone far away on horseback, was slowly drawing closer through freshly falling snow. I knew he was not a stranger, for my heart was pounding faster than the ancient drum skins of war. My voice began to swell above the others' chanting and as it echoed onto the standing stones encircling us, they sang in resonance to the vibration of my longing for him. His companion was some sort of bird of prey, like a falcon I think, for it had soared up into the sky at lightning speed, announcing the imminent arrival of the master with unnerving squeals made even more chilling carried in the bitter wind.

My phone started ringing and when his name flashed onto the screen, my heart pounded so hard, that I thought I would burst with anticipation.

"OMG!" I whispered with delight. It was time to actually hear his voice and to match it with the image of that beautiful face and to the spark of his soul, which was already dancing with mine a thousand miles away.

"Hello?..... Mark"? I could hardly contain the thrill of anticipation in finally hearing the tone of his voice.

"Hello darling. This is me. God you sound wonderful".

His voice was so rich and deep and I tingled all over.

"Oh hello. You're so English aren't you"? I gasped with a giggle.

"Oh Mark, talk to me. Let me hear you. I just looove your voice".

Claire:

He was chuckling and it made me laugh back. His voice was as familiar to me as his photos and I ached with happiness, as we talked and laughed for hours about everything from the magic connection we had made, to our children and past relationships, spiritual lessons, food, sport and other passions, eagerly exploring the only physical aspect of ourselves we could share right now, which was the sound of each other's voices. Everything else had been the exploration of each other's hearts, minds and souls and it was an unforgettable experience of the deepest connection.

"Thank you for seeing in me, that which is sooo you! Mwah! X Goodnight".

"You're off to bed now"?

"I really loved tonight. Thank you for catching me for a little while. I'm already in bed. Tapping on the keys of my laptop with you a thousand miles away. Take me with you into your dreams"…

"Meet you in your dreams".

"Yes. 'Twins' again".

"Yes. That's happened very quickly with you, without even meeting. There is a strong connection".

"It's magic".

"Like the astrology charts were saying……the whole is greater than the two parts".

Mark:

This was still only the second day. Talking on the telephone brought forth a whole new dimension and with real time interaction now we bounced and danced as we talked. At times when we were on the computer, I would be typing a question, and before I had finished, or could even send it, Claire would answer it and I would sit there in awe, wondering how. Coincidence? Anticipation? Possibly, but often I was changing the subject and typing about something completely different to what we had been talking about, and before I could send the new question, there was the answer to it. I would just sit there with my hands hovering over the keyboard and my mouth open wondering how she was doing it.

"Amazing that you do that too. Amazing! Thanks universe. Sometimes we just need an Angel to remind us of who we are. Mwah! So whatever unfolds from here, I just want you to know that you are an angel".

"I often wonder….do the Angels get together and say, 'Hey let's get these two souls together. They are made for each other and should be together??'"

"Omg! We were both talking about Angels and we were both writing at the same time".

"It's happening again".

"When we are ready to meet, they bring us together".

"If you and I were to meet… I think we would blaze into major sexual bliss and miss out on something".

"Do you"?

"WE WEREN'T MEANT TO MEET YET".

"What do you think we'd miss out on"?

"Falling in love. Unless of course, you believe in love at first sight, which is very rare, but I have to tell you"…

"I do actually, but it is very rare. It's often really just lust that soon wears off".

"Yes. Lust is cool though, don't you think"?

"It can happen with the right two people sometimes".

"Yes".

"Lol. I have always said....lust is a critical part of a happy and loving relationship".

"I adore that! I feel the calmest calm I know. I want to.... take you into me... into places that you've never been.... and yet you do know, because it is the place you have known is there always…like the city of Atlantis, like the ancient sighs of Cleopatra and the feeling of coming home again".

"And the feeling of meeting someone you know you will be with forever".

"Yes. You have the x factor Mark. Spirit. Sexual intensity. Energy. Heart. Integrity. Honesty. Courage. Independence".

"You must have picked out guys you thought had all those in the past though, before you met them"?

"No. I picked what I needed to learn about myself. Hopefully I am ready to be with a real man now. A lot of women don't know how to handle a real man, because they are still wrestling with the shadow feminine".

"Like most guys couldn't handle a real woman"?

"Yep".

"What is the 'Shadow feminine'"?

"That's another six hour conversation".

"I'd like to know".

"I have all the knowledge in the world, because she was me.... long, long ago, before I met my beautiful earth angel Kerry-Ann (not to be confused with Kerrie), who showed me that I didn't have to be stuck in the darkness of my shadow anymore. She is the only woman I have ever known, who I do not believe even has a dark side, because she always shines with pure love and laughter, expressing the nature of her Higher Self. Perhaps I'll write a book one day about the shadow feminine. It's the dark side of the feminine, but I don't want to use that energy anymore".

"Dark side"?

Mark:

I quickly searched online expecting another one to add to my list of reading. I was surprised to discover that there really wasn't much written on it to read at all. All I could find was a couple of pages here and there, or an odd reference in the middle of something else. The only writing of significance I found was that Deepak Chopra had written about it and some references to Karl Jung discussing it. So that was another intriguing topic to add to my reading list to delve into when I had time.

"It's stuff locked in the feminine ego that's all fear based".

"Fear of being feminine"?

"It's based in the subconscious. Most women are oblivious that they choose to resonate with this".

"It says it is repressed issues, with the term "shadow" representing the personal unconscious, or the psychological material that we repress, deny, dissociate, or disown (which can be not only the lowest and worst aspects of us, but the highest and best). The shadow feminine is the energy of the smotherer, insecurity, controlling with love, the martyr and the one who never honours one's own needs. When we are out of balance within the feminine it works against us in our lives to create conflict. Helloness"?

"You awake"?

"Yes, I'm still here. Just thinking how to explain it. It's the horrible part of the woman that dumps her crap on you. All her negative, ego based fears. Like in men when they are physically aggressive, women are more manipulative and passive aggressive. I believe we can transform the energy into being more of love and shift into the Higher Self. Feeling so sleepy now".

"Goodnight then darling".

"Goodnight. Xxx. Amazing.... hehe we both said the same thing at the same time yet again".

"Oh, yes. 'Twins'. Lol. ....Not even noticing now! Sweet dreams. MWAH xxxxxx".

It was 2.55AM in the morning.

34 - AN EMOTIONAL HANGOVER

Day 3 - Monday, 13th April 2009

Claire:

I woke up feeling amazing. I was different this morning from yesterday. Younger somehow and lighter, without the heaviness of worry across my forehead, which I could never seem to separate myself from first thing in the morning, or especially last thing at night. It was as if the worry was me and not just a state of mind that I could put aside and forget about whenever I chose to. I felt wonderful and looking out the window and into the day, discovered how late it was, for the sun was already high in the sky.

Why it must be nearly lunchtime!" I scolded myself with a chuckle. How could I have slept in for so long? I remembered his voice and then a rush of excitement filled me up from the inside of me like a warm gush of spirits entering the bloodstream and into my pelvis. My heart pulsed more rapidly and skipped a beat, just as I remembered how he had made me feel. Unbelievable. Could I be falling in love with someone I had never laid eyes upon before? He was different from the others though, this I knew just by instinct. It never crossed my mind that I was stark raving mad to trust a man again so quickly. It just felt so right to bare all and not hold anything back from him. In fact it felt wrong to hold back from Mark. I wanted him to know everything about me. Not just the good things, but all of the bad things as well, like losing my driver's license for drunk driving, having been raped and things like that, which others might keep secret and hide for as long as possible from the other. If I was going to scare him off, it may as well be sooner than later I decided.

I fixed myself a coffee and wandered back to the computer in my bedroom.

My inbox had new messages from other men on RSVP.

"Oh that's it" I decided firmly.

Time to close my profile on RSVP. I don't want to do this anymore. It just doesn't feel right chatting to other men about dating now. I want to give Mark one hundred percent of my attention from now on.

One by one, I replied to each message, saying thank you for their kisses, but I had already met someone special and didn't want to waste their time. I wished them all the best in finding what they were looking for and then copied all of the emails and chats from Mark and closed my online dating profile with a giggle.

I drew heavily on my cigarette and leaned back in the chair. I was beginning a new relationship, only after hearing his voice once on the telephone and getting to know him via the internet for one whole day. "Friends my arse"! I thought.

Yes, it had only been one day and already it felt like we had delved into each other's souls and knew more about each other than some couples do in a lifetime.

How was he feeling right now, I wondered, as I exhaled the smoke high up to the ceiling and watched it curl around the light bulb like a grey winter mist on an English moor? Most men I had known in my life would be uncomfortable with such intimacy and would try to desensitize by running away for a couple of weeks before contacting me again, if at all for that matter. Most men would never give that much in the first place actually and I realised only a man with true inner strength would be able to share his vulnerability with me like Mark had done. How long would it take him to contact me I wondered? All I knew was that I couldn't wait to speak to him again and hear that voice, which gave me goose bumps and made my eyes squint in a faraway trance of delight, when was it again? Oh yeah that's right, only last night.

I began chopping up some vegetables for a Thai green curry when an uncanny urge to go to my computer pulled me out of the kitchen and over to my desk in the bedroom. I clicked on MSN and there was Mark asking if I was there, as if he had tapped me on the shoulder and called me over for a chat at that very moment.

"Afternoon darling, how are you? I'm just about to head out and take my daughter to her friend's house. She's going with them to the Easter Show tomorrow. Then I'm meeting a friend and going to the movies. Do you have an emotional hangover? I can't stop thinking about you. You are deep in me already and I love it Xxxxx".

An emotional hangover? How divine I thought. No one has ever described falling in love like that before. Without censoring my reply, my fingers were tapping back to him excitedly.

"Oh yes I do! You are so inside me. I love it too! Have a gorgeous day beautiful one Xxxxx".

"God, when I talk to you, I actually feel different inside", he added.

"I do too".

"The Angels must be feeling pretty pleased with themselves right now and I thank them".

"Yes", I agreed, hardly believing my eyes and what he was saying to me. Fancy him believing in the Angels too.

"Ok. I'm off. You have a nice day. I'll feel your energy with me xxx".

"Take it with you darling xxx ", I replied in a daze. My heart rate had quickened again. It felt like I was on drugs. How did I know he was online right at that moment? Were we really that connected? God how spooky. How divine. How bloody divine!

For the rest of the day I experienced him telepathically, as waves of emotion quite out of the blue and unexpectedly, as if he were thinking of me at just the same moment too.

11.57PM, my mobile beeped a text message.

"Off to bed now. See you in your dreams Xxxx".

"Funny about that! It's like you've always been there... Good night Mark ~ xoXOo"…

It was 12.26AM on April 14th 2009 and for the first time in my life, my days and nights were starting to merge into one delicious dream. Except that I wasn't dreaming anymore. This was real.

Day 4 Tuesday, 14th April 2009

Claire:

I began to wonder if my inner core was changing somehow or that dormant DNA inside of me was being switched on. It wasn't just the feeling of stress being lifted from me again today, or an overall state of sheer happiness that I noticed being weird about me for the fourth day in a row, but when I looked at something perfectly ordinary, I could see exquisite beauty and design within it. This seemed to be happening to me moment by moment as a deepening spiritual awareness. Even a chore as boring as washing the dishes was a creative experience for me. The bubbles in the detergent gleamed more vividly than usual with all the colours of the rainbow glittering like a kaleidoscope in the sunlight at me. I watched them hiss and pop as if they were alive, picking some up and gazing at them closely as if for the first time. How could something so beautiful and delicate just happen?

The sky seemed bluer, the air sweeter and the breeze softer on my face when I was out hanging the washing on the line and I couldn't stop smiling. My sensitivity seemed heightened as if I could feel Mark living inside of me, because I sensed that he was mysteriously connected to me there. But how could that be? I hadn't even met him yet. It felt like he was physically stroking my heart and I could feel it, just because he was thinking of me right then and there.

Having finished the housework, I sat at the computer staring into a lukewarm cup of coffee and pondered the thought of being zapped into a parallel universe, perhaps having swapped lives with a much lighter and more finely tuned Claire. Yes falling in love with him was definitely changing my frequency, or was making me go nuts. I just hadn't worked out which it was.

"I can check my personal email from work every hour or so, if you've ever around. God I can't get enough of you. :-) xx".

"I wonder why my heart begins to race, whenever I hear from you. Something alters my chemistry and it feels divine xx".

Half an hour later there was another email waiting for me.

"Yes. Do you think it will last? I know very well about 'honeymoon' periods. But believe the fire can last forever with the right connection Xx".

I answered him honestly without holding back my usual fear of scaring men away, daring him in fact to run away as fast as he could without looking back.

"I believe if you have enough space from each other, you don't lose yourselves within the relationship. I think losing oneself is the problem. However, I think I could lose myself in the chemistry of this of you - or should I say ... I could so merge with you, but with lots and lots of spaces and freedom in between. We can hold the secret to being one with ourselves. Yes I think it will last! Mwah! :)) xx".

His next email came almost immediately. My heart had that feeling it was being stroked again and I suspected he was aware of it too.

"As I read your reply, I felt a rush of blood through me...followed by a shortness of breath. No kidding! Merging together is such a turn on ...sexually, emotionally and spiritually Xx".

"Yes" I answered.

"You are so in tune with the essence of me… and I, you!

Euphoria.

Have a gorgeous day! Xx

P.S. Was wondering if you are programming the software at work or moi… LOL x".

I jumped out of my chair and ran outside. 'Whoo- hoo!' I screamed at the top of my lungs.

"You seem happy mum", said Rick sitting in his wheelchair in the courtyard and gazing up from his ship book for a moment.

"I am Rick". "I think I have finally found someone very special and I can't wait to meet him".

"Good for you. What's his name"?

"His name is Mark." I told him, "but he lives in Sydney, so it won't be easy for us".

This man wasn't afraid to show his feelings. I hadn't scared him away, but actually turned him on. He wasn't afraid to talk about his emotions and I had never found a man in my life before, who felt just like me – not just a soul mate, but like my 'Twin'.

For the rest of the day no matter what I was doing, waves of him continued to wash over me. I couldn't think about anything else for very long and at 8.30PM he came back on line at MSN and I asked him how his day was.

"It was wonderful. I couldn't stop thinking about you. : I had a smile on my face all day I think".

"Sometimes I felt you so strongly. Wow. I felt you like some massive wave in the middle of talking to someone about something else. I look at your photos and I just know. It's written all over you. So powerful, that I must say, it scares me a little. The energy I mean".

"You know, on the way to work this morning, I felt I could just quit my job and home and walk out of here to be with you… and KNOW it wouldn't be stupid, because it WOULD work. Am I crazy"?

"It's like you said yesterday… all happening like this… geographically separated… is like an extended brake to slow down the coming together. (A bit at least)".

"Yes. Like we have to experience the soul connection first".

"Yes and we are! How wonderful huh? Truly amazing".

"Don't be scared. The soul connection will always be there and strongest of all. Sex or no sex".

"I've never felt so overwhelmingly intense before. I know me and that's why it scares me, because I know my intensity without you. Now having your energy here with me is almost too much"…

"I think talking on here and the phone is in itself making it slow. I mean, I could just get on a plane up there tomorrow, but I won't, because I'd like to develop at a nice pace too".

"Nice pace…LMFAO! Light years. Nothing about you and I could ever be at a steady pace".

"But it is right now physically… because of where we live….which is allowing us, forcing us, to focus on experiencing this wonderfully strong spiritual and emotional connection".

"Yes it is. We're kind of really lucky actually"!

Mark:

The attraction was so intense, we both knew if we had been within driving distance of each other we would have been in our cars and together physically from the very first night. We both also knew very well that also meant sexually and it would have been intense. Very intense. Being so far apart was forcing us to take things slowly. I realized that when relationships start quickly with massive lust, such as affairs or instant physical attractions do, if they survive at all, later they are often left always wondering if that was all the relationship was fundamentally built on? Was there really anything more beneath the sexuality of it all? Was it actually built on a deep mutual attraction of souls and love? It can often lead to one or other party later starting to question the whole basis of their relationship and then, inevitably, starting to test it and the consequences of the cracks that it brings with it.

I realised for us this wasn't a bad thing at all, in fact it was a godsend. It was a gift to be thankful for. We were in a situation where we would always be able to look back and know that the deep connection between us was there before any physical or sexual dimension existed at all. We would never have to wonder, we would always know our love was deep and true in our souls before we had ever met in the flesh.

"I know you. I read your face. It's that face I have always looked for in a man, but never found".

"How about in a few weeks we arrange to meet up, just to see? Then take it from there"?

"Sure".

"Ring, ring".

"My bloody phone's ringing. Is it you"?

"Know what? Yes".

Mark:

We talked for hours. It turned out we had experienced so many similar things in and out of relationships. We had both been married and divorced, twice. We had both been in relationships where we had been worn down to the point of losing ourselves and ending up totally controlled by the other persons, and made to feel we were being inconsiderate if we ever objected to what they wanted.

We both believed in the soul, and that love is all we are all here for. We entirely resonated with each other. I explained to Claire how resonant frequency worked, from when I studied it in physics. It was as though we both resonated on exactly the same frequency and in perfect synchronicity, raising us up in a way we had never been with anyone else.

Claire:

We were on the phone for three and a half hours. When he spoke, his voice seemed to stroke my heart and my mind all at once. My spine had shivers charging up and down it every time he laughed and there were no uncomfortable pauses or awkward 'no go' zones to negotiate with him. The sound of his voice didn't just float around my ears and waft off into space, it actually had a physical effect on my whole body that lasted a long time after we said goodnight.

Later, lying in the darkness, I saw tiny golden orbs floating in the corner of the bedroom and wondered what they were as I fell asleep, but it only seemed a moment, for I unexpectedly awoke, which wasn't for the normal reason to get up and to have a pee. I puffed the pillows up under my neck with my fist and lit a cigarette, trying fruitlessly to calm my racing pulse down for a little while. Just then my phone beeped that a text message had arrived. It was 2.30AM. "Why is my heart pounding again"? it read.

Oh God, he must be awake too. The same thing must be happening to him as well. I could hardly believe my own boldness, as my finger quickly hit the send button, "Because mine is too and they are making love to each other Xo".

I slipped the phone under the pillows only to drift back into the blackness again, but not before realizing that the extraordinary developments of my own real life outshone any dreams I was having these days or ever in my life for that matter.

35 - DREAMING

Day 5 - Wednesday, 15th April 2009
Mark:

It wasn't long before my alarm went off and I was back up and heading off to work.

I dreamt I had moved to Queensland to live with Claire and in the dream we were looking at a house together. It was a big old wooden Queenslander, on low stilts and surrounded by decking. It stood by itself and was surrounded by open land on all sides. We came out of it, walked across the wooden porch, down the steps and got in our car and drove down a long curved gravel drive around and out onto the main road and turned right. The road winded its way through low lying hills on either side. Trees sparsely covered them and you could see a lot of the bright blue sky through them. Little did I realise that three years later, as we started writing this book, it would be a perfect description of where we lived, an area neither of us had never been to or seen before. In fact, I even worked out the exact spot the dream was from. The house wasn't far away and had a long private driveway off the road, so we couldn't go there to check. But looking around, it was the exact view I dreamt. It makes it more intriguing, as to how I could have a dream from a specific location I had never been to beforehand, nor since.

Day 7 Friday, 17th April 2009

Mark:

Over the weekend without saying anything, I went to Astrodienst.com and had a look at Claire's birth chart. I also ran the compatibility check to see how we were suited. I had done it before about others, and so had she. It was an interesting insight and a bit of fun. It said we were a very potent combination and there were lots more details to read through some other time. So I purchased the full compatibility report to send her as a surprise present.

Before setting off for work the next day I emailed it to her as a surprise.

"I've just finished reading our report! Wow"!

"Yes! And like you said, I think most of the potentially bad stuff we've already gone through and grown from".

"Have you read it already Xo"?

"Yes. Bought it when I got home yesterday Xx".

"Hehe... You blow me away. Are you scared"?

"Scared of"?

"Me!"

"Why? How"?

"Wondering that's all. Oh just after reading the composite – it's so very powerful and I was wondering if you were scared of the power of this"?

"No way. Bring it on".

"You are gorgeous Mark"!

"What is the point of searching for this for an entire lifetime and then after fifty years it arrives and being scared of it"?

"Yep. No point. I love that so much in you…xo".

"I just hope I live up to what you want".

"I want you to be so happy and so free to be exactly what you want to be".

"… and the thing I feel here, is just being me for the first time is what you actually want".

"YES".

"'Twins".

"'Twins".

"Need to book flights, and I want as much time as I can get with you now. "How many days shall I come up for"?

"Forever. Xox. By the way, Rick bought a new pack of angel cards today. He uses them sometimes when he's feeling a bit fearful and they help him to focus on something positive instead. He's actually really very good at pulling out the appropriate one for other people as well. I asked him to pull a card out for us today and I nearly had a heart attack. Guess which card he pulled out"?

"Which one"?

"The 'Twin Flames' one! I didn't even know there was one and I have never spoken to Rick about us being 'Twin Flames' before either".

Mark:

The more we thought about it the more it spun us out. Here it was popping up again from a completely different place.

"I want everyone to be happy around us and share in our love. I'm about to make this booking…. I asked my boss for 2.5 days, but am taking 4 days".

"Yaye"!

"If he has a problem, I will quit. I have quit jobs before that threatened to wreck my personal life. Fuck them".

"Me too. I adore your attitude. 'Twin' xo".

36 - THE SPIRITUAL COUNSELLOR

Day 8 - Saturday, 18th April 2009
Mark:

The day arrived for my appointment with the spiritual counsellor. Christine took me inside and the whole of the ground floor of her two story home was dedicated to her, and her husband's, spiritual work. Downstairs had been converted into large open rooms, obviously to hold group gatherings. We went through to a big room at the back and sat down and she started the reading. She didn't seem to be going anywhere for a while, but I didn't say anything or give any feedback - I just let her go where ever she was taken.

Suddenly she came out and declared that I had just met 'the one'. Interesting. Now that got my attention. Why would she say that, and use that specific phrase? When I had made the booking with her I didn't even known Claire.

She continued, saying this was the woman I had been waiting all my life for, and also I was 'the one' she had been waiting for too. She said we had "finally found each other" and that "this is it". I didn't say anything and she continued on. She described this woman as "wicked", "in fact very wicked", but had been "hurt a lot in the past, badly, very badly, and I needed to be very gentle with her".

Then she suddenly announced this woman was also my 'Twin'. I gave her a puzzled look and innocently asked what a 'Twin' was? "Your 'Twin Flame'. Do you know what 'Twin Flames' are"? I told her I didn't and she started talking to me about 'Twin Flames', explaining they are 'Twin Souls', identical and that everyone has one. She pointed to the walls at either end of the room where there was a large coloured picture of a flame on each wall facing each other. She said they represented her and her husband... they were 'Twin Flames' too. I still didn't mention a word about Claire. She described how we had always been together, always, either in life or in spirit, and now it was our time for both of us to be here together in life at the same time, and finally together physically. She carried on, and came out with quite a number of other things that fitted exactly what Claire and I had been discovering and experiencing, and as just importantly, none that didn't. I wasn't just picking out the bits that did fit and discarding the rest.

For the last part of the reading she picked up her cards and asked me to turn three over. I shuffled them and I turned the first one over. It said 'Wholeness'. I asked her what that meant. She said "You are there. You have done your growing, about fear and love and many other things". I asked what she meant? She said "You are 'Whole'. You are ready to meet your 'Twin'. You can't be together with your 'Twin' in life until you have done the work needed on yourself. It takes many lifetimes".

'Whole'? I'd certainly never considered myself 'Whole', in fact, far from it. Very far from it. I was in shock. What was she saying? Here was the 'Twin Flame' concept being raised again, and I was starting to wonder, maybe, it was real?

After she had finished the reading we talked openly and I told her a bit about my past and where I was coming from. She said it wasn't me who was the problem in the difficult relationships - it was the other person who had issues. They had taken advantage of my forgiving nature in not having to look at themselves and their own behaviour. I started to look back through all of those relationships, and events, from an entirely different viewpoint. They flashed through my head and I thought, "Oh my god, maybe it really wasn't me that was really the issue all along? Maybe it actually was them? Maybe it was their 'baggage' and unresolved issues they had been dumping on me, and I had let them do it by having such low self-esteem"? When I had confronted them, they had pointed the finger at me all the time, to keep them from having to honestly look at themselves? What an idiot I had been for tolerating it for so long each time.

As soon as I came out I texted Claire.

"You really are 'the one'. We've been together before. I love you Xxx".

"OMG! My soul has goose bumps Xo"!

"She said 'Twin Flames'. She knew without me saying anything. Just like her and her husband".

"Take your time. Digest. We both knew Xxx".

"Yes. I already knew Xxx".

"Mark xo I am covered in shivers Xxxxxx".

"Lol. She said to tell you, "This is it. I hadn't told her anything about you and she said that this woman has a wicked sense of humour".

"Really"?

"And she said that I do too. Us two will play with each other – word for word what we were saying on the phone last night...and she said it would never stop. She said that you've been through a lot of really bad stuff. Really bad".

"To be ready for you. Yes. I don't see it as bad. I prefer to see it all as an opportunity for inner transformation".

"She said we've both been through it, but we were both now ready for our true love".

"Yes".

"She said it was just like her husband. They both had lots of bad and unhappy relationships, but learnt their lessons, and when they met it was an instant connection and we have the same. I was told that I've been going into relationships to help others and when I've helped them, they flick me off, but it was meant for me to grow from them as well. Love you".

"Love you too".

Mark:

I drove home slowly contemplating what I had been told. The more I thought about it the more it explained everything. I rang Claire as I drove home. I was in tears. I had been beating myself up for all of these years, relationship after relationship, believing all the darkness that had been blamed on me with no concern for how it hurt me, just to selfishly avoid looking at their own issues. It was despicable.

I spent the rest of the day replaying past events, reliving past relationships, and suddenly finding answers to so many questions and events I remembered living through as they began to make sense. If only there had been a book I could had read that would have even given me a clue, or someone who I could have talked with and shown me another view of what might have been going on, it might have helped me be a bit more objective at the time. It would have saved so much time, so many years. That doesn't mean I didn't need to go through those situations, just that I could have left them sooner when they turned abusive. This is one of the main reasons we have written this book, in the hope it just may help others still back where we once were.

Day 9 Sunday, 19th April 2009

Claire:

"It's all sinking in today".

"Being apart like this has taught us how close we are non-physically 'Twin'. It actually dawned on me....like everything else, I bet that I will be just all you wish for, and you will be all I could wish for, naturally without any effort".

"Just like the first night when I was just being me... talking about seamed nylon stockings".

"It could be tantric without us even trying to be".

"That was just me and having a thing for the stockings was also.... just you. We didn't try. It just happened"!

"I know. That was a major shock for me".

"SEAMED STOCKINGS WAS THE SECRET CODE THAT WE SHARED AT BIRTH WHEN WE SPLIT SO THAT WE COULD RECOGNISE EACH OTHER... HA-HA"

"If I could only describe how I have been mesmerized by black seamed nylon stockings since childhood"!!

"They are my energy too, reminding you of me".

Mark:

The nights dragged on, each evening sitting in our homes alone in the dark we would talk on the phone for hours and hours. We never had any of those uneasy silences, in fact we could never get out half of what we were talking about before we were had moved on to another topic. Sitting in the dark, at times I would see what looked like feint tiny lights in the room, usually high up around the walls. At other times they were small transparent spherical shapes, only a few centimetres across and with no definable edge. Usually they were an off white colour, but sometimes bluish, or red. Sometimes there would be just one, sometimes there would be a few. I would see long hazy strands of translucent light, shaped like a tear in a piece of paper, as if tiny thin rips in the fabric of space, just millimetres wide and about half a meter long, floating there in mid-air in the dark with no clear edge. I had perfect eyesight and at first just thought I was imagining it: adrenalin rush of chemicals in the brain affecting the visual stimulation of the retina, or something like that, as I'm sure some scientific type would try and explain it away with. But I wasn't, they were there. I know I saw them on many occasions. I saw the various lights in different places around the room, so I know they weren't some static reflection, and in different rooms, even upstairs. I checked all the possible reflections and light sources and they weren't coming from outside. They would be there for ages, hours sometimes, so I know they weren't due to something passing by outside like a reflection from a car or plane. If I turned my head they didn't move with my head, so I know it wasn't something on, or in my eyes, or my mind. I don't know what they were, but after three or four times I realised they were something very real and felt benevolent. I didn't say anything about them to Claire, until one night whilst talking to her, she suddenly said she could see little lights in the room where she was. I got her to describe them to me and we went through all the options to eliminate the obvious, and were left with the same conclusion as the ones I had been seeing. When I told her I had been seeing them too, it freaked us both out.

Day 10 Monday, 20th April 2009

Mark:

"Hi my darling. Just got in from work. Going upstairs for thirty minutes to sort out bedrooms for tomorrow's house inspection. xxx".

"Hey darling... xxx".

"I just had to hide away all the dildos, lingerie, whips and chains".

"HA-HA"!

"You think I'm joking ;)".

"Not at all… Am just laughing in anticipation of all that fun we are going to have... I adore you and your decadence! Mark"…

"Decadenceness".

"Decades and decades of itness 'Twinness' and I'm coming at you from behind...but you can't see me… All you can hear are the heels".

"Oh drooooooooooool".

Claire:

There was such a long pause, as I sat gazing at the screen waiting for him to respond and then the computer suddenly went black. I fumbled to reboot it as quickly as possible, but it seem to take ages.

"You there"?

"I don't think we are meant to experience cybersex".

"Why not"?

"Cos the computer just crashed, as I was getting started".

"The anticipation builds then and the electricity keeps sizzling eh? Miss you Claire".

"Miss you too. So when I pick you up, do we have to go straight home, or can we have an adventure"?

"Anything you fancy. What were you thinking"?

"Well I was on the beach today and had some ideas about a little diversion somewhere, just to get to know each other".

"So what's a 'get to know each other' diversion"?

"I would need to create it. I was just wondering if you were open"?

"Claire, I will just be so glad to be with you. I'm happy to do whatever you think would be nice".

"Well I just thought, because this is such a special occasion, we could create a memory"?

"Elope at the terminal"?

"Ok. Nothing tops that"!

"So what were you thinking"?

"Nothing really, just seeing if you were open to an adventure. Not sex. Just, something special".

"I know we'd both like the first time to be very special, affectionate and romantic. We have been gifted with such a special relationship, I want to savour all of the deep love and affection sexually as well".

"xxxxx Yes. Ooooo".

"Sexual fun is GREAT and all the games and variations you and I can think of will give us some great experiences and memories, but primarily, it's about the very special deep love and affection we have".

"Yes darling. I know. I love you Xx".

"I love you too. So what were you thinking"?

"Just maybe bringing a bottle of champagne and sitting on the sand for the first time. It's two minutes from the airport".

"That would be great!! Love it"!!

"Ha-ha Oh God, I hope you can cope with my craziness Mark".

"Why, do you class champers on the beach as crazy"?

"Well yeah, if you were expecting to be picked up from the airport and going straight home"?

"No, I wouldn't class that as crazy. I would call going straight home crazy actually. I was thinking about it today and felt that you would suggest we go somewhere for a coffee, or something anyway. I really don't mind, as long as I'm with you Claire. Whatever you think".

"You are fucking amazing! I just don't want to spend my first hour with you driving the car. I just think it would be gorgeous for an hour or so, to actually spend that time being really together".

"Ok. You know the area. I want to be with you as soon as possible".

"Sameness. Today was deeper somehow".

"Why"?

"I had the realization, that if some reason, we didn't get together, I would be so sad. It hit me in the gut".

"Sad wouldn't be the word".

"Yes and isn't it amazing that we are sharing the dimension of writing to each other before we even meet"?

"I am going to ring you soon. Hey maybe when we meet, we will have nothing left to say".

"NO"!

"We'll just have to kiss each other a lot then ;)".

"I just can't wait".

"Oh yummmmm. I really love lots of kissing and hugs and touching and NEVER grow bored of it. Both giving and receiving".

"I think we are very similar in that regard. My heart is aching for you".

"I don't need to party to be happy".

"Me neither. Just you".

"Sameness".

"It's funny, we even kind of speak the same".

"Yes. 'Twins'".

"Hehehe… yeah. 'Twins' Xx".

"I am totally yours Claire. You have a hundred percent of my heart and future. I have never felt so in love before. Even weirder considering we haven't met".

"My commitment is to you is a hundred percent also. I am exactly the same. Tears now. Sorry Xxx".

"Don't apologize. I love your emotion. Let it flow. Ring ring"…

Day 11 Tuesday, 21st April 2009

Claire:

The first text message of the morning read: "Morning Claire. Hope you have a great sleep in. When I awoke in the night, how did I know that you were awake as well and it was ok to text you? 'Twins'! Have a great day. Love xxxx".

The flame in my soul flickered a familiar warm flash across my heart, skipping a beat, as I replied.

"Darling, I know, I was thinking the same. You must be utterly exhausted. Will let you come to me when you wish. I want to give you some space to sleep. Love xxxo".

One of my piano students and her mum asked what the hell I was doing to look so good today, because my eyes are shining and I told them that I'm in love with you"!

"That's really nice. To think that I am having that effect on you makes me happy".

"Yes. I feel so wonderful. You are so wonderful. You are the best"!!

"Many couples, who do not even have our deep spiritual connection, can keep chemistry there for decades".

"Yes, but I think that you will always make my heart race. God, it's racing now and I can't even see you! I can't wait to see you, touch you, smell you".

"Yes".

"For the first time".

"We have to wait for just over a week though."

"And that will so seem like forever darling".

"Ring, ring"?

"Oh I love it when you do that before you call"!

Claire:

I couldn't get enough of hearing his delicious voice caressing me deeply inside. I would shut my eyes for ages, whilst he wrapped me up inside his voice like a glorious cocoon of bliss, stroking me gently in ways, which I didn't know had even been invented yet. We weren't trying to be sexual on purpose, yet this was our tantra, our sacred worship of one another, without touching flesh or even being in the same room together. So much for candles and incense and black satin sheets we both discovered. We could tease and please each other for hours, just by listening to the other's voice instead. On the phone, we played like this for ages and the miles between us faded until there was no distance left between us at all. We were merging. One of us would seem to notice the clock shouting out 11:11 at us again and we would giggle in amazement of how special the numbers had become for us.

I had to keep swapping the phone over to the opposite ear frequently though, because it would start to ache like hell after a while from pushing the phone up so hard trying to get a bit closer to him. I didn't mind though. My arms ached as well from lifting the phone up to my face for hours and hours in the same position, but I still didn't care. I was in love. I was in heaven. I was with my 'Twin Flame', 'the one' I'd longed for all of my life. Secretly, I was more than a bit nervous though, about whether Mark would really fancy me in the flesh or not, that's all. We hadn't even talked about body image or height and weight or anything yet. How weird is that? It didn't matter to either of us though it seemed, because it never came up in our conversations. Photos are one thing, but people are all different to how you might perceive them when you actually meet them in the flesh. His only remark pertaining to looks, was something about bringing his apple box to stand on at the airport, so that I could see him above everyone else. He just cracked me up. Was he really that short or was he just being funny with me? I loved him however he looked. Inside he was my 'Twin' and outside I knew I would love him as well, because a body is just a house for the soul to live in right? Anyway, his soul and my soul were definitely burning like crazy for each other, even sizzling with the same intensity and that feeling was pure bliss.

Day 12 Wednesday, 22nd April 2009
Mark:

"I totally believe that neither of us will stuff this up".

"No. You embody everything I've ever dreamed of in a man Mark. You're classy, sexy, and bold, as well as being both brave and vulnerable at the same time. You're fucking so funny and intelligent and"….

"Demented".

"Hahahaa, no! You're spiritual, intuitive and you're intense, and tall! We'll be here all night if I'm going to finish writing this. It's just the combination of your aspects, which is so overwhelmingly delicious. I just had little snippets of you in each lover".

"You know Claire, it's the same for me with you, but I'm a bit overwhelmed to believe it myself at times. I know you're everything I've ever wanted and it brings tears of joy to my eyes".

"Oh Mark, I feel the same. I have experienced feelings so intense with you that is all so new to me. Like you are my inner code to switch on now. I'm all on, all go and there's absafuckinglutely no way back anymore. I can't switch it off. Hey, I just realized the other thing that we do is phrase things in the same way. Who else uses the word 'twas? Or says I love you so"?

"The past is gone Claire".

"Forever".

"It's just you and me forever now".

"Yes Xx".

"You've suffered enough. It's now time to enjoy and be blissfully happy".

"This time next week, when we're together alone on the couch, I will anchor that thought in. You and me forever".

"We will anchor it into each other".

"Blood rushing everywhere now lol".

"Is your mind in that gutter again"?

"As far down as the gutter and as high up as heaven".

"Like you said in your first email, 'from lust to spiritual in one sentence' remember? Yes. 'Twins'".

"Yes. 'Twins'. I'm allowing myself to feel so much. You're divine Mark. Just fucking divine".

"That deep emotional connection will always be present no matter what we do."

"I need a cold shower. Every cell in my body is pumping blood for you. I think my heart is bashing me up".

Day 13 Thursday, 23rd April 2009

Mark:

I had Liana for the weekend and had also bought my Mom an air ticket and flown her over from Adelaide to spend some time together. Claire and I, as usual, spent all day texting and emailing. After work Liana and I picked my Mom up from the airport and had some quality time together in the evening. After they both went to bed I was straight online to Claire. We joked how we were having separation anxiety already, from just not communicating for a few hours. It was a nice problem to have. We also joked about how we could write a book one day about all this, but, nah, couldn't see that happening somehow.

Claire:

"Tonight we travelled another light year into each other. Every day and every night seems packed with more and more intensity, more and more overwhelming emotion and more and more oneness. You are so deep. No wonder I will need forever with you. Sending you a hug".

"We will be doing that for real soon. Hey, I just remembered something the physic said. She said that she was about to wish us luck, but that we don't need it now".

"How wonderful. I can't wait to fall asleep in your arms darling. Sweet dreams. Xx I love you".

"I want you here now in my bed with me and every night Xxxxx".

"Forever".

37 - TITANIC AND JACK AND ROSE

Day 15 - Saturday, 25th April 2009

Mark:

After another ten hours straight talking on the phone, we eventually dragged ourselves apart to get some sleep. Three hours later we were awake and back talking again. It felt like time was running at a different rate now, for the speed at which things seemed to be moving between us seemed dreamlike, not to mention where we had reached emotionally in such a short space of time. It felt as if time was flying by in light years and we joked about time being bent by some means. We just hung on and kept on going, it was a wild ride, yet it was also so easy.

I started to wonder if there was more to this than we had already recognized. We had already talked about resonance, energy, frequencies, and even by the second day were talking about speed and light years. Its common knowledge Einstein linked those all together through E=mc2, energy equals mass multiplied by the speed of light squared. Something about it all still seemed baffling and niggled away at me in a manner I couldn't quite put my finger on.

Claire:

"I remember when I watched the Titanic. I bawled my eyes out".

"I realised that I wasn't with 'the one' and I decided to leave so that I could find you".

"What do you mean leave"?

"I left my husband".

"Really? Watching Titanic was the trigger then"?

"Yes. It reminded me of what I wanted more than anything in this world. When I watched it with my husband, it was like someone was shaking my whole essence from long, long ago. I bawled my eyes out, not for Rose and Jack, but for myself and for 'the one' who I had called out to when I was just a little girl – my one true love. It was a defining moment for me. I knew what I really wanted and it wasn't with my husband anymore. I wanted to feel alive and adored by someone only my soul knew existed somewhere out there with the moon. I decided to leave him. I would rather be alone than be stuck in a lie a moment longer. I didn't know when I would leave and I didn't know how, but I knew it would happen one day soon. And it did not long after and here I am".

"I remember that as well. I think everyone was transfixed with Jack and Rose's love story. I think we were all left desperately wanting what they found. I see it now as a love story of 'Twin Flames', each finally meeting 'the one', and they just had to be with them, regardless of the consequences. That's the way it is when 'Twin Flames' meet. It's not just fiction. We are all looking for that, and I believe we can all have it. We just need to do the spiritual work on ourselves first, as they did theirs, then our 'Twin' will walk into our life".

"In fact it is really interesting that their fictional story inspired you so deeply, deep enough to walk out on your marriage. I wonder how many others out there were inspired to do the same? I wonder if we were to ever tell our story, what it might inspire? No-one should stay in a relationship they are not blissfully happy in".

"Yes. I too, wish those things, for I have experienced the same lessons. I thought it was my responsibility to keep forgiving, time after time, even when my ex- husbands promised not to be violent with me ever again. I learnt that forgiveness is not always the answer. There is a time to forgive and a time to leave".

"God I love your mind and the way you think".

"Sameness".

"Sameness 'Twin'. Come play with me".

"I live for this Mark".

"For us"?

"For us Xxxx".

"It's the most important thing in my life as well".

Claire:

No matter how much time we spent talking on the phone together, it was never enough. By the time I got into bed after talking to Mark, the birds were tweeting and sunlight was flooding into my bedroom. Rick was up boiling the kettle and as I brushed my teeth and grabbed my phone, I slipped under the covers, whilst flashing him a goodnight text. The time was 8AM in the morning and I could hardly believe that we'd talked all night again, for it had only felt like a couple of hours. Time had flown faster than ever before.

"Ten hours of you is such a tease Mark. Sleep tight my 'Twin' xoxo".

Claire:

Even though I was in bed alone with only my mobile phone tucked underneath the pillows, it felt as if Mark was actually wrapped around me like a weightless, silken cocoon and that we had only to listen to the silent voice of instinct, for us each to hear one other's thoughts. It was as if the physical boundaries between us had dissolved completely and we were free to float in a golden fluid dream of each other's inter dimensional garden, no matter where our actual physical bodies were located. We couldn't be any closer if we were together in the flesh.

"Sending you me now for your dreams to hold. Mwahness Xoxox".

I received a text from him just as I hit the send button, so we both must have been typing at the same time. I read his reply only to find that my eyelids had become so heavy that I could not open them again for some time.

Mark:

Claire must have dropped off to sleep and as I couldn't get the notion of 'Twin Flames' off my mind, I decided it was time to do some more reading up on it. We had both stumbled across it and bounced about it, but I wanted to research more about it. There was so much information out there I was surprised I'd never come across anything about it before Claire telling me about it. I read and read, but I really needed some sleep. It was mind blowing. Everything I read seemed to be was happening with us, yet in some ways our story seemed to go beyond somehow. What did it all mean? I was so tired I collapsed into sleep.

Claire:

My eyes were open again three hours later, but I was too excited to lie in bed any longer. Where was I getting all of this energy from? I lit a cigarette and hovered over the computer to check my inbox, whilst waiting for a fresh pot of coffee to brew in the plunger. Mark was messaging me on MSN already and so I poured the coffee and sat at my desk to focus better on what he was saying. Apparently when I had fallen asleep, he had researched some material on Twins Flames and I was mesmerized by what he had learnt.

"Some of the other articles I read on 'Twin Flames' talked about there being a good reason for connecting before actually meeting physically as well. It's intriguing how the mechanics of that are playing out for us don't you think"?

"Totally. It's a big advantage the internet gives us all, enabling couples with an intense connection, who would never otherwise meet in person, be able to find each other and connect on a soul level before any physical meeting, like us".

"Yes. I wonder if that's why many people online are saying 'Twin Flames' are coming together all over the planet right now? I was actually having goose bumps rush right through me whilst I was reading articles. I know from experience goose bumps are always relevant for me and an alert system telling me to pay close attention to something".

"For sure. I think goose bumps are the voice of the soul telling us to take note of something real and special. I have read a fair bit about 'Twin Flames' now also, but the one thing I find questionable, is how there is strong opinion about not confusing passionate, romance and roses with 'Twin Flames'. It is meant to be about the spiritual aspect of raising the vibration of the planet for ascension, by breaking down duality into oneness. It seems that you and I do not fit into that agenda entirely, because the chemistry is so strong between us".

"Not all 'Twin Flames' are the same though are they? We are both so deeply passionate and sexual as well as having a strong spiritual mission. You can be all at the same time. There is no mention of anything out there on a sexual level in relation to 'Twin Flames'. Strange, as I thought there would have been. I have read in the past that deep loving sex, divine tantric sex, can open up higher levels of consciousness and spirituality. About how balancing our masculine and feminine energies breaks down barriers and frees us to experience even more. When we are honest, we all have both masculine and feminine sides and we just need to balance them. That is why we all get such a thrill and adrenalin rush when it's of pure love, we are unlocking doors to another realm of consciousness and are meant to go there. It's so unfortunate that so many people have issues and hang ups about sex, and so to appease their own baggage they lecture others that it is bad, intentionally brain washing people that uninhibited loving sex is 'dirty' or 'sinful'. They are just manipulating people because of their own abuse or bad experiences and so many people are missing out on experiences of extreme pleasure. Maybe we should write about it one day, if we get there".

"Funny how you described the male attributes and I the feminine, yet both of us share both male and feminine aspects. It's the Yin and Yang. I'm very passionate and sexual as well and you are also sensitive and romantic. It's like everything we have talked about previously. We are all aspects of the male and female energies. Now together we can both fine tune the balance".

"I know Claire and that comment resonates deeply, probably more so than any other. We live in a world where little boys are often taught that they shouldn't cry, and should go and punch someone if they are not happy about something, and girls should be submissive and not ambitious. And what do we get? Aggressive alpha males running the world, with constant wars, and aggressive males who can't run the world instead murdering someone who looked at them the wrong way, or gutlessly trying to hold it to ransom by terrorism. If males worked on their feminine side, and that doesn't mean becoming weak or a cissy, and worked on becoming more empathetic, kinder, genuinely friendly, giving and being loving, and not being embarrassed about it, the world would become a much more peaceful loving place to live".

"Amen to that".

"I read a number of times that without your 'Twin', we can all hide issues from partners, even soul mates, for years, decades, forever even. But when you are with your 'twin', you can't hide anything. They are you, and see right through everything you are and do. You are totally transparent to them. So those issues we have all been able to hide from others all of our lives, we now have to finally face up to and work on and resolve. In fact, you can only address those final issues with your 'twin'.

Perhaps in time, all of the answers will unfold for us, but some articles said that 'Twin Flames', or 'Twin Souls', are literally the same soul. We each have only one 'Twin', and generally after being split the two go their separate ways, incarnating over and over to gather human experience before coming back together. Ideally, this happens in both of their last lifetimes on the planet so they can ascend together.

Some of the writings seem to conflict in some places. For example many say twins always stay together. As one incarnates into a life, the other is with them on the other side, watching over them and helping them on their journey. Then next time it might be the other way around.

I want to ring you. I want to hear your voice again".

"Oh I can't wait"!

"Ring, ring"...

38 - OUR LAST DAY APART

Day 16 - Sunday, 26th April 2009

Claire:

"I was just wondering what I was going to wear to the airport".

"So what did you decide"?

"Lingerie under a trench coat. Ha-ha. With my hair up in a bun, black rimmed glasses and black sheer silks with seams running perfectly down the backs of my legs. Dark red rose lips blowing you kisses, whilst killer heels echo provocatively, as I slowly walk towards you".

"You must have found one of my favourite websites. Lol".

"Ha-ha. Love your energy. You know I can see it searing through that photo. We may NEVER have had the courage to go all the way into each other's core if we had met at the beginning of us, the chemistry would have just been so strong".

"Yet what we have now, is knowing what we have done that without sex playing any part".

"Isn't that fantastic? I love that French trance music you just sent through for me to download. I'm listening to it right now and it inspires me so much".

"That sounds intriguing"?

"Well, imagine a French boudoir filled with a huge four poster bed, all covered in masses of sumptuous linen and a ceiling all dressed in layers and layers of beautiful ruched nylon with a crystal chandelier dangling down and sparkling like diamonds from the centre".

"Mmmm. And what else"?

"You are sitting on a gilt chaise lounge sipping French champagne with a devastating smile on your face, for you're waiting for me, as I dress up in the lingerie you've chosen and hung over one of the panels of the vintage dressing screen for me".

"Mmm"...

"There's candles flickering in the reflection of a floor to ceiling antique gilt mirror and incense wafts into our senses like a musty, heavy drug, preparing us for the anticipation to follow… I emerge from the screen behind a bohemian, black feather fan and your alluring eyes begin glittering with stars, which shoot at me in delight and so I make a wish upon them"…

"Ring ring"...

"Bonjour"?

"Bonjour mon Cherie. Je t'aime".

"Oh, je t'aime Monsieur. Hehee".

"I love French movies".

"I've never seen a French movie, except with Jacques Cousteau exploring the sea, but I love everything French".

"Really? They have the best, most original stories in their films".

"Do they"?

"They are mostly about relationships and do such a great job of exploring them".

"Oh you'll have to share some with me. You know the sweetest dreams are not in sleep, but with you in every moment Mark just like right now".

"Nightness. I love you too darling. Only two sleeps to go. Yaye".

"Oh now I'll never sleep. I'm so excited".

Day 17 Monday, 27th April 2009

Claire:

"Just gazing at the beautiful new moon. Make a wish with me".

"Ok, but I'll have to think of a new one".

"Hehe… Sameness".

"Ring, ring"…

"Oh helloness. I'm surprised that you're still awake. You must be so exhausted".

"Hello. I slept on the train coming home from work".

"I had a power nap on the couch. Are you excited"?

"Hehe. Yes. Are you"?

"Yeah. Just use your magic on me. This time on Wednesday, we'll be entwined"?

"We'll be fast asleep"!

"I've connected with many people, as I'm sure you have, but I've always needed to take my space from them. I've never experienced this oneness I have with you before. It's the most divinely calming balm to me, which I know will never go away".

"Yes. There's only one day to go now. It sounds better than two sleeps".

"Yes. It's even more exciting than the day before I've ever been married".

"This is a divine union. Marriage has nothing on it. Marriage is just a piece of paper".

"I know. Are you tired"?

"No. I'm not tired. You lift me up".

"Sameness".

"Wow. I'm sure that I just saw something white swirl around me and they've got all of the bright lights on in here".

"I wonder if it's our energy or the Angels taking photos from another dimension? Lol".

"I have a great DVD to play you one day called Flatland, about the fourth dimension. If you get what its saying, it opens your mind right up to other dimensions around us all the time. I'd better go and be sociable, then we can head off to bed at a reasonable time tonight and I'll phone you for another fix of my favourite drug 'Clairenol'".

"Mwah. I'll light the candles for us".

"Ok. I'll ring you from bed in five to ten minutes time".

"Bring the wine. I'll chill the glasses. We should drink in bed and we could have a specific drop as our thing".

"Ok we'll find it. Chateau Clairemark"?

"Twin".

"Clairemark Valley"?

"Chateau Clairemark it is and we should design our own labels too".

"Spirit of Clairemark"?

"Mount Clairemark"?

"We are so in sync".

Claire:

We planned to retire to sleep at midnight, but we couldn't help talking for hours. It was a quarter to two in the morning before we said our goodnights and finally settled into the pillows to go to sleep. I sent him a text, before allowing myself to close my eyes.

"See you tomorrow at "the airport" Heart of Hearts Xxxxx".

"Yes. Promise you'll be there? I need you in my life now Xxxx".

"I cross my heart and never hope to die Mark, 'cause I want to live with you forever. Only love xxxxx".

"Oh yes. I've waited so long in this life for you and your love. I want to be able to give you mine, forever Xxxx".

"In the big picture of eternity, what's fifty years amongst 'Twin Flames'? Hehe. Sleep now my Darling... In bliss Xxxx".

"I think the last few weeks has shown that fifty years apart is like an eternity for us. We have so much to remember about us. Love you Claire Xx".

"Oh Mark. You are truly 'the one'. You are my oneness and completeness and I am yours always. Clairemark xo".

Day 18 Tuesday, 28th April 2009

Claire:

"My heart is pounding so hard for you. This will be the last day of my life without knowing your scent, your touch, the feeling of your eyes, the hunger of our mouths searching for our first kiss, the way your body feels when we hug and the presence you command, as you walk into the room. There are so many things about you that I will know, even without us whispering a word and I am trembling with sheer excitement. Enjoy this my 'Twin'. Claire xo".

"I know. My stomach is knotted from the anticipation I know we are both feeling. The end of a journey and the beginning all in one. It really does feel more like we are reuniting, rather than meeting for the first time. Do you feel the same Xxx"?

"I feel the sameness exactly and have from the beginning. You are loved with everything I am Xxxxx".

"Sameness darling Xxx".

"But I'm so happy that it's you Mark and nobody else Xxx".

"It was always going to be me. Woohoo. Finally out of work and my manager still hasn't approved my leave. Managers. They always make sure they quietly get their leave without issue, then dither and make a huge fuss when their staff want some".

"Yaye! Mark at last, can fly away to his Claire, where he belongs Xxx".

"My goddess. That is such a turn on, telling me I belong with you".

"My heart hasn't stopped pounding all day".

"Let's stay up all night and there will be no sleeps to wait Xx".

"LMFAO! You are so like me and then what? I pick you up and we have to sleep all day. No way! Hehe... Anyway, I'm going to sleep now. Mwah! Xox".

39 – THE AIRPORT

Day 19 - Wednesday, 29th April 2009

Claire:

"At least four new senses to discover with you today: - touch, smell, taste and visual. No wonder I'm nervous. Yet I know we are only adding to the perfect alchemy of us. Mwah X"!

"Running very late that's all. Leaving now Claire. Won't be long. Love you Xxx".

"Drive carefully my darling. See you soon. I love you Mark Xxxx".

"Parked car. On way to check in Xxx".

"Enjoy this. I am... We're about to find out what finally happens at 'The Airport' I can't wait Xxxxx".

"I am. Doesn't matter really anyway...it's the next fifty plus years of love together I am looking forward to most of all".

Mark:

The day was racing past in a slow hazy out of focus blur. The rest of the world around me seemed to go into slow motion, as if it was a giant 3D video inching past a frame at a time. Nothing else mattered to me at that point in time and space. Nothing. I had my apple box with me and was about to board.

I boarded the plane. We taxied for miles across the airport out to the third runway and soared up into the air. Just over an hour later we were touching down.

I waited for all the usual people who jump up as soon as a plane stops, pushing and shoving to get their carry-on luggage out, only to then be stood blocking the aisle so no-one else can get their things. When the aisle finally cleared I got up and grabbed my bag, and disembarked.

Walking along through the terminal I thought to myself, "this is it, will it, or won't it be"? I knew it would be ok, but had to be realistic by keeping one foot on the ground. I wondered how the next few minutes were going to play out, it would either be the biggest buzz of my life, or the biggest let down.

My heart was pounding, as I walked through the terminal and drew closer to the exit. I walked down the last short corridor and pulled over to the side, stopped, and stood there for a moment to gather myself. Could I really be in love with someone I had never met before? Was I being stupid? Could she really be as crazy about me without ever seeing what I actually looked like? Or feeling my energy? What if she didn't even show up? Can you really love someone on purely a soul level with no physical dimension involved at all?

I took a deep breath and walked on and out through the security exit, which was surrounded by huge glass partitions. I scanned the whole crowd looking for her. I'm pretty good at that sort of thing and don't miss much. I noticed a single woman right at the back with jet-black hair, heavy makeup and a white jacket on, who stood out right across the arrivals hall. I wondered if that was Claire and hoped it was.

I walked out and through the crowded barrier exit and suddenly she emerged from the crowd. There she was, standing right in front of me, only yards away. Our eyes met for the very first time, hers burning right into me, into my heart and into my soul. Her bright pink lips broke into a smile, as she slowly walked towards me. She was fucking gorgeous. Her smile grew bigger and the closer she got to me, the faster she walked. In the cramped busy arrivals terminal she ran into my arms, giving me the biggest hug and we wrapped our arms around each other like a couple of long lost boa constrictors.

We held each other so closely, savouring for the very first time the aroma of each other, the warmth of each other's bodies, and our energy sparking. Our bodies fitted together like they were made for each other. I was in a daze, but also soon aware of a sea of faces around us that were now all staring with wide eyes right at us. She slid the palm of her hand into the palm of mine, sliding each of her fingers between each of mine, and our hands just locked together into place without any pressure being applied, as though they were perfectly designed to fit together. It was just like interlocking my own two hands together. Her soft feminine skin felt like sliding into silk sheets. The feeling of already knowing each other so deeply, emotionally, spiritually, and now finally being together physically was the most intense drug.

As we began to walk over towards the baggage collection chute, she leaned over and whispered in my ear, "You're gorgeous". I couldn't believe it. She must have forgotten to put her contacts in. She was the one who was gorgeous, I know I'm not. Still I held back until we were alone, just in case, when she could tell me honestly if I wasn't what she had quite expected, as if I was just waiting for the first hints to be delivered. It felt like a mixture of relief and excitement all blended together in one big infusion. It felt like I had just returned home to my own reflection, my beloved, as the warm soft electricity flowed and crackled between us with everyone else in the terminal still staring at us, but fading into a 360 degree blurry painting.

We stood there gripping each other's perfectly interlocked hands, grinning away at each other and looking down at the amazing feeling coming through them. It was electric. I leaned over to her and told her I thought she was gorgeous too. Other than that, we barely talked. We were just together, and there was a knowingness I had never experienced before. We just knew. It felt like we were just meant to be. No words were needed.

My bag came through and we walked out of the terminal, hand in hand. The rest of the world didn't exist anymore, because we had just left the planet for a higher plain. We crossed the pedestrian crossing and weaved our way down through the rows of the car park towards her car. I hadn't even seen it, yet she kept apologising for it in advance. I told her I didn't care, it's not important (and it isn't). We eventually reached her beat up old car she was so embarrassed about, an old light blue Datsun with plenty of rust. I put my bag in her boot, turned to her, took her hand, pulled her close, wrapped my arms around her and we kissed slowly and deeply. It was heaven.

We headed out and onto the highway and turned north. She kept looking at me, her right elbow on the door of the open window and right hand wiggling the steering wheel with two fingers, the other arm changing gear. She had masses of chunky bracelets on both wrists constantly clinking away, sitting in her skin tight leggings, one foot up on her seat in a half lotus position, grinning in every direction and saying 'fuck', over and over, with a very wicked looking grin on her face. Telling me how good looking she thought I was. I found it really hard to believe and it took me a while to realise she was serious. We eventually stopped at Mermaids bar right on the beach at the Gold Coast for a drink. It was daytime and mid-week, so it was nice and quiet. We walked in and sank into a comfy leather sofa together, with a view of the beach and to the sound of waves roaring in from the Pacific and ordered French champagne. She plonked her left leg over my right thigh and between my legs and nestled her head into my shoulder. It was like it was always meant to be. We sat there in bliss, there was no need to say anything, silently both just knowing this was the beginning of forever.

We put our hands together and suddenly realised they were the same. Exactly. The same size and the same shape. I put my right hand against her left one and it looked like we were looking at a mirror. It looked as if they were one person's hands, one hairy and the other hairless. Claire said I wouldn't be able to match the spread of hers from all her years of piano playing, as she splayed hers fingers out to their limit, and was shocked when I stretched mine just as far. It was freaky.

We eventually prised ourselves away and headed slowly off back onto the highway north and up to her unit at Hope Island. She had left her previous home with no money and had to take the cheapest unit she could find, and a friend had had to pay her bond for her she was so broke. Although it was set in a marina near the water, it was off the beaten track and well away from the main towns and highways. I walked in and it was immaculate. She had gone to a lot of trouble for my arrival.

We sat and drank and just talked and talked. Claire had prepared one of her specialities, a huge platter of all sorts of delicious food, and we feasted on that and talked and drank wine on through the evening and into the night. I was all prepared to sleep on the couch, but Claire just said "No way. You're sleeping with me". It was as simple as that.

We spent six blissful days together at Hope Island. We sat and talked, and drank and made love. We would go down to the main marina, which had a large bar and restaurant built over the water. We would sit outside on the decking over the water for literally hours and hours and hours, occasionally popping inside to get more drinks, or a pizza. The staff were highly amused, and we would see them obviously talking about us, pointing, grinning, wondering, why we were there for so long, and every day.

We didn't live by any clock; sometimes we would sleep half the day and be up all night. One night we drove all the way over to the coast before dawn and sat on the beach wrapped in a blanket to watch the sun rise over the Pacific Ocean. It was very appropriate, a new dawn for us both. It was as though our lives had just started, we had both been on long, separate, often painful journeys, but had now finally reached our destination. Everything felt right about each other, and for the first time in both of our lives we were both truly adored for just being ourselves. I didn't have to put on any act, or be on best behaviour. I was able to just be me, and Claire truly loved me for who I really was. It was so liberating, being able to be loved for just being who I really am.

Rick would take off in his wheelchair to give us a couple of hours alone each day. He would put his leather jacket back on and each time I would hear those metal rims of his wheels grating along the concrete and gravel paths. I thought it must be hard work pushing on a flat tyre and indeed he would always come back pouring of sweat. So I went out and bought a puncture repair kit and fixed the tyres for him. He would inevitably come back within a couple of days with a new puncture and repairing them became an ongoing job.

Claire had told me about the strangest cat she had ever seen that appeared one night not long before meeting me. It was white and had a black and white hooped tail and a black patch around one eye and just didn't look the shape of a normal cat. It had come to the glass sliding door of her bedroom, madly purring away, and when she opened the door it had raced in, snuggled up to her and wouldn't get off her bed for ages.

We were sitting there in her bed one night, when suddenly the same white cat appeared again at the glass sliding doors, frantically meowing away. It did look very strange and was demanding to be let in. If it wasn't for the fact it clearly was a cat, I would have said it looked more like a racoon. Claire got up and opened the doors and it shot past her, leapt up on the bed and raced right up onto my chest, madly meowing away. It was so affectionate and sat there purring with its head nuzzled right up under my chin. It was so strange for a cat to be like that with a complete stranger. It was exactly as Claire had said it had been with her. It stayed nestled up with us on the bed for ages, purring away, going back and forth between the two of us, until it decided it wanted to go. So we opened the door and off it went. Claire had never seen that cat around there before, and we never saw it again. It was all very weird.

Eventually six days of bliss came to an end. We both had no hesitation, we knew deep in our hearts and souls we were going to be together, permanently, as soon as we possibly could. We didn't want to waste another minute of our lives not being with each other physically.

Claire said straight out I should come and live with her. There was no work for me in the area where she lived, so we weren't sure where we could get together for the longer term, just that we would. We decided the best thing would be first for me to just get up there, and then take it from there. Our Angels would help us find a way. For the longer term, it looked like Brisbane would probably be the best option. Rick had to go to the Oncology department at the hospital in Brisbane at least once a month to have his blood treated for his bone marrow transplant, and it was also the hospital that had managed all his Leukaemia treatment, and he would have to be taken back to if there were any issues. It was also the nearest city where there was at least a reasonable chance of me finding IT work there, so it chose itself.

We drove back down to the airport. Getting on that plane after six amazing days together was hard though. We didn't want to be apart ever again. I kissed Claire goodbye and gave her a massive hug, and reluctantly boarded my plane. I sat buckled up waiting to take off feeling as though we were now joined, and going away from her was like having something ripped out of me from inside. It felt like a big piece of me was now missing, a piece that had been missing all my life and had been briefly back for the last six days where it truly belonged, and was now gone again. As the plane took off and the ground sunk away and disappeared below the clouds, it felt like an elastic rope from inside me was being stretched longer and longer, thinner and thinner, until it was as thin as a hair the further apart we became.

40 – MERGING

Claire:

In the darkness I fumbled for my phone, which was lying just underneath my pillows and saw that it was 3.24AM, I had actually been asleep for eight full hours. It was the longest sleep in one night since our connection eighteen days ago. I began to send him kisses, only to discover before the hitting send button, that another text message was coming in. He was sending me three kisses at exactly the same time in the middle of the night. I giggled out aloud and a rush of blood whooshed through me, as my heart quickened. This was amazing. It happened too often with us to be a coincidence now. We were so in tune I thought. How wonderful. How sexy. How scary. I tapped out another message, "It's today already… I'm fucking shitting myself xxx"…

"Why"?

"In case you really don't fancy me. Did I wake you"?

"Why wouldn't I fancy you? You might not fancy me".

I thought how hideous that would be after everything we'd shared, after everything we had said to each other. Of course I'd fancy him. It didn't matter what he looked like. I was in love with him. Let him bring his apple box. It didn't matter.

"I love you X".

"I thought last night when you said you were going to sleep, you meant a nap. I missed talking to you".

"Oh I knew I needed sleep. I was washed out completely. Miss your voice. Miss you".

God if I hadn't had that sleep, I would look terrible today with big black bags under my eyes and no energy. I wanted to sparkle with him today. I wanted to be at my best. Thank God the black under my eyes was only smudged eye makeup from yesterday.

"So are you up now"?

"Yes Mark. Need to wash my hair and get ready for you darling".

Claire:

It was still only 5AM and the seagulls calling to each other in the first light of the morning reminded me to look outside to see what kind of day it was shaping up to be. It was bright and clear blue already, the perfect one I decided for meeting my darling at last and also a brilliant day for the beach. My heart caught in my throat, as I realized I had not even touched his face with my own bare fingers, or tasted his kisses or his skin, or danced with his eyes across a crowded room and yet in just a few short hours all of these experiences were about to happen. At least four new senses were waiting to be explored with him. Touch, smell, taste and sight. I knew though. I just knew that I loved him and that he was 'the one'. I wondered what I would do if he did not feel the same way about me? Oh God, what if this knowingness about him was all wrong? What if it was all just my overactive pineal gland foreseeing the perfect romance like a teenage schoolgirl does when she begins falling in love with love for the first time? But this was not the first time for me. I was fifty years old. I was practically a grandmother with my daughter Emma carrying her first child already.

I crushed my thoughts, snatching at the sheets and ripped them off the mattress in one huge tug. It was high time to cool my head off under the shower and so, as I lathered up the shampoo, I could not help but feel a wave of sheer excitement rise and wash over me with electric intensity. I was feeling so alive in my bare skin that I let out a thrilling "whooo hooo", drying myself off and taking care to cover every inch of my body with moisturizer and layering it as well with Chanel No 5, my favourite perfume. I wanted to smell delicious. It was all for him you know, and it was definitely all for me too.

What would he really look like I wondered? Which photograph captured his true likeness? He seemed to look different in every single snap, just like my photos seemed to capture a different aspect of myself in the same way. Not one of them looked like me at all really. Mark's photos reminded me of something deeper and more mysterious though, which I did not quite know how to put my finger on exactly and yet the images were intrinsically familiar to me. When I looked at his photos, I would have flashbacks. It was like gazing into an old, old memory, of my own faded world of sepia in an ancient photograph album of another lifetime. Who were the ghosts rising out of parchment paper like a waft of fine sandalwood incense I wondered? Where did the Egyptian paraffin candle wax come from that melted the seals to my heart and to my soul, leaving me hypnotized into a trance devoid of all other lovers and memories? I was stuck in a fog totally captivated by his images and seeing him in the flesh would soon tell me why.

I put on my favourite little black dress adding a little chic with a nineteen fifties style cream jacket which swung at the bottom like something Audrey Hepburn would have worn in the old movie 'Breakfast at Tiffany's', except at least four sizes smaller. When I had finished applying my makeup, I sat for a while just gazing into the mirror and imagined what the swish of black seamed nylon stockings brushing against each other would really sound like on me, and how they would feel against my bare skin under my little black dress. I would love to have had the guts to meet him all dressed up in them with suspenders and the six inch killer black heels as well, but I realized that it would probably be all too much greeting him like that for the first time, just to pick him up at the airport. Besides, I did not even own a pair of real nylon stockings from the 1950s anyway. It was just a fantasy.

I threw back my head and laughed, catching a brief reflection of it in the mirror and recognized a piece of uncut diamond shining through my eyes untouched by any man before and certainly never seen in myself until now. I wanted Mark to touch that part of me there as well. Was this the reflection of the famous Medusa with twisting slithering snakes crawling in her hair? To me, she would be the most frightening woman of all my wildest dreams and to every man as well I think, yet I wanted to share her with him and not just show him the lovely, positive, happy Claire that everyone else knew outside of my bedroom.

I was rather afraid that this darker shade of me would try to consume Mark and decided to try and tone down my energy of pure sex with him somehow, so I threw on some black leggings under my dress and a pair of flat ballet shoes to make the overall first impression less formal and more casual. I thought my demeanour was already intense enough to frighten him away and so was my face covered in all of this makeup, which defied my mother's last request to be plain and unattractive.

Then I remembered his voice. To me it felt as familiar to me as a waft of velvet soap, carrying me far back in time to one of my earliest memories when I was a baby in Melbourne, having a bath in the laundry trough, which was as yellow as the colour of English buttercups. I would splash about and have to hold my breath at the same time, so that the soapy water didn't go up my nose. The sound of Mark's voice took me back to that place, before I had any knowledge of something sinister going on in the darkness. There was something so pure and innocent about my love for Mark and something so damned primal and erotic about it as well. So this was lust and this was love entwined at last. "How utterly so divine", I whispered to the lady in the mirror. "Bring it on Medusa"!

My phone started beeping again at 7.05AM.

"Running very late that's all. Leaving now Claire. Won't be long. Love you Xxx".

"Drive carefully my darling. See you soon. I love you Mark Xxxx"!

Better pop on the jangle bangles and make this raven hair dead straight I suppose. Time to throw the dishes in the dishwasher, change the sheets, and have one last walk through the place to check everything looks good, smells good, is good. Better plump the cushions on the couch up again and light more incense before I'm off. Yes the flowers look beautiful on the piano, or would they look better on the dining table? No matter. The candles are ready, champers is chilling. Another squirt of Chanel and two layers of lipstick, plus another sweep of mascara over the lashes will do it. Cool! Time to go. Oh my God. I was so nervous and so excited all at the same time.

My phone started beeping again. I grabbed it and searched for unread messages in my inbox.

"Parked car. On way to check in. Xxx".

Oh my heart again. It was off pumping me with more blood, more fix. More Mark.

"Yesss"! I texted him. "Enjoy this. I am. We're about to find out what really happens next".

"I am. Doesn't matter really anyway. It's the next fifty plus years of love together I'm looking forward to. Xxx".

Oh my 'Twin' I thought. He doesn't really care how I look after all. Just fucking chill Claire!

"'Twin'", I replied.

"See ya", Rick called, as I marched through the back door.

"Good luck with Mark today. You look beautiful mum".

"Thanks love. Make your bed ok"? I yelled as I took off and into the day down to Coolangatta airport three quarters of an hour's drive away in my rusty old light blue Corona, rather wishing it was a black 911 Porsche with the wind wafting through my hair instead. Shut up ego, I screamed in my head. I don't need you anymore! I don't need to impress him and I don't want to either. It's ok now. I am really being my true self at last. Just fuck off ok?

I watched the people spilling out of the gangway and into the arrival area at the airport with my heart jumping madly like a pony. The information screen had told me that his plane had landed five minutes earlier and he would be amongst the next batch of passengers walking through at any moment now. I placed myself far enough away to get a really good look at him, as he came through the entrance, giving myself time to prepare for the surprise of seeing his face and then to quickly contain my nerves somehow before saying hello. I knew this was it. There was no turning back, not that I wanted to for a second mind you.

More people started to come through now. Their bodies swarmed around me like busy bees droning for honey and my eyes darted everywhere searching the empty faces for him, but there were only blank unfamiliar expressions, whilst their shoulders bumped into me accidently amidst the buzz. I could not recognize anything of the feeling of him anywhere at all. Maybe he had missed the plane? Maybe he wasn't coming? But he had texted me and rung me at the airport to say that he had parked and was on his way to check in. Maybe he had changed his mind? I started to bite the insides of my bottom lip and my eyes returned to the gangway again. People were dribbling out now and I searched each face for even a tiny spark of recognition from someone. Anyone, but they were just ordinary people not matching my feelings or my anxiety in the slightest possible way.

And then my heart stopped. Oh please God, please make that gorgeous man him coming out of those doors right now. Make him please be 'the one'? He was tall, devastatingly handsome, wearing a nice suit and a devilish grin and was slowly walking straight towards me. My chest started to burst inside the walls of my heart, as if a thunderstorm was looming there. I started to walk slowly towards him too. Then faster and faster as the warm rush of blood rose to my cheeks and then flashed down into my stomach in a bolt of lightning. I hurried faster towards him now, as another rush of blood gushed into my groin in a hot tropical throb of rain. My head was spinning. Oh God this was it. Could this really be him? His curls were tousled down over his forehead, as he paced towards me, whilst more locks of hair bounced up and down across those strong broad shoulders with each step approaching closer to me. I glanced behind me to see if he was making his entrance towards someone else, but the beautiful woman I braced myself to see and envied so much was nowhere in sight, instead those electric blue eyes were melting into mine as if they were pieces of decadent Belgian chocolate. It must be him. He was so gorgeous! Oh thank you God. Thank you. Thank you. Thank you.

He paused in his path about ten paces away from me and my fear was just an old demon exorcized by his eyes and his smile and his beautiful carriage. Something sizzled about him, his energy, his soul, crackling, burning into mine in an invisible embrace. I ran to him, reaching up on tip toes and threw my arms around his neck and his were enfolding me as well, as if our bodies were made for each other, holding each other dissolving and softening into oneness. I caught his aroma, breathing him in for the first time, tasting his skin, as my lips brushed his neck and covered me in goose bumps and happiness, as if we had known each other for eternity and been ripped apart forever and ever until now. He was heaven. I knew I'd been right about him all along. He was 'the one' and it was mutual in that very first moment I know, because that oneness told me so.

"Hello", we both said simultaneously smiling to the brim of happiness, so that I did not think there was room for any more to be contained inside. It was overflowing now from both of us and people were staring, but I couldn't care less, the only face my eyes embraced was his. It was obvious to me now, why his photographs had triggered so many visions and memories of my past. He was every man that I had ever loved or had wanted to love. I had fallen for each one of them, recognizing an aspect of Mark's being and he was the epitome of them all put together.

"Oh Mark you are so gorgeous".

Our hands slid together as if they had been choreographed to soaring violins, exactly sculpted to entwine perfectly.

"I think you're gorgeous too Claire".

Mysteriously, Sleeping Beauty awoke from within and I thought it strange how I never knew that she was even there before. I was too overawed for words and nothing more was said. We just beamed at each other, filling up and overflowing on the reality that our souls had already known the truth before our bodies could ever imagine the depth of intensity of the secret flame we shared.

Another conversation had started going on between us without words now, whilst our senses deliciously began discerning everything about each other that neither of us had spoken about. We made our way to the baggage area smiling and squeezing each other's hands, tripping high on the cloud of euphoria and being vaguely aware of many other staring eyes around us, who were captivated by that electricity invisibly buzzing and sparking between us. Strange how the unspoken is more potent than a three dimensional conversation and how some of us still mistrust the silent language that we are all so familiar with, yet find so unbelievably naïve to take seriously.

We strolled to my car, still hand in hand, me apologizing for picking him up in such an embarrassing old heap and he just chuckling sweetly and telling me it really didn't matter to him one bit what sort of car I drove. How refreshing I thought and how very polite for him to be so nice to me and I believed him. Maybe only certain types of people with massive egos were concerned about what sort of cars people drove these days and before I could jump into the driver's seat, he had laid the luggage in the boot. Then with an unexpected advance, he caught me up in his arms, gently lifting my face up to drown in those dreamy eyes of his all over again. For a moment he held me there, leaning me up against the back of the car, so that only the anticipation of his lips on mine was all that came between us. Waves of bliss swelled out from my heart and then he kissed me. Deeply, passionately, honestly and I decided that every tinge of pain that I had ever suffered in the world could be entirely wiped away in that unexpected blaze of our first 'Twin Flames' kiss, followed closely behind by a tremendous flood of belief in the new and wondrous beginning of us .

Whilst we drove up the coast road, the rapture of finally being together began to sink in. I could not stop beaming across at him and he would not stop beaming at me as well. He was beyond the wish list I had made a few months earlier and yet he was everything on it. His photos hardly resembled what he was like in the flesh. He was even better and I was already so in love with him.

"Fancy a drink by the sea"? I flashed as my eyes turned to flirt with his raised brow.

"Of course. Why not"?

He was driving little shivers up and down the back of my neck and all the way up and down my spine just by the way he was looking at me. A tango, I mused would be way too subdued for that untamed rebellion in those eyes. Yet all I could think of to say to him was, "Fuuuuck"!

We stopped at Mermaids bar right on the ocean at Burleigh Heads. The sand seemed more pure white than usual and the water a more intense aquamarine. We sat on a sumptuous couch and he ordered French champagne. I naturally just flung a leg over his and curled up into his chest, feeling like we had sat like this a thousand times before, because it simply felt so comfortable and so right.

"Here's to us Twin", he whispered raising his glass to mine.

Our glasses clinked and I suddenly realized that I was no longer alone in the world anymore. I wiped away an unexpected tear, before letting it remind me how far I had travelled over so many huge potholes in the road of my life. I did not feel older than him as I had with the others. We were the same and I was feeling utterly soft and feminine and very much loved by him.

"Yes, here's to us Twin".

Everything was alive with delicious sensual tension, whilst another puzzling chemistry was happening through the electricity between our hands. Something unusual was definitely going on between them, because it was not just the warmth of being close, which held both of our fascination. We had noticed this remarkable energy at the airport when they locked together for the first time and had never experienced this sensation ever before with anyone else. We held them up so that each palm was flat against the each other's and perceived in awe that they were exactly the same, as if someone had deliberately cut them out from the one mysterious template of flesh and blood. I stretched mine right out saying I had a pianist's stretch with a chuckle, but incredibly he could stretch his out exactly the same. As they entwined, an electrical current flowed between us creating a power source much greater than the feeling of our own separate charge. There was that sacred feeling between us, which I experienced as humility and nobility all in the same shard of a second, which kept pulsing in greater increments as time passed together.

We slowly drove back to my place at Hope Island, not experiencing the nervous pauses in conversation or the chasms of awkwardness, which is sometimes felt with people when they first meet. It was like reuniting with an old friend on that level and yet it was also like a chemistry lesson bubbling away on another. When we arrived, Tchaikovsky's Swan Lake was wafting out into the lounge room from underneath Rick's bedroom door. Then the familiar sound of his wheelchair entering the room briefly distracted our attention away from each other's fascination.

"One of my wheels has a puncture again mum", he groaned as the ship book he was nursing on his lap slipped off onto the carpet.

"Hi Rick. This is Mark darling", I said.

"Oh Hi there Mark. The 'Twin Flames' are finally together now at last, just like on my angel cards hey"? Rick beamed.

"Hi Rick", Mark grinned back, diving down to the floor to retrieve the book for him.

"I see you're into ships as well", he continued.

"Wow do you like them too Mark"?

"Yes, ships have always been one of my favourite things Rick, ever since I came over to Australia on the Fairsky from England a long time ago. One of my distant relatives was a radio operator on the Titanic too. How are you? It's really good to meet you".

"I had only just finished building the RMS Titanic before I contracted Lymphoblastic leukaemia in 2004. There were over one thousand, five hundred souls who perished on that fateful night of April 15 in 1912 you know Mark".

"Yes I know Rick. It must have taken you ages to build your model".

"Yeah it did. It took twenty four months. Every week I would walk an hour and a half up to the newsagent to buy some of the pieces for it, and then another hour and a half back home again. I couldn't wait to put the bits together. I loved it. What was your relative's name? I know all the names of the crew. Even Captain John Smith".

"Phillips. He was one of the radio operators I believe. My Gran told me about him when she was alive".

To me it was yet another hint that Mark was meant to be with us. Another thread to the fabric of our destiny.

"I'll fix that wheel for you later Rick. Have you got a pump somewhere"?

"Yeah but don't worry about it now, I'll just leave you two lovers alone for a while and go down to my favourite spot at the marina. See ya".

"Ok, see you Rick. It was really good to meet you at last".

Rick was already out the back, thumping the screen door as he went, whilst his wheelchair rim clunked down the back path nursing the flat tyre.

Mark cracked a nice bottle of champagne, whilst I threw together an antipasto platter to nibble on. We snuggled up on the couch and our bodies seemed to be weaving a magic spell. It felt like we were a silken cashmere blanket from an exotic Persian market amongst the pyramids of Egypt. We lit the candles and more incense, even though it was still broad daylight, because it just seemed like the perfect atmosphere to honour our celebration.

We both saw the odd pinhead orb of light, so bright that it was not possible to be imagined. We wondered what they were. Every now and then one of us would comment about seeing one somewhere in the peripheral vision and then the other about the strange phenomenon of shooting stars falling down over the piano. To me, the energy in the room felt like the night I spoke to 'the one' when I was just a little girl on that cot mattress in my mother's bedroom. It was the same feeling reminding me that this was the magic of true love resonating from the beginning of my soul. Perhaps they were the Angels celebrating, we marvelled.

As I went into the bedroom to freshen my makeup, I felt his arms reaching for me from behind. I turned my face, so that I could look straight up into his eyes again. He was unwinding me, teasing me, unleashing a desire that I never truly allowed to soar in me before, lest I be caught just being true, just being me, being free.

I was spellbound inside the mystery, as my heart quickened to the rhythm of a primal dance. His tongue was calling me to ride on waves of euphoria inside the deep blue ocean of those electric eyes. That smile was slowly melting into me, devouring me, adoring me and arousing the whole of me along with the caress of his sighs, as they tingled like kisses across my hips. He was provoking me, calling Medusa with his mind to follow him into his secret place. I screamed from the core, whilst our bodies trembled like the earth shifting in each other's kundalini, smashing together every particle of our existence into one glorious new energy. I saw the divine in the ethereal light of his smile. I saw a galaxy of stars shining through from the beginning of time. I saw myself and my God, revealed in the liquid blue of those beautiful eyes on that beautiful face.

We had remembered the music and the familiar pounding of the drums from a distant past. We had evoked the ancient tango of 'Twin Flames', dancing and merging from duality into the oneness of a lake of fire exploding from a volcano. Our souls somehow emerged and became the molten lava of a new world. Our new world. So this was tantric sex unleashing the mind, body and soul all at once and by the thrusting of twin flaming arrows, we had anchored the promise of true love into each other's secret places.

All of the others were just rehearsals he had said, as we lay in each other's arms overflowing with heaven, speechless, breathless and laughing until falling asleep with our bodies naturally entangled together in weightless ecstasy. Our legs were also entwined around each other, so that our entire bodies were totally wrapped up as one. Both of us felt that there was something sacred about it that neither of us had previously experienced before. We slept like this, tightly wrapped, not just for a couple of hours, but for that entire first night, blissfully in exactly the same position. It was the best night sleep either of us had in years, but it was not just the first night, the second night was the same, as was the third and the fourth and so on. We quickly came to refer to the way we slept as 'The Wrap' (and wrote about it at 'www.twinflameskiss.com/Articles/The-Wrap'). Before long, we added sleeping cheek to cheek to this position. Wrapped up, our cheeks would rest upon each other's and we would fall asleep like that, instantly and gloriously for the entire night.

During one of those nights in The Wrap, I awoke to hear Mark making a beautiful type of crying sound in his sleep. It was not words, it was not breathing or snoring and when I tried to mimic the sound, I found it impossible. The best description I could come up with is that it sounded like the song of the whales when they are calling to each other; a long soulful cry that comes from deep within. As soon as Mark awoke, the sound stopped and he listened with astonishment as I told him about it. It happened again a number of times over the following nights, and one night Mark woke up to hear me making the same sounds. We can only wonder if it is our souls crying to one another in our sleep, but neither of us have ever heard others speak of it happening before to them, so we really can't be sure ('www.twinflameskiss.com/Articles/Crying-Souls').

We spent so much time in each other's arms talking about everything we could think of to try and find where we differed in our opinions from each other. Even on spiritual issues we noticed that we had both come to the same conclusions about lessons learned though painful experiences. We came to see that everything stems from love or fear and that we had both experienced more of fear than love. We were amazed at how many of the same problems we had both endured with ex's, often feeling like we had been the giving ones in the relationship only to be taken advantage of, yet here we were realising that being together was nothing like that anymore. We were so similar. I felt so soft around him. I could also be so strong around him. Feminine and Masculine, Yin and Yang, all rolled into one. I just could not get enough of him or those beautiful eyes and we never stopped touching each other, whether it be holding hands or lying in each other's arms. Even when we went out to dinner, his hands would be having a private conversation with my legs underneath the table.

One evening around dusk we had an unexpected visitor. My bedroom had a door connecting straight onto the veranda and I'd often leave it open with just the screen locked to keep the insects out. A strange snow white cat with distinct markings like that of a raccoon around its eyes, ears and tail paraded up this night, as if he owned the place and started meowing relentlessly at the door until I let him in. When I opened the door, he immediately raced in and jumped up onto the bed and onto Mark and started purring frantically, as if he had always known us both. He nudged us incessantly, taking turns with one and then the other, whilst purring wildly with both paws wrapped around our necks and rubbing his head into our faces adoringly. We had the impression that he was earnestly trying to tell us something, as if he was a long lost family member making himself at home after years of separation from us. It was amazing, because not even our own much loved pets had behaved so affectionately to either one of us before. Finally when I had to put him outside, we started to wonder if it was actually a cat at all, for he possessed none of the aloofness of other felines.

It was almost like the soul of the cat was saying, "See, you are with your twin now. Everything is going to be alright for both of you from now on".

I told Mark that I had only ever seen him once previously, just two months earlier, when he had come to visit me with the same familiarity. I had recalled having the distinct impression that it was trying to tell me something by the outpouring of affection to me even then and felt that there must have been a special reason for his visit, because it seemed so bizarre for a strange cat to be so demonstrative with me and then to just vanish into thin air as if he were invisible. I wondered where he lived, for I had never seen him wandering around anywhere before as stray cats do.

Out of the blue the next day, the much older man I had been seeing suddenly broke up with me because he said that he wasn't in love with me. I hadn't seen that one coming, because he had always been so kind and generous to me and we had always had such a lovely time together. Not a passionate time mind you, but a happy time. He had been more like a friend to me I suppose, preparing me for Mark by treating me with genuine care and respect. At the time I chose to use the white raccoon cat's visit as a positive reminder that I was truly made of love and not to let the rejection make me feel afraid of ever being loved again.

Mark and I searched online for the raccoon features of him to see if there is an actual breed of cat that displays such an affectionate disposition, but we couldn't find anything that resembled him at all. We wondered if perhaps departed souls have the ability to use an animal's body to communicate with us, or even the Angels, because the whole experience was so bizarre to both of us. Then mysteriously the raccoon cat just disappeared and sadly we never saw him again.

I do not think I could have ever been ready for Mark to leave, no matter how long he had stayed with me for. I wanted him beside me forever and since our six days had flown away in such a romantic cloud of bliss, it came as a shock when it was suddenly time for him to go back to Sydney. Neither of us wanted to mention the inevitable goodbye at the airport and we even booked a return ticket for him to come back the following weekend, so that saying goodbye never held the anxiety of when we would ever see each other again. I knew that we couldn't be separate anymore, even if we were thousands of miles apart, for we had merged into a divine oneness, where the soul abides forever young.

When we arrived at the airport, he held me so tightly that I knew it would be the memory I would recall when I was alone after the plane had taken him back to Sydney. My heart felt like it was in a vacuum being sucked out of my chest and into his. And then Mark was gone.

I so wanted to breathe again, but how could I? And then I remembered about the heart he had so generously left behind for me to treasure and so I touched it and it made me smile from the inside out.

"I love you! I love you! I LOVE YOU!" I screamed, as I watched his plane take off into the rain, whilst the lump in my throat grew and my heart fucking ached like hell, so that nothing could have prepared me for how badly I was missing him already. Yet in my soul he remained, like a brilliantly coloured rainbow after all of the pouring rain of my life.

41 - OUT OF DARKNESS COMETH LIGHT

Mark:

I flew back into Sydney and went straight to pick up Liana. Back home I sat her down and we had a big talk. I explained honestly to her what was happening. She knew the awful mess I had been through in my last couple of relationships, for she had suffered with me, and she really wanted me to be happy.

The only issue could have been her schooling, but her grades were down and she was hanging out with the wrong crowd, the crowd the school had warned me they got rid of in the final couple of years. The headmaster at Cumberland had labelled it 'releasing non-academic students early', but it was really about increasing the schools average grades by kicking out all the kids who would pull their average down, the very ones who actually needed their help the most. I had already been formally summoned to the school to be told she was being given her first official warning for wearing slip on shoes instead of lace up ones - that's how low they were prepared to stoop to end a child's education, and so the writing was on the wall. It wasn't what I hoped for her educationally, especially after all the effort I had put in over the last few years, but it made it easier for me to be with Claire.

The next day I walked into work and took my manager to a meeting room and handed my resignation in. I told him I had met the woman of my dreams and yes, I knew I was leaving a highly paid 'dream' job, and yes I had no other job, or home, to go to, but we had to be together and we would find a way to make it work, so I was leaving. It was way outside his comfort zone and he just sat there in shock, with his mouth open in complete disbelief not knowing how to respond.

I submitted my one month's notice of moving out of my home, breaking my lease in the process, and started to pack. Some would call it crazy. We had known each other less than four weeks, and had only met once. But when you truly meet 'the one' you just know, as it is unlike anyone else you have ever met, and nothing will stop you from being together. You just have to have faith and go for it.

I had thirty days left at work and we counted down every one. It felt so right. There was no doubts at all, neither of us hesitated, not even once. We were averaging about two hours sleep a night, yet still could not spend enough time together. We could not bear to be physically apart any longer. We just had to be together now. 11:11 kept catching my attention and running through my mind. I had read 'Twin Flames' were somehow connected to that number. Talking one night we realised that we had connected on the 11th day of the month and the day we physically met was the 29th. When you add the two together, they come to 11as well. Hence our relationship began with 11:11. I suddenly started seeing those numbers everywhere, wondering if it was just that I hadn't noticed them before, or it was now actually appearing more often?

I booked flights to fly up every weekend to see Claire until I moved up, so we would at least have the weekends together until then. During the week we would message all day via texts or email, talk on the phone at lunchtime, and then we would be on the phone all evening and through the night until the early hours. Most nights I would only get three or four hours sleep, and even during those we would be texting each other. I don't know how I functioned. I was living on pure adrenalin.

Each Friday I would drive straight to the airport from work and fly up to the Gold Coast and we would have a weekend of eating, drinking, celebrating and decadent wild fun and planning our future together. In the daytime we would go back to the pub at the Marina and sit there talking for hours. We had a lifetime of each other's past to catch up on, and a lifetime of the future to plan. Some evenings we would walk back over to the local marina and sit on a bench in the dark right by the water. We would see tiny shooting stars high up flashing past overhead against the background of thousands of stars, as they entered the atmosphere and broke up.

Monday morning Claire would take me to the airport to fly back to Sydney and go straight to work when I arrived. Catching that plane back on a Monday morning was awful. Every week, I would sit there after boarding, feeling like part of me was being ripped out again and again.

One weekend I took Liana up with me up to meet Claire. As we walked through the gate at the airport, Claire raced over and threw her arms around both of us. Straight from the airport we drove for 90 minutes up the Pacific Highway to Brisbane and to a series of rental houses open for viewing. We had to find somewhere to live, and quick. The first house we saw was gorgeous, off the road, buried at the back of other houses and it was as though it was set in its own tropical micro rainforest. The only downside was the only way in was via steep and winding steps, which would be a major issue for Rick in a wheelchair. We talked it over with him and he was all for it. We agonised about whether we should, but as he only went out once a month for his trip to the hospital, we decided we could cope and decided to go for it. We applied, offering to pay all I had in the bank as six month's rent in advance to secure it.

In the evening the four of us went down to the local marina near Claire's flat. It was a wonderful clear cloudless night as we sat outside under the stars, drank, ate and talked and laughed. As we were walking back to Claire's, something to the left in my peripheral vision caught my attention up in the clear night sky. I turned to the left, looked up and saw what looked like a comet streaking overhead with sparking brilliant white light trailing behind it, only this one was low, lower than I had ever seen before, probably only around a few thousand feet. I've spent many hours watching aircraft land and take off, and it was at about the same altitude as commercial aircraft are on their final approach to land. It was awesome. I quickly shouted out to Claire and she looked up and to the left and saw it too. We stopped and stood there holding hands in awe. As we followed it fly from left to right. It looked like it had broken into two main pieces, both sparking brilliant white light and leaving white trails as they flew along side by side. Behind they were followed by smaller pieces that had broken off, sparking in brilliant purple, green or white light. It was amazing. I have never seen anything like it before, even on television. In a couple of seconds it was right above us, so close we had to turn our heads to the right to watch it pass over us and off to the right. We stood there in utter disbelief. Claire said it was a 'sign', as though it was there just for us, two trails of white light blazing across against the dark sky, together, side by side. We will never forget it.

A few days later Claire rang me and said the property agents had rung her about our house application and were about to go through and do all the reference checks. Within about an hour we got another call saying the house was ours. We found out later that they had taken one look at Claire's music website and that was enough for them, and that they had never actually checked any further at all. Woohoo. Thank you Angels. We now had a home to go to.

We made the final plans to be together. We each booked our furniture removalists and arranged an air ticket for Claire to fly down and help me pack my home up for the last couple of days before I left. Liana had changed her mind at the last minute about coming with us, and had instead decided to go and live back with her mother, which was a worry, but it was her choice.

One week to go and Claire picked up the keys to the house and I flew up for the weekend to help her move. The removals guys loaded her grand piano and all her and Rick's belongings into the truck and we moved Claire and Rick from the Gold Coast up to Brisbane and into the house. To get Rick down the steps I would first have to carry his wheelchair down the steps, and then we would get Rick to put his arms around each of our shoulders, and we would support his weight to get him down the stairs one step at a time, very slowly. He always had a backpack with him, which weighed a ton. When I asked him what on earth he had in there, it would always be the same answer... a dozen of his ship books. He was obsessed. He wouldn't go anywhere without his backpack full with big heavy ship books in it. It didn't matter where we were going, he had to take them with him. We used to joke about how we would be in trouble if ever we were in a rush, or if there was a snake around, little realising how prophetic that would be one day.

At last I flew back down to Sydney for the last time.

In that final week I had a dream. Claire and I were sitting on a train, unlike any train I had ever seen before. It had lime green hard seats and a cream coloured plain inner décor. The outside of it was dark blue metallic, with a light blue stripe, black windows and was of a futuristic design. We were speeding along across the fresh open countryside, knowing the route well, for we had both travelled it many times before. We looked out across the flat and lush green countryside, across to low lying hills in the distance, whilst being completely engrossed in each other. Very. We wanted to unleash our desires, but even though we noticed our carriage was otherwise empty, were afraid someone else might walk through.

I looked out of the windows and could see in the distance behind us a very big city right on the horizon. It felt familiar as though I had seen it before somewhere. All I could see was the outline of the tallest skyscrapers right on the horizon peering through the haze, but this time there was something strange about it. There were two huge mushroom shaped clouds rising above it, as though it had just been nuked. Strangely though, we were far away from it and speeding off in the opposite direction, so it didn't faze us.

I suggested I have a walk down the train to the refreshments carriage and check out along the way how many people were in the adjoining carriages, and what the chances of us being left alone were. We were sitting near the front, so I started walking back along the train. I walked through the next carriage and it was totally empty. There was no-one in it at all. Then through the next carriage, and that was empty too, and the next, and the next. Every carriage was empty. I reached the back of the train and still hadn't found the refreshments carriage, for there wasn't one, neither was there anyone else on the train at all. We were completely all by ourselves.

I made my way back through the empty train towards the front. It was surreal. What was going on I wondered? I got back to Claire and started to tell her about how the train was completely empty and so the coast was clear for us to unleash our desires. That was all we cared about. We looked up and out of the window saw that we were approaching a very tall black glass skyscraper and the train was slowing down. Where had it come from? The train was on tracks about 4-5 stories up high above the ground in mid-air now, and we were approaching a big hole in the side of the building we could see ahead. As we entered there was a big wide platform on the one side and realized that this was the station. Strangely, we had never been to this train station before, but knew instinctively that this was our destination - our final destination and we were there.

To us it was a dream of leaving all of our past crap behind us and of the now in being just the two of us together, not caring what anyone else thinks of us, for the ride will be over before we know it. We should enjoy every minute whilst we can, and that is how we now live our lives.

Finally, the last few days apart were over and Claire flew down to be with me forever. I drove down to the airport and picked her up and we stopped for dinner on the way. We got to my home and I showed her there wasn't really much left to do regarding packing, I had done 95% of it already, so we headed off to bed. She came out of the bathroom looking absolutely stunning in a black see through girdle, black seamed nylon stockings, black high spikey stilettos and a long see through black negligee. It was a vision of countless fantasies over many years. We immersed ourselves in each other and drowned in the most intensely passionate love making, which was more like a spiritual experience, as though our souls were making love, entwined as one ascending into some sort of divine experience. I had read a number of times about how Tantra can unlock the highest realms of spiritual existence, and now I was starting to see what they meant. Eventually we fell asleep in each other's arms in The Wrap and had the most divine night's sleep, the first for a long time without texts going back and forth.

The next morning was my last day at work. I woke up and there was the woman of my dreams in my bed. Was she real or was I about to wake up again and discover it had all been a dream, a fantasy? It was so hard to believe. I touched her to check and no, she was real.

I headed off to work and Claire helped pack up the remainder of my things during my last day. In the evening we picked up Liana, and took her out to dinner. We made it very clear we both really wanted her to come and live with us, and she could come anytime if she changed her mind. I knew how things worked with her mother, and it would not be long before they fell out again. Yet more prophetic words.

Saturday finally came. The removals company arrived with a shipping container and we loaded all my belongings in and the container left. We cleaned the house through and were finally finished. We headed over to a local hotel, checked in and had showers. We were nearly there. The work was done and we were clean and could finally relax together. We should have been exhausted, but how could we be when we were on such a high, so spent the afternoon merging into oneness. We went and had a lovely early dinner, as we had to make an early 4am start the next morning for the long interstate drive north. Then it was back to our room, where we explored more of the mysteries of Tantra and collapsed in each other's arms in 'The Wrap' and fell blissfully asleep.

The next morning we rose at 4am for an early start and the 1,000km drive that lay ahead of us. We packed up, checked out and drove out and onto the highway, turning north just as the first light of dawn was broking through the horizon. We both sat there grinning away at each other as we drove off up Highway 1. We had done it. It was so true, Out of Darkness Cometh Light. We weren't driving off into the sunset, we were driving off into a new dawn, to a new beginning, one we had both been searching for all of our lives and had finally found.

It had taken me fifty years of searching and getting it wrong, to finally get it right. My quest for that golden relationship with 'the one' had taken me to many places, both light and dark, and had to face many demons along the way, trying to learn and to grow from them.

I shudder now when I hear people say 'all that matters is family'. Try telling it to someone who has been abused regularly by a relative who has gotten away with just because they are family, and so people don't want to face up to it. Having the same genes, the same blood as someone, does not give them a right to abuse us, sexually, physically, emotionally in any way, and expect us to keep going back for more. They should be treated the same as if they were a stranger and expunged from our lives just as quickly and permanently, as I was eventually forced to do with my father and brother. We have had so many comments and emails about this on our website from people realising the same, and feeling guilty for having to split from their family because of abuse when they keep people hearing 'all that matters is family', and thanking us for talking about it.

For many years I had believed a relationship could only work with compromise, but eventually was forced to accept that was wrong, for it only served to keep me in bad relationships way too long. It was just another a form of self-abuse.

You can only control what you choose to do in life, not what others may choose with theirs. It is not the way to find true happiness. If we aren't in a relationship in which we are truly happy, blissfully happy, then we are with the wrong person and should leave, whatever the cost. We should free ourselves to journey on and do the work we need to on ourselves to be ready for 'the one' to come into our life.

In all my relationships, with both family and partners, I had always been loving and given all I could and shared all I had. With partners I had shared all I had with them, worked long and hard hours to earn an income, and loved them in every way I could. I had taken on their children whose fathers had deserted them as my own, cared for their upbringing and welfare as my own, only to be instantly cut from their lives as though I was nothing when I separated from their moms.

Regardless, I always gave because that is who I am and cherish kindness in people. People who do not appreciate it, or reciprocate, do so because of their own issues, we should not let them change who we are. I always honoured my own integrity and could walk away from a relationship, with my head held high and a clear conscience, knowing I had always given all I could and not taken advantage of anyone. I believe the world would be a better place if we all did that. It would be even better if we all shared all we had, looked after each other in a spirit of love and harmony, not restricted by borders or economies or religion, but while there are still people who believe they deserve more than others, sadly, it won't.

I have always been honest with others and can honestly say I have never done anything to intentionally hurt another person, and are proud of that. Honesty is about actions, not words. Many may say one thing, but do a different thing, or nothing at all. I learnt if you want to know the truth about something, ignore what a person may say and watch what their actions are instead. If there is anything after death, any form of the Life Review we often hear of, then I will be able to stand there and feel proud in that I always tried to be love. For those who have surrounded themselves in a wall of lies in not having to face the despicable way they have treated others during their time here, well, they will probably just have to hope there isn't anything after death.

The only thing that transcends this earthly life is our soul. It defines who we really are, and I believe, it is the only part of us that lives on after death. If we learn to listen to it, nurture it during our short time here, it will always help us to choose love over fear, and all that matters is love. Just ask anyone who has faced death, in a war, through accident or illness, clinically died and returned. They nearly all come back with the same life changing revelation: all that matters is love. Nothing else matters.

When I met Claire, the contrast to all that had gone before completely changed my view of life. I suddenly saw that I had been on a journey without even realising it at the time. I realised I wasn't the nasty bad person others had made out. Those people were only afraid of looking in at themselves, honestly, and so repeatedly twisted the blame onto me, or others.

I realised in each of my previous relationships that there had been more and more elements of who Claire was in them, as though I had been following a trail of clues my whole life. She loves me totally for being who I really am, without any need to compromise. The spiritual counsellor was right. Claire had used her past to transform herself into love and is truly wonderful to be around. Not only does she pick me up when down and make me feel loved like never before, but not only me, she does it to others, complete strangers, in little ways on a daily basis. She is love - pure light, it radiates from her. I treasure every minute I am with her. I am so lucky. There is no feeling like finding your 'twin', as once you meet them you are together forever, and nothing will stop it.

If passing our experiences on in this book helps even just a few in the sorts of abusive relationships we have endured, to realise sooner than we did to leave theirs and do the work to find 'the one' for them too, then it was worth writing. We believe 'the one' is out there for everyone, but not until we have each journeyed inwards, faced our demons, and learnt to choose to be love. Once we do that, 'the one' will suddenly appear in our life, as it has for so many other couples before us, and will continue ever after us also. It's true, going through the darkest of darkness only makes the light that emerges afterwards all the more brighter. Out of darkness cometh light.

42 - TWIN FLAMES KISS

Claire:

I was amazed when Mark told me that he had simply walked into his office at work the morning he returned back and handed in his resignation, without even having a home or a job up here beforehand to go to, or waiting a bit longer to see if things definitely worked out with us. It made me laugh. He was just like me. It showed me what he was made of and just how much he believed in us. This was the man I had always dreamed of and now we just had to be together no matter what. Nothing was going to keep us apart anymore.

I went into the office where I paid the rent at Hope Island and told the property manager the news about falling in love and needing to break the lease to move out. To my amazement, instead of having to pay four more month's rent to honour the rental agreement, she said that Rick and I could leave whenever we wanted to without incurring any further costs. Mark and I felt so grateful. It was a blessing from the Angels we were sure and I soon found a gorgeous home five minutes away from Brisbane city centre, which Mark, Liana and Rick thought was beautiful also.

Every weekend Mark would fly up to be with me and every Monday morning we would have to tear ourselves away from each other so that he could catch a plane to go back to Sydney and then drive straight to work. I was in total awe of his ability to make our coming together happen so effortlessly and he gave me a deep sense of knowing not only that I had found 'the one' in my heart and soul, but that I was his true love too.

One evening, on one of his visits up to see me, Mark pointed to the biggest shooting star soaring across the heavens that we had both ever seen before. The size of it and the amount of time that it appeared streaking across the sky was truly phenomenal. It was more like the size of a planet than a small star and we gazed in wonder with mouths agape, as it lit up and fell for as long as ten seconds, flashing over and over and bursting again like a fireworks display as it went, especially for us.

He turned to face me clasping both of my hands in his. We both knew that this was a special moment and so we both instinctively closed our eyes to make our wishes, but burst out laughing simultaneously instead, realising without speaking that we had both had the same wish to make, but it had already been granted. All we had both ever dreamed of was finding each other.

"Thou hast melted mine heart into thine to beat eternally as one..." I whispered into his ear as we wrapped our arms around each other.

"Thine soul and mine are one. And in your eyes I see your soul, my soul, our soul, a single us. Our oneness is a sacred gift that we shall never stop loving each other or being together. I love you always Claire Buchholz".

It was like being in an old black and white movie where the end credits start to roll, as the two lovers melt into each other's kiss, for that is exactly what happened next.

It was thirty more days before we could be together forever, which gave me time to ponder the rollercoaster of my life and the lessons I had learnt to prepare me for it. I realised that none of us are any better than anyone else. It is just that we each are on different stages of the journey and sometimes we just have to move on from a relationship when we are no longer happy. Learning to love ourselves and accept ourselves is the hardest lesson that we come here to do. Whenever we mindlessly just react to a negative situation, instead of responding with the voice of our Higher Self, we make it harder for others to learn their lessons too.

There is no experience so traumatic that it can supress the soul from transforming it into something magnificent. Even after being abused sexually, physically and emotionally, I have come to realize that choosing to be love is the most beautiful and powerful way to transcend all of the darkness that has ever happened to me and that nothing but love really matters anyway.

My own life lesson has been to learn that love is not outside myself, as in where my upbringing taught me to find it, but within my own centre. For so long, I believed that it was selfish to love myself and so I focused on my parents or my friends and then my lovers instead, hoping to find that elusive drug which would magically complete me and make me whole. I yearned for approval, to be good enough for them, forever putting them first, whilst enduring their sheer abuse of me in the process. I thought I was being unselfish by putting up with it. I thought I was doing the right thing and becoming a better person by forgiving them. Yet all of the time, I was simply being foolish by basing all of my relationships on fear.

If I had learnt my lesson sooner, I would have saved myself from reacting to all of that so called bad stuff so deeply, in knowing that nobody can really hurt me. Pain is only how we each perceive our own experiences and I was contributing to other's fears by believing that I was suffering. In reality, I was growing. When I finally learnt the lesson, I started being responsible for my own happiness, focusing on how to go about loving myself instead. This is not selfishness as I was once taught. This is love. Only then, was I ready to meet my twin.

So what is selfishness anyway? Sorry to sound like a broken record, but I think it too is based on fear. Fear of not having enough or being enough and trying to take others choices and power away from them. Greedy people can never get enough can they? If only they realized that they could get what they wanted from feeding from the love that is already there within themselves. They *are* love.

Everyone is suffering in some way. Suffering from fear based thought processes of some kind or other and until we all learn how to love ourselves, we will continue to live in a reactive world of war instead of responding to our problems in peace. Imagine our potential, when the whole world realizes that we are all made of love.

Those negative aspects of my relationships have actually been my teachers in giving me the opportunity to grow and heal. That is why some toxic relationships are actually soul relationships, because they trigger a spiritual awakening to heal what is broken about ourselves, waking us up so to speak. There is always a private story going on between two people in a relationship and nobody can understand what is really going on except the two people involved. There is often a bigger picture at play for them, and that is why it is important not to judge others who are in so called toxic relationships. The other is working knowingly or not knowingly on the soul, inspiring a transformation into being more of who we really are, so that we can move more into love and away from fear. In my case at least, both of my husbands were my soulmates, shaking up my frustrations and triggering my unhappiness so much, until I discovered layer by layer why I was so unhappy in the first place and was able to finally stand up and become the person I really am, instead of just being a 'programmed zombie', which my parents had created.

Each of us go through difficult times of conflict in our relationships, so that we can address what needs to be healed and grow more whole from them. Some say that we simply need to change, yet I believe that unless you get to the core of the problem to reprogram the way you think about it, nothing ever changes and the lesson remains unlearnt. Some of this deep work can be done whilst we are single, but the deepest work can only be accessed in our relationships with others. Soul mates are not just our perfect partners, more often than not they are the ones who trigger the most conflict, so that we can face up to what needs to be healed into love within ourselves. Soul mates can be our partner, our children, or other members of family and friends. These are our angels, who allow us to discover the joy of life and what being here is all about.

Whenever rain clouds gather and lightning strikes, or the wind blows cold sending shivers to the bone, I am no longer afraid when I remember who I am in the story of my life anymore. Even when the thunder rumbles and shakes me to the core sometimes, amongst the earthquakes and tsunamis, or the cyclones and hurricanes that I have experienced as part my inner journey home towards my 'Twin Flame', no disaster can separate me from who I really am now.

For so long I believed that I was the actual disaster or contributed to the magnitude of it, yet now I realise that it is all just an illusion, no matter how much my parents and especially my ex-husbands have attempted to tell me otherwise. I am not the cause of the catastrophe. I am not the crisis. I am only the mirror allowing the other to recognize something within themselves that needs work, as they are to me also.

We are here to reflect the essence of our core which is pure love. Our minds get caught up in that illusion of life where the ego creates so much fuss and fear about everything. Are we rich enough? Are we clever enough? Are we famous enough? Are we strong enough or sexy enough? Are we slim enough or are we just enough period? And are we brave enough to accept our feelings or opinions even if someone else does not like them for whatever reason? It's ok being real, even if that means sometimes just having a bad day and not blaming anyone else for it.

Whenever I remember who I really am, the illusion disappears in the blink of an eye; I am simply a little white daisy bobbing about in the storm with Mark, my beloved 'Twin Flame', who is my rainbow after all of the rain. Finally I am with 'the one' and here we are actually living happily ever after with our children, and their children shining brightly around us too, like all the stars twinkling brightly in a heavenly crown. This is how I am no longer separate from everything anymore, but part of that great oneness which everything is.

Meeting Mark has inspired me to begin writing music once again, and he has learnt how to engineer and produce. Where else was there to start writing music again, other that right here, searching for each other and finally when we met our merging into oneness. One track is called 'Visited By Angels' and is the music I heard from the Angels that day many years ago, as close as is possible in our limited physical world. We called the album 'Twin Flames Kiss' and they are pieces that go right along with many of the chapters in this book. It is available online on

Amazon, iTunes or at CD Baby. You can always find it via our website, www.twinflameskiss.com/music, or Claires music website www.clairebuchholz.com.

You may be lucky enough to have reunited with 'the one' already. If not, no matter how long it takes, your 'Twin Flame' will be journeying towards you at the same pace as you are to them. Be gentle with yourself, for it is a bumpy road with many potholes, but you are sure to find a jewel if you look very carefully along the way. I know, because Mark and I have already been there too…step by baby step. The fifty year journey towards each other as we merge rapturously into sacred oneness, is our 'Twin Flames Kiss'. Somewhere out there with the moon, someone else is on a journey and making their way home too.

The question is, are you ready?

www.ingramcontent.com/pod-product-compliance
Lightning Source LLC
Chambersburg PA
CBHW071142300426
44113CB00009B/1054